Gramsci and
Marxist Theory

D1553158

Gramsci and Marxist Theory

Edited by
Chantal Mouffe

Routledge & Kegan Paul
London, Boston and Henley

First published in 1979
by Routledge & Kegan Paul Ltd
39 Store Street, London WC1E 7DD,
Broadway House, Newtown Road,
Henley-on-Thames, Oxon RG9 1EN and
9 Park Street, Boston, Mass. 02108, USA
Set in Times by
Computacomp (UK) Ltd, Fort William, Scotland
and printed in Great Britain by
Whitstable Litho Ltd, Whitstable, Kent

British Library Cataloguing in Publication Data

Gramsci and Marxist theory.
   1. Gramsci, Antonio
   I. Mouffe, Chantal
   335.4'092'4   HX288.G7   79–40935

ISBN 0 7100 0357 9
ISBN 0 7100 0358 7 Pbk

Contents

Acknowledgments

For kind permission to reprint several of the essays contained in this reader the editor and publishers wish to thank Editori Riuniti, Giangiacomo Feltrinelli Editore, *Mondoperaio*, *Telos* and *Dialectiques*. They also wish to thank Lawrence & Wishart, Publishers, London, for permission to quote from the following works by A. Gramsci: *Selections from the Prison Notebooks* (1971), edited and translated by Q. Hoare and G. Nowell Smith; *Selections from Political Writings 1921–26* (1978), edited and translated by Q. Hoare; and *Selections from Political Writings 1910–20* (1977), edited by Q. Hoare.

Introduction: Gramsci today

Chantal Mouffe

If the history of marxist theory during the 1960s can be characterised by the reign of 'althusserianism', then we have now, without a doubt, entered a new phase: that of 'gramscism'. For some years now we have been witnessing an unprecedented development of interest in the work of Antonio Gramsci and the influence of his thought is already very extensive in several areas of marxist enquiry. This phenomenon, which has developed in the wake of the events of 1968 is certainly linked to a renewal of interest amongst intellectuals in the possibilities of revolutionary transformations in the countries of advanced capitalism. Following a period of pessimism which had caused intellectuals to turn to the countries of the Third World, seeing these as the weakest link in the imperialist chain and the natural starting point for the revolutionary process, there is now emerging some sort of consideration of the specific conditions in the West. More recently, the rise of 'eurocommunism' has played a very important role in the extension of this phenomenon, though we have to acknowledge that opinions are very divided on the legitimacy of attributing the theoretical paternity of this movement to Gramsci, as the debate currently taking place in Italy on hegemony and pluralism would suggest.

This divergence concerning the political significance of Gramsci's work is by no means the first to arise. In fact, since his death in 1937, Gramsci has been subject to multiple and contradictory interpretations, ultimately linked to the political line of those who claimed or disclaimed him. So we have had the libertarian Gramsci, the stalinist Gramsci, the social democratic Gramsci, the togliattian Gramsci, the trotskyist Gramsci and so on. For an analysis of the way in which Gramsci has been taken up in direct relation to a political line the development represented by Palmiro Togliatti's interpretation is very important: from

Gramsci the national anti-fascist hero we move to Gramsci the leninist; an indication that the 'Gramsci question' has never been dissociable from the strategy of the Italian Communist Party (PCI).[1] This is still the case today, but an important new dimension was added by the quality of the debates on this question towards the end of the 1960s.

During the whole of the earlier period, in fact, the majority of interpretations of Gramsci presented him as a purely Italian figure whose influence was strictly national. The most advanced form of this in the PCI (Togliatti's second version) involved the application of leninism to Italy. But the question of Gramsci's contribution to marxist theory was never posed. This can be partly explained by the fact that the official philosophy of the PCI at that time – historicism – emphasised the importance of analysing a situation in its particularity and insisted upon the specific nature of the Italian situation. It was only when this historicism was confronted with a crisis in the 1960s with Italy moving into a new phase – the high point of neo-capitalism – that the analysis shifted from the particular in order to understand the more general characteristics of the capitalist mode of production. It was at this point that the scientific aspect of marxism became a central issue.

The critique of historicism, in which Galvano della Volpe played an early and important role with his *Logica come scienza positiva* in 1950, was central to the debate among Italian marxist philosophers during the 1960s. It was to result in a rejection of Gramsci's thought since he was considered to be the historicist philosopher *par excellence*. We had to wait until the questioning of the official interpretation of Gramsci's historicism developed by the PCI for the problem of Gramsci's relation to marxist theory to be effectively approached in any objective way, and for his important contribution to be assessed. Since then different points of view have been put forward concerning Gramsci's contribution to marxist theory and it is the aim of this reader to familiarise the English-speaking public with them. The debut for this new stage in Gramsci studies was the Cagliari Conference of 1967, for it was here that the new type of approach was expressed for the first time in the intervention by Norberto Bobbio, 'Gramsci and the conception of civil society'.[2]

Gramsci: theorist of the superstructures

Basing his intervention in part on the different meanings of the concept of civil society in Hegel, Marx and Gramsci, and in part on the difference between the conceptions of hegemony in Lenin and Gramsci, Bobbio puts forward the thesis that in Gramsci's work there is a double inversion in relation to the marxist tradition:

1 the primacy of the ideological superstructures over the economic structure;
2 the primacy of civil society (consensus) over political society (force).

For Bobbio, Gramsci's importance for marxist theory lies in this double inversion and in spite of Gramsci's differences from Marx, Bobbio claims that he should none the less be considered marxist for the reason that any theory which accepts a dichotomy between structure and superstructure warrants this title.[3]

This interpretation, which is a typical example of the sort of relationship that liberal democratic thought attempted to establish with Gramsci's work, was criticised by those marxists who insisted upon Gramsci's 'orthodoxy'. For Jacques Texier,[4] there is no divergence between Marx's theoretical problematic and Gramsci's since for both it is the economy which is determinant in the last instance. The only difference for Texier resides in the fact that Marx is above all concerned with the structural conditions while Gramsci is more specifically interested in the role of the superstructures, thereby completing Marx's project. The influence of Bobbio's interpretation was nevertheless very extensive and opened the way to a whole series of 'superstructural' interpretations of Gramsci, presenting him as the marxist theorist whose principal contribution was to have broken with the economic determinism of Marx and the authoritarianism of Lenin and to have insisted upon the role of human will and ideas.[5] As Biagio de Giovanni has recently shown,[6] a fundamental element of Bobbio's approach required the presentation of Gramsci's thought as profoundly inscribed within the tradition of Western political philosophy and the establishment of a determinant relation with the highest points of idealist culture from Hegel to Croce. Gramsci was thereby reduced to a chapter in modern political philosophy and all the elements of his thought which represented a break with this tradition were ignored. Furthermore, this type of 'philosophical' reading of Gramsci is a constant factor in all the superstructural interpretations of his work which isolate his thought from its political context and treat his works as if they were philosophical texts like any other.

This type of reading has been radically questioned by the most recent work which takes as a common theme the notion that it is impossible to understand the very problems posed by Gramsci and his importance for

marxist theory if his writings are not related to his practice as a political
leader, and if his thought is not situated in the theoretical and political
context of the struggles of the working-class movement at the beginning
of the century. It is from this standpoint that Paggi[7] studies the
development of Gramsci's thought up to the formation of the
Communist Party at Livorno in 1921 and shows the influence on
Gramsci of figures such as Barbusse, De Léon, and Tom Mann as well as
the *Clarté* group and the English Shop Stewards Movement. Badaloni[8]
discusses the relationship between the problems posed by Gramsci
and the debate on revisionism and emphasises the influence of Sorel
on Gramsci's thought. For her part, Christine Buci-Glucksmann[9]
established leninism and the Third International as a primary point of
reference. Finally, Franco de Felice[10] situates Gramsci within the context
of Italian socialism, contrasting his positions with those of Serrati and
Bordiga.

From all of this work a much richer and more complex picture of
Gramsci emerges which can neither be reduced to the dimensions of
traditional philosophy nor limited to the context of Italian politics. In
fact, Gramsci emerges as a political theorist who has radically distanced
himself from speculative philosophy and whose reflections on politics
have an importance which goes beyond the limits of the Italian
experience.

Gramsci: theoretician of the revolution in the West

It is now generally accepted that at the heart of Gramsci's thought there
is an elaboration of a series of concepts crucial to a theory of politics. The
realisation of this forms the main axis of the most recent work on
Gramsci. But there are a number of divergences concerning the status
that should be conferred on this theory of politics; divergences which
arise partly from the different theoretical problematics from which the
problem is approached. Thus we paradoxically find authors of such
different formations as Christine Buci-Glucksmann, influenced by
althusserianism, and Biagio de Giovanni, one of the principal
representatives of the hegelian–marxist tendency of the Bari school, both
insisting on the 'epochal' nature of Gramsci's thought which was able to
grasp the profound modifications in the forms of politics appropriate to
monopoly capitalism.[11] These changes result from the ever-increasing
intervention of the state in all areas of society, instituting a new form of
relation between masses and state/masses and politics. In this

perspective Gramsci's 'integral state' comes to be identified with the monopoly capitalist state which is not restricted to political society but permeates civil society. This latter becomes the private 'network' of the state through which it organises the whole of social reproduction, permeating all forms of organisations and mass-consciousness and provoking a 'diffusion of hegemony' at all levels of society. It is this 'enlargement of the State' (Buci-Glucksmann) which establishes its general contact with the masses, the consequence of which is that politics ceases to be a specialised and separate activity and we begin to see its 'expansion through the whole of society' (de Giovanni). The attainment of power can no longer consist, therefore, in a frontal attack on the state apparatus but will be the result of a long 'war of position' involving the gradual occupation of all those positions occupied by the state in social institutions. In this interpretation this is the meaning given to the gramscian notion of the struggle for hegemony whose object must be the control of the whole process of social reproduction. As de Giovanni states, 'Gramsci's political theory, therefore, becomes a theory of the struggle of the masses in the network of the state where the social reproduction of the whole system is effected'.[12] What is involved, therefore, is a strategy which has been thought out in terms of the advanced capitalist countries and Gramsci is presented as the 'theoretician of the revolution in the West', inaugurating 'a new chapter in marxist political theory'.[13]

Marxism as science of history and politics

A different interpretation of the theoretical significance of Gramsci's elaboration of a theory of politics is that offered by Leonardo Paggi.[14] Paggi suggests that this theory of politics is not limited to the typical situation of the Western countries since it throws into a critical light a whole mode of economistic readings of historical materalism and therefore has important implications for marxist theory in general. Paggi proposes that from the heart of Gramsci's project there emerges the necessity for an elaboration at the theoretical level of the implications of Lenin's political practice. The aim of this would be to develop an adequate theoretical instrument enabling both the knowledge and the mastery of the historical process. This, Paggi declares, would involve a complete change in our modes of analysis:[15]

it meant primarily the abandonment of the traditional interpretation of historical materialism which had shown itself inadequate not only in the East but also in the West: not only had it failed to understand the October Revolution, but it had also failed to develop a political strategy adequate for those capitalist countries where all the conditions seemed to be ripe. ... In the East as well as in the West, Marxism had to reject the interpretative scheme based on the relation of cause and effect between structure and superstructure.

Only on this condition will marxism be able to theorise the role played by politics in the social formation. But for Gramsci this was not simply a question of adding a supplementary field of research − politics − to a historical materialism which would continue to be understood as a general sociology. In fact, any interpretation of historical materialism which reduces it to a simple methodology of sociological research and which separates it from praxis, is considered by Gramsci to be a form of economism. It is, therefore, of prime importance for him to re-establish the link between theory and practice lost in the economistic interpretations of Marx's thought and to formulate an interpretation of historical materialism which would relocate it as a mode of intervention in the course of the historical political process. This new interpretation of historical materialism as 'science of history and politics' which, for Paggi, forms the principal axis of Gramsci's thought, necessitates a break with the positivist conception of science which reduces its role to the establishment of laws. The form of scientificity appropriate to marxism must be different since, as a 'theory of contradictions' it must enable us to establish a correct analysis of antagonistic forces and the relationships of force which exist between them at a determinate historical moment, but it can only indicate the way in which the antagonism may be resolved. In fact the resolution of contradictions could not be realised without a political intervention by the forces present. If this latter dimension is lacking then the result will be periods of stasis, or even regression, as the history of the working-class movement at the beginning of the century shows.

This *political* reading of marxist theory which enabled Gramsci to answer the criticisms of the revisionists by showing that the role of ideas and organised forces (Croce's 'ethico-political') was not excluded from the marxist conception of history, but that on the contrary they established their real effectivity within it, provides us with a mode of analysis and transformation valid for any historical process. This is why, according to Paggi, Gramsci does indeed provide us with 'a general theory of marxism'. In this sense, then, his theory goes far beyond simply a theory of revolution in the West.

Historicism and philosophy

In the light of this 'general theory of marxism' in Gramsci, a reconsideration of his 'historicism' is necessary. Gramsci's contribution to marxist philosophy has in fact been generally neglected as a result of the particular interpretations given of those texts where he declares that marxism is an 'absolute historicism'. From this it was hastily concluded that Gramsci should be located within the hegelian–marxist tradition of Karl Korsch and Georg Lukacs who considered philosophy to be the conscious and critical expression of the present. This tendency, qualified as 'historicist' by Althusser,[16] should be criticised for the reduction it operates between the different levels of the social formation, reduced by it to a single structure in the mode of the hegelian expressive totality. This conception prevents the levels from being thought in their relative autonomy and permits no notion of the effectivity of the superstructures. This type of interpretation explains why, for many years, Gramsci's philosophical ideas were considered 'dated' and why the profound originality of his philosophical position has taken some time to be recognised.

The identification which Gramsci establishes between history/ philosophy and politics and which provides a target for his critics, takes on a completely different meaning when we grasp the importance of his conception of marxism as science of history and politics and when we understand the consequences of this. In this light, far from designating the theoretical status of marxism, Gramsci's historicism enables us to re-establish the indissoluble link between theory and practice at the heart of marxism – its status as the philosophy of revolution. As Badaloni emphasises,[17] with the concept of absolute historicism Gramsci is pointing to the necessity for marxism to become history: to concretely realise this socialisation of the economy and of politics which, as a theory, it enables us to envisage as a real historical possibility. The union of history and philosophy should not, therefore, be conceived of as some new method of reflective knowledge, but as the necessity for philosophy to become history. This becomes possible when ideas acquire this 'mass and unified form which makes them historic forces'.[18]

Far from extolling a new philosophical system comparable to previous ones, Gramsci aims to show, when he declares that an original and integral conception of the world is to be found in Marx, that marxism must provide the basis for a new civilisation. It is not just a new philosophy then but, as Paggi points out,[19] a new *practice* of philosophy breaking completely with traditional modes. This 'becoming history of philosophy' is possible for Gramsci because of the link he establishes between philosophy and politics. Rejecting the traditional division between philosophy and common sense, Gramsci shows that both express, at different levels, the same 'conception of the world' which is always the function of a given hegemonic system expressed in the whole culture of a society. In effect, what is involved here is a certain 'definition of reality' of which philosophy constitutes the highest level of elaboration and through which the intellectual and moral leadership of the hegemonic class is exercised. This is what gives it its political nature and indicates the necessity for any class which wants to become hegemonic to struggle on the philosophical front in order to modify the common sense of the masses and realise an intellectual and moral reform.

Gramsci's struggle against all interpretations which reduced marxist philosophy to materialism must be understood within this context. As Christine Buci-Glucksmann emphasises[20]

> any reproduction in a hegelian or materialist form, of the classical location of philosophy which renders it alien to the conjuncture in which it intervenes, cannot fail to reproduce directly or indirectly a division of specialisations and tasks which Gramsci contests: that of 'philosophers on the one hand and masses on the other'.

The identification of marxist philosophy and materialism is considered by Gramsci to be a form of economism and it was because of this that marxism lost its revolutionary character and was recuperated within the problematic of bourgeois philosophy. What is at stake, then, is a particularly strategic concern and in this light we can establish Gramsci's importance for a non-economistic refounding of marxist philosophy.

Politics and hegemony

There is a whole area of Gramsci's work which has not been considered by the interpretations hitherto discussed, but which is at the very centre of his theory of politics: this is the whole problematic elaborated around the concept of the 'national popular' and the relationship established, through hegemony, between a fundamental class and the 'people-nation'. As Hobsbawm and Luporini emphasised at the 1977 Conference in Florence, this is a very original aspect of Gramsci's thought which opens up a whole new terrain of marxist research. Hobsbawm put it in this way: the fact that Gramsci conceives of the working class as part of the nation 'makes him the only marxist thinker to provide us with a basis for integrating the nation as a historical and social reality within marxist theory'.[21] The 'national question' is in fact one of the areas where marxist theory is most seriously lacking and it is urgent, today more than ever, that the question be posed correctly.

Luporini[22] considers that the origin of this weakness must be sought in Marx himself. Marx, he states, always operated with two diverse and non-unified conceptual 'couples' which he never managed to integrate. On the one hand the structure/superstructure couple in the analysis of the mode of production in *Capital* and on the other the state/civil society couple in the historical and political analyses (i.e. at the level of the social formation). But this second couple always remains descriptive in Marx and he never manages to integrate the two types of analysis at the same conceptual level in articulating the analysis of the mode of production with that of the social formation. This explains for Luporini why the question of the state remained conceptually unresolved in Marx, constituting an absence at the heart of his theory. It is for this same reason that the question of the nation is also unresolved. Gramsci's great originality, therefore, lies in his attempt to answer these questions and to conceptually unify Marx's two oppositional couples by establishing a link between 'politics – class – state' and 'people – nation – state', thereby recuperating within marxist theory a whole series of elements which has been excluded from it.

This is one of the most interesting areas of Gramsci's work and its implications for his theory of politics clearly show that it is not limited to the context of Western capitalism. In this context we can locate the origin and principal meaning of the concept of hegemony, a concept which provides Gramsci with a non-revisionist answer to the problems encountered by marxist theorists and militants when it became clear that the development of capitalism was not going to cause the disappearance of those social groups which were not strictly the bourgeoisie or the proletariat and that the working class would have to pose the problem of the transition to socialism in terms which were not strictly class-based.[23] In relation to these problems, Gramsci considered the relations between class and nation and the forms of the bourgeois revolution, a line of enquiry which led him to postulate that 'the supremacy of a social group manifests itself in two ways, as "domination" and as "intellectual and moral leadership" '.[24] Hegemony, therefore, becomes, in its typically gramscian formulation, 'political, intellectual and moral leadership over allied groups'. It is by means of this formulation that Gramsci articulated the level of analysis of the mode of production with that of the social formation in the notion of the 'historical bloc'. This hegemony, which always has its basis, for Gramsci, in 'the decisive function exercised by the leading group in the decisive nucleus of economic activity',[25] operates principally in civil society via the articulation of the interests of the fundamental class to those of its allies in order to form a collective will, a unified political subject. In this way Gramsci recuperates a whole dimension of politics understood as the expressive form of the common general interests of a society; a conception present in the young Marx but lost in the elaboration of marxist thought.[26] This non-instrumental conception of politics, no longer considered as exclusively an activity of domination, but permeating all the superstructures and serving as an articulating principle, is linked in Gramsci to the notion of the integral state (coercion + hegemony). But if hegemony is related to the state then this is only in so far as the latter is defined as 'the entire complex of practical and theoretical activities with which the ruling class not only justifies and maintains its dominance but manages to win the active consensus of those over whom it rules'[27], which clearly indicates that it is always in the fundamental class that hegemony has its primary point of reference. So the concept of the integral state must not be understood as designating simply the enlarged state of monopoly capitalism. For Gramsci it serves primarily to demonstrate that civil society, which in liberal thought is presented as an autonomous sphere having no relation to class interests, is in fact the place where the hegemony of the bourgeoisie is exercised. This notion plays a role which is doubly critical; of the instrumentalist conception of the state and politics which reduces them to the single dimension of the expression of class interests, and of the liberal conception which presents them as completely independent of those interests. For Gramsci it is important to emphasise that the dimension of the expression of general interests does exist but that it is always linked, through a hegemonic system, to the interests of a fundamental class.[28]

It would seem, therefore, that without seriously limiting Gramsci's thought we could not identify, as de Giovanni does, hegemony with the phenomenon of state intervention in the social sphere such as takes place under monopoly capitalism, and present the strategy of hegemony as the elaboration of a model for the transition to socialism based on this form of 'enlargement of the state'. If this is indeed an 'enlargement of the state' it is not what Gramsci had primarily in mind when he defined the integral state; in fact this notion is crucially related in his work to the state since the bourgeois revolution.[29]

Having established that, however, it is clear (and here de Giovanni's analyses are extremely enlightening) that the increasing intervention of the state in the countries of monopoly capitalism has led to an increasing politicisation of social conflicts. In fact it has multiplied the forms of confrontation between masses and state and created a series of new political subjects whose demands must be taken up by the working class. In this sense the struggle for hegemony is at each stage more pressing and more complex under monopoly capitalism, but we should not forget that it is posed in all historical situations which are never reducible to a pure and simple confrontation of two antagonistic classes. The concept, therefore, possesses a wide range of application.

Passive revolution and theory of transition

For Gramsci, hegemony does not refer only to the strategy of the proletariat. It is, as we have already indicated, a general interpretative category which applies to all forms of the articulation of the interests of a fundamental class to those of other social groups in the creation of a collective will. Consequently, there are several possible forms of hegemony according to the modes of articulation through which a class assumes a leading role. The category of 'passive revolution' is often used by Gramsci to qualify the most usual form of hegemony of the bourgeoisie involving a mode of articulation whose aim is to neutralise the other social forces.[30] But the category is not limited to this situation: it assumes a central role and a strategic function as a crucial element in the science of politics. As Paggi suggests, it provides us in effect with 'an adequate representation of the complex historical process resulting in the definite supersession of an entire mode of production'.[31] The concept of passive revolution, to the extent that it indicates a possible form of transition from one mode of production to another, has a general theoretical value for a political theory of transition.[32] It enables Gramsci to establish a non-determinist relation between crisis and revolution by which he manages to avoid any interpretation of historical development and of the transition from one mode of production to another solely in terms of the development of productive forces. As Franco de Felice notes,[33] there is a direct link between passive revolution, the primacy of the political and the analysis of society in terms of the relationships of forces in the work of Gramsci, which enables him to throw into question the idea of a linear historical development. For Gramsci, the objective conditions render the subjective conditions possible but the development of the latter depends on political organisation. If this political organisation is lacking on the part of the working class then capitalism in crisis will be able to reorganise itself on new bases as both the experiences of fascism and Roosevelt's 'New Deal' show.

Gramsci bases this non-economistic interpretation of the historical process on a reading of Marx's 1859 *Preface to a Contribution to the Critique of Political Economy* which breaks with traditional conceptions of the necessary relation between the capitalist development of productive forces and the numerical, organisational and political growth of the working class. For Gramsci, when Marx declares that no social order ever perishes before all productive forces within it have developed, and that mankind only sets itself those problems for which the solutions already exist, the aim is not to establish a law of causality; Marx wants to show quite simply 'that a given structure gives rise to a field of possibilities which relatively permanent and countervailing forces seek to utilise in opposite ways'.[34] For Gramsci this is a fundamental text for the critique of any fatalist or catastrophe theory since it provides the theoretical basis for establishing the fundamental role played by politics in any historical process. In fact, as Paggi points out[35]

in Gramsci's interpretation, the first part of the 1859 Preface emphasises the possibility of survival of a capitalist society, the second part points out the historically necessary, organic and irreversible character of the birth and development of political and economic organisations of the working class. This entails the possibility of elaborating, not only the theory of the political party, but also the two major interpretative categories of the forms of development of the revolutionary process in a capitalist society: the concept of the 'relationship of forces' and that of 'passive revolution'.

For Buci-Glucksmann,[36] with the concept of 'passive revolution' Gramsci effectively adds something new to Marx's Preface because he theorises an element which was absent from it: the study of the political form of transition. In Buci-Glucksmann's reading, passive revolution designates a potential tendency in any process of transition in which the state plays the dominant role. It is a political form of transition in which the problems of the transformations of society and the establishment of hegemony are effected through the state apparatuses.[37] This, for Buci-Glucksmann, is what happened in the Soviet Union and the concept of passive revolution can, therefore, be of great value in enabling us to analyse and clarify the problems of the construction of socialism in the non-Western formations.

Even more relevant for us is the vital importance of this category for the revolutionary process in the West. In fact, Buci-Glucksmann insists that an understanding of the dangers and consequences of the passive revolution can infirm our conception of a form of democratic transition to socialism. In this sense the strategy of the working class in the West must be a strategy of 'anti-passive revolution', that is, we must realise and effect an active, democratic revolution in which the masses and not the state, play the fundamental role.

Gramsci and eurocommunism

Is it not precisely this form of active revolution and of democratic transition to socialism which is proposed by eurocommunism? And is it possible in this context to establish a direct line of descent between Gramsci and the political line of the Italian, French and Spanish communist parties? This question is currently the object of a debate in Italy between communists and socialists. The consideration of the theoretical bases of the PCI which is an expression of the revival of the 'communist question' following the success of the Italian Communist Party in the elections of June 1976, began with a discussion on the relation between democracy and socialism started by Norberto Bobbio with his article 'Esiste una dottrina marxista dello stato'.[38] Following a debate on the possible alternatives to representative parliamentary democracy which took place principally in the Socialist Party journal *Mondoperaio*, attention has more recently been focused on the question of the relation between the current line of the PCI and Gramsci's thought. More concretely, the question posed was that of whether it was possible to reconcile the line of the hegemony of the proletariat – at the heart of Gramsci's strategy – with the pluralist line of the PCI's 'historic compromise'.

One of the principal interventions from the socialist side was that of Massimo Salvadori. In his article 'Gramsci and the PCI: two conceptions of hegemony',[39] Salvadori suggests that there is a complete break between the current strategy of the PCI and the leninist tradition to which, for Salvadori, Gramsci fully belongs. He is at pains to show how the PCI gives a certain interpretation of Gramsci which functions as a hinge between leninism and the current strategy, thereby establishing a link of continuity between its policies and those of Lenin and Gramsci. In opposition to this, Salvadori defends the 'structural leninism' of Gramsci which, far from representing a meeting point of leninism and post-leninism must be considered as 'the highest and most complex expression of leninism'.[40] (This can be contrasted with the position put forward by Luciano Gruppi who sees in Gramsci the starting point for a new conception of the revolutionary process in terms of hegemony.) According to Salvadori, Gramsci's conception of hegemony is unambiguously located within the leninist problematic of the socialist revolution conceived as the dictatorship of the proletariat, and is incompatible with any form of pluralist transition.

Against this thesis it was argued from the PCI side that Salvadori was offering a tendentious reading of hegemony based on the political writings in which the concept had not yet received its typically gramscian formulation, and thereby ignoring the modifications which it underwent in the *Prison Notebooks*. In an article rich in theoretical implications, Biagio de Giovanni[41] undertakes to show, on the basis of the conception of hegemony developed in his earlier works, how the concept is decisively post-leninist since it reveals an awareness at the theoretical level of fundamentally different structural conditions from those known by Lenin. The transformations of monopoly capitalism after the 1929 crisis which form the context for Gramsci's theoretical elaboration imply a completely new form of politics and demand a different strategy for the transition to socialism based on pluralism. This strategy, far from being alien to the revolutionary working-class movement is 'From Gramsci onwards ... *necessarily an organic part of it*',[42] de Giovanni declares in conclusion. The issue for him is not the opposition of Lenin to Gramsci on points of orthodoxy, but the understanding that both figures made a marxist analysis of two structurally different situations and that it is from this that the differences in strategies emerge. As we can see, it is again the concept of hegemony which is at stake. Neither of these interpretations seem really convincing, however, Salvadori's because he gives a truncated version of the concept of hegemony which evades the real originality of its gramscian formulation and presents it in a totalitarian light. Hegemony, in this version, excludes pluralism since it involves the imposition of marxism as a total and integral conception of the world upon society and leaves no room for other conceptions. Salvadori's mistake is in his failure to grasp the radically new character of the conception of ideology implied in the gramscian problematic of hegemony.[43] In fact, once we have understood that intellectual and moral leadership does not consist in the imposition of a ready-made world-view, but in the articulation, around a new hegemonic principle, of the fundamental ideological elements of a society, we can see that hegemony does not exclude pluralism. This, of course, does not mean simply any form of pluralism and certainly not a liberal pluralism for which all elements exist at the same level, democracy resulting from their free concurrence. The gramscian conception of hegemony is not only compatible with pluralism, it implies it; but this is a pluralism which is always located within the hegemony of the working class.

In relation to de Giovanni's interpretation, we have already indicated the limitations of a definition of the concept of hegemony in terms of the state's permeation of the social. To this we should add that if this notion does in fact enable us to give some theoretical foundation to a concept of pluralism, then it only does so at the risk of displacing the link established by Gramsci between hegemony and fundamental class, and it is in this way that an undifferentiated conception of pluralism emerges.

What is it, then, about the relation between hegemony and democratic transition? Once the gramscian concept of hegemony is located in its original context and meaning as political, intellectual and moral leadership of the working class over all anti-capitalist sectors, a leadership which demands a real democratic relationship within the hegemonic system and which therefore implies a democratisation of the institutions through which it is exercised, it provides us with the basis for a strategy of democratic transition to socialism: a 'possible' euro-communism which avoids both the perils of stalinism and of social-democracy. This is a strategy which, in Christine Buci-Gluckmann's words, must be an '*anti-passive revolution*' which, far from being limited to the developed capitalist countries, provides the basis for any real struggle for a democratic socialism. Gramsci has left us much more than a theory of politics: in fact his legacy to us is a new conception of socialism.

Notes

This chapter was translated into English by Colin Mercer.

1 For a discussion of Togliatti's interpretation and a general presentation of the ways in which Gramsci has been appropriated in Italy see Chantal

Mouffe and Anne Showstack Sassoon, 'Gramsci in France and Italy – A Review of the Literature', *Economy and Society*, vol. 6, no. I, February 1977.

2 To date there have been three Conferences on Gramsci studies; the first in Rome in 1958, the second at Cagliari in 1967 and the third in Florence in 1977. The contributions have been published by Editori Ruiniti, Instituto Gramsci, Rome, in three collections entitled respectively; *Studi Gramsciani* (1958), *Gramsci e la cultura contemporanea*, 2 vols, (1967) and *Politica e storia in Gramsci*, 2 vols, (1977). Norberto Bobbio's intervention is reproduced in the present collection on pp. 21 ff.

3 N. Bobbio, 'Gramsci and the conception of civil society', op. cit.

4. J. Texier, 'Gramsci, theoretician of the superstructures' included in this volume, pp. 48 ff.

5. The most serious work along these lines is by Jean-Marc Piotte, *La pensée politique de Gramsci*, Paris, Editions Anthropos, 1970.

6 B. de Giovanni, 'Critica organica e Stato in Gramsci' in *Politica e storia in Gramsci*, op. cit.

7 L. Paggi, *Gramsci e il moderno principe*, Rome, Riuniti, 1970.

8 N. Badaloni, *Il Marxismo di Gramsci*, Turin, Einaudi, 1975.

9 Christine Buci-Glucksmann, *Gramsci et l'État*, Paris, Fayard, 1974.

10 F. de Felice, *Serrati, Bordiga, Gramsci e il problema della rivoluzione in Italia 1919–20*, Bari, De Donato, 1971.

11 If we place within the same rubric here the positions of Christine Buci-Glucksmann and Biagio de Giovanni this is not in ignorance of the differences which are far from being minor, but because in relation to the precise point we are dealing with here – the conception of Gramsci as theorist of the revolution in the West and the conception of the state – their points of convergence are more important than their differences.

12 De Giovanni, op. cit., p. 253.

13 Ibid., p. 253.

14 L. Paggi, 'Gramsci's general theory of marxism', included in this volume, pp. 113 ff.

15 Ibid., p. 153.

16 L. Althusser, *Reading Capital*, London, New Left Books, 1970. See especially the chapter 'Marxism is not a Historicism'.

17 Badaloni, op. cit., ch. 12.

18 N. Badaloni, 'Gramsci and the problem of revolution' included in this volume, pp. 80 ff.

19 Paggi, op. cit., p. 115.

20 C. Buci-Glucksmann, op. cit., p. 264.

21 E. Hobsbawm, 'La scienza politica', *Rinascita*, nos 50–1, 23 December 1977, p. 19.

22 C.Luporini, 'Marx e Gramsci: le categorie strategiche', *Rinascita*, nos 50–1, 23 December 1977, p. 29.

23 Gramsci stated at several points that he had found this concept in Lenin. Perry Anderson has shown that it was a notion frequently used by Russian

social democracy and which enabled the theorisation of the role of the working class in a bourgeois democratic revolution ('The Antinomies of Antonio Gramsci', *New Left Review*, 100, 1977). But we cannot agree with Anderson when he declares that this concept became redundant with the onset of the socialist revolution and that Gramsci takes up the notion to use it in a different way by applying it to the mechanisms of bourgeois domination: 'the problematic of hegemony shifted away from the social alliances of the proletariat in the East towards the.structures of bourgeois power in the West' (p. 25). I would say, in fact, that there is no real change in the problematic since hegemony continues to be thought by Gramsci in terms of alliances. What we find in Gramsci is an extension of the concept, for hegemony ceases to be considered as a strategy which is necessary because of the weakness of the working class due to the backward stage of development of capitalism in Russia and which would serve as a palliative for this weakness. On the basis of a non-reductionist and non-economistic interpretation of marxism, Gramsci arrives at a conception of the impossibility of reducing every contradiction to a class contradiction and of the necessity to articulate the level of the struggle between antagonistic classes to that of other sections of the nation. The struggle for hegemony thereby acquires a fundamental character for every political struggle. This extension of the concept of hegemony in Gramsci is accompanied by an enrichment in comparison to its use by Lenin. On this subject see my own article in this volume, 'Hegemony and ideology in Gramsci', pp. 168 ff.

24 A. Gramsci, *Selections from the Prison Notebooks*, ed. and trans. Q. Hoare and G. Nowell Smith, London, Lawrence & Wishart, 1973, p. 161.

25 Ibid.

26 This is an aspect emphasised by Leonardo Paggi in *Gramsci e il moderno principe*, op. cit., pp. 398 ff.

27 Gramsci, op. cit., p. 244.

28 According to Gramsci the distinction between civil society and political society must be methodological and not organic. It is from this point of view that he criticises Gentile who ignores the distinction since for the latter force and consent are equivalent.

29 Gramsci, op. cit., p. 257.

30 This is the method which Gramsci calls transformism and which consists in 'the gradual absorption, achieved by methods which varied in their effectiveness, of the active elements produced by the allied groups', Gramsci, op. cit., p. 59.

31 Paggi, 'Gramsci's general theory of marxism', p. 151 in this volume.

32 This is brought out by Christine Buci-Glucksmann in her essay in this volume, 'State, transition and passive revolution', p. 207 ff.

33 F. de Felice, 'Rivoluzione passiva, fascismo, americanismo in Gramsci' in *Politica e storia in Gramsci*. op. cit.

34 L. Paggi, op. cit.; Gramsci's anti-economistic reading of the 1859 Preface is extensively discussed by Paggi from whom several ideas have been taken up here.

35 Paggi, op. cit., p. 150.

36 Buci-Glucksmann, op. cit., p. 220.
37 Ibid., p. 228.
38 This article by Professor Bobbio as well as the main interventions in the debate have been published by *Mondoperaio*, in *Il marxismo e lo stato*, Rome, 1976.
39 Salvadori's article as well as the other interventions on the relation between Gramsci and the PCI are collected in the volume *Egemonia e Democrazia · Gramsci e la questione comunista*, *Mondoperaio*, Edizioni Avanti, Rome, 1977.
40 M. Salvadori, 'Gramsci and the PCI: two conceptions of hegemony', included in this volume, p. 237 ff.
41 B. de Giovanni, 'Lenin and Gramsci: state, politics and party', included in this volume, pp. 259 ff.
42 Ibid., p. 285.
43 This aspect of Gramsci's contribution to marxist theory is the subject of my own article in this volume, 'Hegemony and ideology in Gramsci'.

Part one

Structure, superstructure and civil society

1   Gramsci and the conception of civil society

Norberto Bobbio

1   From society to the state and from the state to society

Modern political thought from Hobbes to Hegel is marked by a constant tendency – though with various solutions – to consider the state or political society, in relation to the state of nature (or natural society), as the supreme and definitive moment of the common and collective life of man considered as a rational being, as the most perfect or less imperfect result of that process of rationalisation of the instincts or passions or interests for which the rule of disorderly strength is transformed into one of controlled liberty. The state is conceived as a product of reason, or as a rational society, the only one in which man can lead a life which conforms to reason, that is, which conforms to his nature. With this tendency, both realistic theories which describe the state as it is (from Machiavelli to the theorists of the 'reason of state') as well as the theories of natural law (from Hobbes to Rousseau, to Kant) proposing ideal models of state, and defining how a state should be in order to reach its own end, meet and combine together. The process of rationalisation of the state (the state as rational society), which is characteristic of the latter, merges with the process of statisation of reason, which is characteristic of the former (the reason of state). With Hegel, who represents the disintegration as well as the completion of this process, the two lines become interwoven in such a way that in the *Philosophy of Right* the rationalisation of the state reaches its climax and is at the same time represented not simply as a proposal for an ideal model, but as an understanding of the real historical movement: the rationality of the state is no longer just a necessity but a reality, not just an ideal but an event of history.[1] The young Marx was able to capture fully this characteristic of Hegel's philosophy of right when he wrote in an early comment 'Hegel is not to be blamed for depicting the nature of the modern state as it is, but for presenting that which is as the *nature of the state*'.[2]

The rationalisation of the state came about through the constant use of a dichotomic model, where the state is conceived as a positive moment opposed to a pre-state or anti-state society, which is degraded to a negative moment. One can distinguish, even if in a rather schematic way, three principal variants of this model: the state as a radical negation therefore eliminating and overthrowing the natural state i.e. as a renewal or *restauratio ab imis* compared to the phase of human development which precedes the state (Hobbes–Rousseau's model); the state as a conservation–*regulation* of natural society and therefore no longer seen as an *alternative* but as an actualisation or a *perfectioning* compared to the phase which precedes it (Locke–Kant's model); the state as the conservation and *supersession* of pre-state society (Hegel), meaning that the state is a *new* moment and not only a perfectioning (which differs from the model of Locke–Kant), without, however, constituting an absolute negation and therefore an alternative (which differs from the model of Hobbes and Rousseau). The state of Hobbes and Rousseau completely excludes the state of nature, while Hegel's state *contains* civil society (which is the historicisation of the state of nature or the natural society of the philosophers of natural law). Hegel's state contains civil society and goes beyond it transforming a merely formal universality (*eine formelle Allgemeinheit, Enc.,* para. 517) into an organic reality (*organische Wirklichkeit*), differing from Locke's state which contains civil society (still shown in Locke as a natural society) not to overcome it, but to legitimate its existence and its aims.

With Hegel the process of rationalisation of the state reaches the highest point of the parabola. In those same years, with the works of Saint-Simon, which took into account the deep transformation of society resulting not from political revolution but from the industrial revolution, and predicted the coming of a new order which would be regulated by scientists and industrialists against the traditional order upheld by the philosophers and military men,[3] the declining parabola had begun: the theory or simply the belief (the myth) of the inevitable withering away of the state. This theory or belief was to become a characteristic trait in the political ideologies which were dominant in the nineteenth century. Marx and Engels would have used it as one of the basic ideas of their system: the state is no longer the reality of the ethical idea, the rational *in se et per se*, but according to the famous definition in *Capital* it is the 'concentrated and organised force of society'.[4] The antithesis to the tradition of the philosophy of natural law which is brought to its culmination in Hegel could not be more complete. In contrast to the first model, the state is no longer conceived as an elimination of the state of nature, but rather as its conservation, prolongation and stabilisation. In the state, the reign of force has not been suppressed, but has been perpetuated, with the only difference that the war of all against all now has been substituted with a war of one side against the other (class struggle, of which the state is the expression and instrument). In contrast with the second model, the society in which the state is the supreme ruler is not a natural society which conforms to the eternal nature of man, but is a historically determinate society characterised by certain forms of production and by certain social relations and therefore the state, as a committee of the dominant class, instead of being the expression of a universal and rational need, is both the repetition and reinforcement of particularistic interests. Finally, in contrast to the third model, the state is no longer presented as the supersession of civil society, but merely as its reflection: such is civil society, such is the state. The state incorporates civil society not in order to change it into something else, but to keep it as it is; civil society, which is historically determined, does not disappear into the state, but reappears in the state with all its concrete determinations.

From this threefold antithesis one can derive the three basic elements of Marx and Engels' doctrine of the state:

1 The state as a coercive structure or, as we have said before, as 'concentrated and organized violence of society' i.e. an instrumental conception of the state which is the opposite to the ethical or finalistic one.

2 The state as an instrument of class domination, where 'the executive of the modern State is but a committee for managing the common affairs of the whole bourgeosie',[5] i.e. a particularistic conception of the state as opposed to the universalistic conception which is characteristic of all the theories of natural law including Hegel's.

3 The state as a secondary or subordinate moment as regards civil society where 'it is not the State which conditions and regulates civil society, but it is civil society which conditions and regulates the State',[6] i.e. a negative conception of the state which is in complete opposition to the positive conception of rationalistic thought.

As a coercive, particularistic and subordinate apparatus, the state is not the final moment of the historical process: the state is a transitory institution. As a consequence of the inversion of the relation between civil society and political society the conception of historical process has been completely turned upside down: progress no longer moves from society to the state, but on the contrary, from the state to society. The line of thought beginning with the conception that the state abolishes the state of nature, ends with the appearance and consolidation of the theory that the state itself must in turn be abolished.

Antonio Gramsci's theory of the state – I am referring particularly to Gramsci's *Prison Notebooks* – belongs to this new history where the state is not an end in itself, but an apparatus, an instrument. It does not represent universal interests, but particular ones; it is not a separate and superior entity ruling over the underlying society, but it is conditioned by society and thus subordinated to it. It is not a permanent institution, but a transitory one which is bound to disappear with the transformation of the underlying society. It would not be difficult to find amongst the many thousands of pages of the *Prison Notebooks* extracts which refer to the four fundamental themes of the instrumental, particular, subordinate and transitory state. Even so, anyone who has acquired a certain familiarity with Gramsci's works knows that his thought has original and personal features which do not allow easy schematisations – almost always inspired by polemical political motives – such as 'Gramsci is marxist-leninist', or 'he is more of a leninist than a marxist', or 'he is more of a marxist than a leninist', or 'he is neither marxist nor leninist'; as if 'marxism', 'leninism', 'marxism–leninism' were clear and distinct concepts where one can sum up this or that theory or group of theories without leaving any uncertainty whatsoever, and one could use them like a ruler to measure out the length of a wall. When doing any research on Gramsci's thought, the first task is to look for and analyse these personal and original features, not worrying about anything else, except to reconstruct the outlines of a theory which seems fragmentary, dispersed, unsystematic, with some terminological uncertainties which are, however, compensated (especially in his writings from prison), by a deep unity of inspiration. This sometimes over-zealous claim of orthodoxy to a given party line, has provoked a strong reaction which has led many to seek out any sign of heterodoxy or even of apostasy; this excessive defence is generating, if I am not mistaken, an attitude which can even be called iconoclastic and which is still latent, but which can already be perceived through some signs of impatience. But as orthodoxy and heterodoxy are not valid criteria for a philosophical critique, so exaltation and irreverence are deceiving attitudes for the understanding of a particular moment of the history of thought.

2 Civil society in Hegel and in Marx

To reconstruct Gramsci's political thought the key concept, that is, the one from which it is necessary to start, is that of *civil society*. One must begin with the former rather than with the latter because the way in which Gramsci uses it differs as much from Hegel as from Marx and Engels.

From the time when the problem of the relations between Hegel and Marx moved from the comparison of methods (the use of the dialectic method and the so called overturning) to the comparison of *contents as well* – for this new point of view the works of Lukacs on the young Hegel have been fundamental – the paragraphs where Hegel analysed civil society have been studied with greater attention. The larger or smaller quantity of Hegelianism in Marx is now *also* assessed according to the extent in which Hegel's description of civil society (more precisely of the first part on the system of needs) may be considered as a prefiguration of Marx's analysis and criticism of capitalist society. An opportunity to understand this connection between Marx's analysis of capitalist society and Hegel's analysis of civil society was given by Marx himself in a famous passage from his *Preface to a Contribution to the Critique of Political Economy*, where he writes that in his critical analysis of Hegel's philosophy of right his[7]

> investigation led to the result that legal relations as well as forms of state are to be grasped neither from themselves nor from the so-called general development of the human mind, but rather have their roots in the material conditions of life, the sum total of which Hegel, following the example of the Englishmen and Frenchmen of the eighteenth century, combine under the name of 'civil society', that, however, the anatomy of civil society is to be sought on the political economy.

But, as it turned out, on the one hand interpreters of Hegel's philosophy of right had a tendency to focus their attention on his theory of state and to neglect his analysis of civil society, which only became important in research on Hegel around the 1920s. On the other hand, the scholars of Marx had, for a long time, a tendency to consider the problem of the connections with Hegel exclusively from the point of view of Marx's acceptance of the dialectical method. It is well known that in the works of the most important Italian scholars of Marx such as Labriola, Croce, Gentile and Mondolfo, some of whom were followers or scholars of Hegel, there is no reference to Hegel's concept of civil society (even though we find it in Sorel). Gramsci is the first marxist writer who uses the concept of civil society for his analysis of society with a textual reference, as we shall see, to Hegel as well.

Yet, differing from the concept of state, which has a long tradition behind it, the concept of civil society, which is derived from Hegel and comes up again and again especially in the language of the marxist theory of society, is used also in philosophical language, but not in such a rigorous or technical way and has varying meanings which need a careful confrontation and some preliminary explanations when used in a comparison. I think it is useful to establish certain points which would need a far more detailed analysis than it is possible to do here or that I am capable of doing.

a   In all the tradition of the philosophy of natural law, the expression *societas civilis* does not refer to the pre-state society as it will in the hegelian-marxist tradition, but it is a synonym, according to the Latin use, of political society and therefore of state: Locke uses one or other term indifferently; in Rousseau *état civil* means state; also when Kant who, with Fichte, is the author nearest to Hegel, talks in his *Idee zu einer allgemeinen Geschichte in weltbürgerlicher Absicht* of the irresistible tendency whereby nature pushes man towards the constitution of the state, he calls this supreme aim of nature concerning the human species *bürgerliche Gesellschaft*.[8]

b   In the tradition of natural law, as we know, the two terms of the antithesis are not, as in the hegelian-marxist tradition, civil society–state but by the one of nature–civilisation. The idea that the pre-pre-state stage of humanity is inspired not so much by the antithesis society–State but by the one of nature–civilisation. The idea that the pre-state or natural state is not an asocial state i.e. one of perpetual war, is being upheld also by writers of the philosophy of natural law, and it is seen as a first example of a social state, characterised by the predominance of social relations which are controlled by natural laws, in the same way as family or economic ones were, or it was believed they were. This transformation of the *status naturalis* into a *societas naturalis* is very clear in the transition from Hobbes–Spinoza to Pufendorf–Locke. Whatever Locke finds in the state of nature i.e. before the state, together with family institutions, work relations, the establishment of property, the circulation of wealth, commerce, etc., shows that even if he calls the state *societas civilis*, the conception he has of the pre-state phase of humanity anticipates far more Hegel's *bürgerliche Gesellschaft* than it continues the *status naturae* of Hobbes–Spinoza. This way of understanding the state of nature as *societas naturalis* reaches the threshold of Hegel both in France and in Germany. The opposition of *société naturelle*, meaning the seat of economic relations, to *société politique* is a constant theme of the physiocratic doctrine. In an extract from Kant's *Metaphysic of Morals*, the work from which Hegel starts his first criticism to the doctrines of natural law, it is clearly said that the state of nature is also a social state and therefore 'it is not the social state that is in opposition to the state of nature, but it is the civil (*bürgerliche*) state, because there can very well be a society in the state of nature, but not a civil society', where the latter means political society i.e. the state, a society, as Kant explains it, which guarantees what is mine and what is yours with public laws.[9]

c With respect to the tradition of natural law, Hegel makes a radical innovation: in the last edition of his laborious and painstaking system of political and social philosophy, which can be found in the 1821 edition of his *Philosophy of Right*, he decides to use the term civil society, which up to his immediate predecessors was used to indicate political society, to mean pre-political society, that is, the phase of human society which up to that time had been called natural society. This is a radical innovation *vis-à-vis* the tradition of natural law, because Hegel, when representing the whole sphere of pre-state relations, abandons the predominantly juridical analyses of the philosophers of natural law who have a tendency to resolve economic relations in their juridical forms (theory of property and of contracts), and he is influenced from his early years by the economists, especially the English ones, for whom economic relations constitute the fibre of pre-state society and where the distinction between pre-state and state is shown increasingly as a distinction between the sphere of economic relations and that of political institutions. We can go back, for this subject, to Adam Ferguson's *An Essay on History of Civil Society* (1767), (translated into German the following year and certainly known to Hegel), where the expression *civil society* (translated into German as *bürgerliche Gesellschaft*) is more the antithesis of primitive society than the antithesis of political society (as in Hegel) or of natural society (as in the philosophers of natural law) and it will be substituted by Adam Smith in a similar context with the term *civilized society*.[10] While the adjective 'civil' in English (as in French and in Italian) also has a meaning of non-barbaric, i.e. 'civilised', in the German translation *bürgerliche* (and not *zivilisierte*) the ambiguity between the meaning of non-barbaric and non-state is eliminated, though it leaves the other more serious ambiguity which Hegel's use of the term gives us, which is between pre-state (as antithesis of 'political') and state (as antithesis of 'natural').

d   Hegel's terminological innovation has often hidden the true meaning of his substantial innovation, which does not consist, as has often been said, in the discovery and analysis of pre-state society, because this discovery and analysis had already been introduced at least since Locke even though under the name of state of nature or natural society, but it consists in the interpretation which the *Philosophy of Right* gives us: Hegel's civil society, differing from the conception of society from Locke up to the physiocrats, is no longer the reign of a natural order which must be freed from the restrictions and distortions which bad positive laws imposed on it, but, on the contrary, it is the reign 'of dissoluteness, misery and physical and ethical corruption',[11] which must be regulated, dominated and annulled in the superior order of the state. With this meaning and this one only, Hegel's civil society, and not the natural society of the philosophers of natural law from Locke to Rousseau to the physiocrats, is a pre-marxist concept. Nevertheless, one must still point out that Hegel's concept of civil society is from a certain aspect wider and from another one more restricted than the concept of civil society as it will later be taken up in the language of Marx and Engels, and which will then be commonly used. Wider because in his civil society Hegel includes not only the sphere of economic relations and the formation of classes, but also the administration of justice as well as the organisation of the police force and that of the corporations, that is two facets of traditional public law. More restricted because in Hegel's trichotomic system (not the dichotomic one of the philosophers of natural law), civil society constitutes the intermediate stage between the family and the state, and therefore does not include all the relations and pre-state institutions (including the family), as do on the contrary the natural society of Locke and civil society in its most common use today. Civil society in Hegel is the sphere of economic relations together with their external regulations according to the principles of the liberal state, and it is at the same time bourgeois society and bourgeois state. It is in civil society that Hegel concentrates his critique of political economy and of political science, the first being inspired by the principles of natural liberty and the second by the ones of the state of law.

e   The meaning of 'civil society', extended to the whole of pre-state social life, as a moment in the development of economic relations which precedes and determines the political moment, and constituting therefore one of the two terms of the antithesis society-state, is established by Marx. Civil society becomes one of the elements of the conceptual system of Marx and Engels, right from Marx's early studies such as *The Jewish Problem*, where the reference to Hegel's distinction between *bürgerliche Gesellschaft* and *politischer Staat* constitutes the ground for Marx's criticism to the solution given by Bauer to the Jewish problem,[12] up to Engels' later works such as the essay on Feuerbach where we can find one of his most quoted extracts for its simple and striking clarity: 'The State – the political order is the subordinate, and civil society, *the realm of economic relations*, – the decisive element.'[13] The importance of the antithesis civil society-state, must also be related to the fact that it is one of the forms through which the fundamental antithesis of the system is expressed, that is the one between structure and superstructure: if it is true that political society does not exhaust the superstructural moment, it is also true that civil society coincides with – meaning that it extends itself as much as – the structure. In the same extract from the *Critique of Political Economy* where Marx refers to Hegel's analysis of civil society, he specifies that 'the anatomy of civil society is to be sought in political economy', and immediately after he examines the thesis of the relations between structure and superstructure in one of his most famous formulations.[14] With this, we should quote and have continually within our reach one of Marx's most important extracts on the subject:[15]

> The form of intercourse determined by the existing productive forces at all previous historical stages, and in its turn determining these, is *civil society.* ... Already here we see how this civil society is the true source and theatre of all history, and how absurd is the conception of history held hitherto, which neglects the real relationships and confines itself to high-sounding dramas of princes and states. ... Civil Society embraces the whole material intercourse of individuals within a definite stage of the development of productive forces. It embraces

the whole commercial and industrial life of a given stage and, in so far, transcends the State and the nation, though, on the other hand again, it must assert itself in its foreign relations as nationality and inwardly must organise itself as State.

3   Civil society in Gramsci

This brief analysis of the concept of civil society from the philosophers of natural law to Marx[16] leads to the identification, which came about in Marx, between civil society and the structural element. Well, this identification can be considered as the starting point to the analysis of the concept of civil society in Gramsci, because – precisely in the individuation of the nature of civil society and of its placement in the system – Gramsci's theory introduces a profound innovation with respect to the whole marxist tradition. *Civil society in Gramsci does not belong to the structural moment, but to the superstructural one.* In spite of the many analyses that have been made in these last years of Gramsci's concept of civil society, it seems to me that this fundamental point, upon which the whole of Gramsci's conceptual system is based, has not been sufficiently stressed, although a few studies have shown the importance of the superstructural moment in this system.[17] It will be sufficient to quote a famous extract from one of the most important texts in the *Prison Notebooks*:[18]

> What we can do, for the moment, is to fix two major superstructural 'levels': the one that can be called 'civil society', that is the ensemble of organisms commonly called 'private', and that of 'political society' or 'the State'. These two levels correspond on the one hand to the function of 'hegemony' which the dominant group exercises throughout society and on the other hand to that of 'direct domination' or command exercised through the State and 'juridical' government.

And he also adds to this a great historical example: for Gramsci, civil society in the Middle Ages is the church understood as '... the hegemonic apparatus of the ruling group. For the latter did not have its own apparatus, i.e. did not have its own cultural and intellectual organisation, but regarded the universal, ecclesiastical organisation as being that.'[19] To paraphrase the passage of Marx quoted above it would be tempting to say that for Gramsci civil society includes not 'the whole of material relationships', but the whole of ideological–cultural relations; not 'the whole of commercial and industrial life', but the whole of spiritual and intellectual life. Now, if it is true that civil society is, as Marx says 'the real home, the theatre of all history', doesn't this shift in the meaning of civil society in Gramsci induce us to ask the question if, by any chance, he has placed 'the real home, the theatre of all history' elsewhere? We can present the problem of the relations between Marx (and Engels) and Gramsci in this clearer way as well: both in Marx and in Gramsci, civil society, and not the state as in Hegel, represents the active and positive moment of historical development. Still, in Marx this active and positive moment is a structural moment, while in Gramsci it is a superstructural one. In other words, what they both stress is no longer the state, as Hegel had done concluding the tradition of the philosophers of natural law, but civil society, meaning that they entirely reversed, in a certain way, Hegel's conception. But with the difference that Marx's reversal implies the transition from the superstructural or conditioned moment to the structural or conditioning one, while Gramsci's reversal happens within the superstructure itself. When one says that Gramsci's marxism consists in the revaluation of civil society *vis-à-vis* the state, one neglects to mention what 'civil society' means for Marx and Gramsci respectively. Let it be made clear that with this I do not want to deny Gramsci's marxism, but I want to point out the fact that the revaluation of civil society is not what links him to Marx, as a superficial reader might think, but what distinguishes him from Marx.

In fact, contrary to what is commonly believed, Gramsci derives his own concept of civil society not from Marx, but openly from Hegel, though with a rather slanted or at least unilateral interpretation of his thought. In a passage from *Past and Present*, Gramsci speaks of civil society 'as Hegel understands it, and in the way in which it is often used in these notes', and he immediately explains that he means civil society 'as the political and cultural hegemony of a social group on the whole of society, as ethical content of the State'.[20] This brief extract brings into focus two very important points: 1 Gramsci claims that his concept of civil society derives from Hegel's; 2 Hegel's concept of civil society as understood by Gramsci is a superstructural concept. A great difficulty arises from these two points: on the one side, Gramsci derives his thesis on civil society from Hegel and sees it as belonging to the superstructural moment and not to the structural one; but on the other hand, as we have seen, Marx also refers to Hegel's civil society when he identifies civil society with the whole of economic relations, that is with the structural moment. How can we explain this contrast? I think that the only possible explanation is to be found in Hegel's *Philosophy of Right*, where civil society includes not only the sphere of economic relations, but also their spontaneous or voluntary forms of organisation i.e. the corporations and their first rudimentary rules in the police state. This interpretation is enhanced by an extract where Gramsci enunciates the problem of 'Hegel's doctrine of parties and associations as the private woof of the State',[21] and resolves it by observing that Hegel, stressing particularly the importance of political and trade union associations – though still with a vague and primitive conception of association, which is historically inspired by a single example of organisation i.e. the corporative one – surpasses pure constitutionalism (that is a state in which individuals and the government are one in front of the other with no intermediate society) and he 'theorized the parliamentary State with its party system'.[22] The assertion that Hegel anticipates the parliamentary state with its party regime is inexact:[23] in Hegel's constitutional system, which is limited only to the representation of interests and refuses political representation,[24] there is no room for a parliament composed of representatives of the parties, but only for a lower corporative house (alongside an upper hereditary house). But the brief annotation where Gramsci, referring to Hegel, speaks of civil society as of 'the ethical content of the State'[25] is almost literally exact. Literally exact, if we recognise that Hegel's civil society, which Gramsci refers to, is not the system of needs (from where Marx began), but is of economic relations, but the institutions which rule them and which, as Hegel says, along with the family, constitute 'the ethical root of the State, which is deeply grounded in civil society'[26] or from another extract 'the steady foundations of the State', 'the corner stones of public freedom'.[27] In short, the civil society which Gramsci has in mind; when he refers to Hegel, is not the one of the initial moment, that is of the explosion of contradictions which the state will have to dominate, but it is that of the final moment, when the organisation and regulation of the various interests (the corporations) provide the basis for the transition towards the state.[28]

4 The moment of civil society in the relation structure–superstructure and leadership–dictatorship

If Marx identifies civil society with structure, then the transference operated by Gramsci of civil society from the field of structure to the one of superstructure, can only have a decisive influence on the gramscian conception of the relations between structure and superstructure. The problem of the relations between structure and superstructure in Gramsci has not received up to now the attention it deserves, given the importance that Gramsci himself gives to it. I think that to identify the place of civil society allows us to adopt the right perspective for a deeper analysis. I consider that there are essentially two fundamental differences between Marx's and Gramsci's conceptions of the relations between structure and superstructure.

First of all, of the two moments, although still considered in reciprocal relations to each other, in Marx the former is the primary and subordinating one, while the latter is the secondary and subordinate one. This at least is the case as long as one refers strictly to the text, which is fairly clear and does not question the motives. In Gramsci it is exactly the opposite. We must not forget Marx's famous thesis in the *Preface to a Contribution to the Critique of Political Economy*: 'The sum total of these relations of production constitutes the economic structure of society, the real foundation, on which rises a juridical and political superstructure, and to which correspond determinate forms of social consciousness'.[29]

Gramsci was quite aware of the complexity of the relations between structure and superstructure, and was always opposed to simplistic deterministic interpretations. In an article of 1918, he wrote:[30]

Between the premise (economic structure) and the consequence (political organization), relations are by no means simple and direct: and it is not only by economic facts that the history of a people can be documented. It is a complex and confusing task to unravel its causes and in order to do so, a deep and widely diffused study of all spiritual and practical activities is needed.

And the following extract already anticipated the problematic of his *Prison Notebooks*: 'it is not the economic structure which directly determines the political action, but it is the interpretation of it and of the so-called laws which rule its development'.[31] In the *Prison Notebooks* this relation is represented by a series of antitheses, among which the following are the most important: economic moment/ethical-political moment; necessity/freedom; objective/subjective. The most important passage, in my opinion, is the following:[32]

The term 'catharsis' can be employed to indicate the passage from the purely economic (or egoistic-passional) to the ethico-political moment, that is the superior elaboration of the structure into superstructure in the minds of men. This also means the passage from 'objective' to 'subjective' and from 'necessity' to 'freedom'.

In each of these three antitheses, the term which indicates the primary and subordinating moment is always the second one. It should be observed that of the two superstructural moments, that of consent and that of force, one has a positive connotation while the other has a negative one, and in this antithesis it is always the first moment that is considered. The superstructure is the moment of catharsis, that is the moment in which necessity is resolved into liberty, understood, in a hegelian way as the awareness of necessity. This transformation comes about as a consequence of the ethico-political moment. Necessity, which is understood as the whole of material conditions which characterise a particular historical situation, is assimilated to the historical past, which is also considered as a part of the structure.[33] Both the historical past and the existing social relations constitute the objective conditions which are recognised by the active historical subject which Gramsci identifies in the collective will. It is only when the objective conditions have been recognised that the active subject becomes free and is able to transform reality. Furthermore, the very moment in which the material conditions are recognised, they become degraded to an instrument for whatever end is desired: 'Structure ceases to be an external force which crushes man, assimilates him to himself and makes him passive; and is transformed into a means of freedom, an instrument to create a new ethical-political form, and into a source of new initiatives'.[34] The relation between structure and superstructure, when considered from a naturalistic point of view, is interpreted as a relation of cause–effect, and it leads to historical fatalism.[35] But, when considered from the point of view of the active subject of history and of the collective will, it turns into a means-end relation. It is the active subject of history who recognises and pursues the end, and who operates within the superstructural phase using the structure itself as an instrument. Therefore, the structure is no longer the subordinating moment of history, but it becomes the subordinate one. The conceptual transition of the structure–superstructure antithesis can be schematically summarised in the following points: *the ethical-political* moment, being the moment of *freedom* understood as consciousness of *necessity* (that is of material conditions), dominates the *economic* moment through the recognition of *objectivity* by the active subject of history. It is through this recognition that the *material conditions* are resolved into an *instrument* of action and with this the *desired aim* is reached.

In the second place, Gramsci adds to the principal antithesis between structure and superstructure a secondary one, which develops within the sphere of the superstructure between the moment of civil society and the moment of the state.[36] Of these two terms, the first is always the positive moment and the second is always the negative one. This is clearly shown in the list of opposites where Gramsci comments on Guicciardini's statement that the state absolutely needs arms and religion:[37]

Guicciardini's formula can be translated by various other, less drastic formulae: force and consent; coercion and persuasion; state and church; political society and civil society; politics and morality (Croce's ethical–political history); law and freedom; order and self-discipline; or (with an implicit judgment of somewhat libertarian flavour) violence and fraud.

Gramsci certainly referred to Marx's conception of the state when, in one of his letters from prison (that of the 7 September 1931), he said, on the subject of his research on intellectuals, that:[38]

This research will also concern the concept of the State, which is usually thought of as political society – i.e., a dictatorship or some other coercive apparatus used to control the masses in conformity with a given type of production and economy – and not as a balance between political society and civil society.

It is true that in Marx's thought, the state – even though understood exclusively as a coercing force – does not occupy the superstructural moment on its own, and that this moment embraces the ideologies as well. But it is also true that in the above quoted extract from the preface to *A Contribution to the Critique of Political Economy* (which was well-known to Gramsci and to which he could have found a confirmation in the first part of the *German Ideology*, if ever he could have known it),[39] ideologies *always* come *after* institutions, as a secondary moment within the same secondary moment, because they are considered as posthumous and mystified–mystifying justifications of class domination. This thesis of Marx had had an authoritative interpretation, at least in Italian theoretical marxism, in the work of Labriola. Labriola had explained that the economic structure determines *in the first place and directly* the rules and the forms of subjection between men, that is the law (the ethics) and the state, and *in the second place and indirectly* the objects of imagination and thought, in the production of religion and of science.[40] In Gramsci, the relation between institutions and ideologies is inverted, even within the scheme of a reciprocal action: the ideologies become the primary moment of history, and the institutions the secondary one. Once the moment of civil society is considered as the moment in which the transition from necessity to freedom takes place, the ideologies, which have their historical roots in civil society, are no longer seen just as a posthumous justification of a power which has been formed historically by material conditions, but are seen as forces capable of creating a new history and of collaborating in the formation of a new power, rather than to justify a power which has already been established.

5 Historiographical and practico–political use of the concept of civil society

The really singular position that civil society has in Gramsci's conceptual system causes not one, but two inversions as regards the traditional interpretation of the thought of Marx and Engels: the first consists in the prevalence of the superstructure over the structure; whereas the second consists in the prevalence, within the superstructure itself, of the ideological moment over the institutional moment. As regards the simple dichotomy civil society-state, which has become the current conceptual scheme for the historical interpretations of Marx, Gramsci's scheme is more complex. In fact, it makes use – although the reader might not always realise it – of two dichotomies which only partially overlap: the one between necessity and freedom, which corresponds to the dichotomy between structure and superstructure; and the one between force and consent, which corresponds to the dichotomy between institutions and ideologies. In this more complex scheme, civil society is both the active moment (as opposed to passive) of the first dichotomy, and the positive moment (as opposed to negative) of the second dichotomy. It seems to me that this is the real core of his system.

This interpretation can be proved by observing the consequences that Gramsci draws from his frequent and varied use of the two dichotomies in his reflections from prison. I think that it would be useful and give a clearer understanding if we were to distinguish two different uses of the dichotomies: a merely historiographic one, where the dichotomies are used as canons of historical interpretation–explanation; and a more directly practico-political one, where the same dichotomies are used as criteria to distinguish what must be done from what must not be done.

In general, I think we can say that in Gramsci's historiographic use, the first dichotomy, the one between the economic moment and the ethico-political moment, serves to individuate the essential elements of the historical process; the second dichotomy, the one between the ethical and the political moment, serves to distinguish the phases of ascent and the phases of decline along the process of history, according to the prevalence of the positive moment or the negative one. In other words, moving from the central concept of Gramsci's thought, that of 'historical bloc' – by which Gramsci means the totality of a historical situation, which includes both the structural and the superstructural element – the first dichotomy serves to define and to delimit a determinate historical bloc, while the second one serves to distinguish a progressive historical bloc from a regressive one. Let me give some examples: the first dichotomy is the conceptual instrument with which Gramsci singles out the Moderate Party and not the Action Party as the movement which led to the unification of Italy (this is one of the fundamental themes of the notes on the Risorgimento); the second dichotomy explains the crisis of Italian society after the First World War, where the dominant class had ceased to be the leading class; a crisis which, because of the fracture between rulers and ruled, can be resolved 'only by the pure exercise of force'.[41] The major symptom of the crisis, that is of the dissolution of a historical bloc, consists in the fact that it is no longer able to attract the intellectuals, who are the protagonists of civil society: the traditional intellectuals preach morals and the untraditional ones build up utopias; in other words, neither have any link with reality.[42]

Under the practical aspect, that is of political action, the use which Gramsci makes of the first dichotomy constitutes the grounds for his continued polemics against economism, that is against the claim to resolve the historical problem which the oppressed class has to face, operating exclusively within the sphere of economic relations and of the antagonistic forces that they generate (the trade unions). The use of the second dichotomy is one of the greater, if not the greatest, source of reflection from the *Prison Notebooks*, where the stable conquest of power by the subordinate classes is always considered as a function of the transformation which must first be operated in civil society. The two directions towards which Gramsci's criticism moves can be explained only through a complete understanding of the idea that the two dichotomies continually overlap. His criticism is against taking into account the structure only, because this leads the working class towards a sterile and unresolved class struggle, and it is also against considering the negative moment of the superstructure only, because this too does not lead to a stable and resolute conquest. This battle on two fronts takes place once again in civil society. One front is concerned with the supersession of the material conditions which operate within the structure; the other presents a false resolution of these conditions (i.e. one which would be pure domination without consent). An improper use, or no use at all of one or other element of the dichotomy leads to two opposite errors in theory: the confusion between civil society and structure generates the error of trade unionism; the confusion between civil society and political society generates that of idolatry of the state.[43]

6 Political leadership and cultural leadership

While the first polemic against economism is connected to the theme of the *party*, the second one against dictatorship – which is not accompanied by a reform of civil society – brings forward the theme of *hegemony*. The analyses which have just been made put us in the best position to understand that the themes of the party and of hegemony occupy a central place in Gramsci's conception of society and of the political struggle. They are, in fact, two elements of civil society, opposed both to the structure inasmuch as it represents a superstructural moment, and to the negative moment of the force-state inasmuch as it represents a positive moment of the superstructure. Party and hegemony – along with the theme of the intellectuals which is connected to both – are the two major themes of the *Prison Notebooks* and, at the same time, they are the ones which allow a comparison between Gramsci and Lenin.

During the elaboration of the concept of hegemony, which Gramsci carried out in his reflections from prison, he frequently paid homage to Lenin, whom he saw as a theorist of hegemony.[44] But he does not realise generally that the term 'hegemony' does not belong to Lenin's usual language, while it is a characteristic of Stalin's who, if we can say so, has virtually sanctified it. Lenin preferred to speak of *leadership* (*rukovodstvo*) and of *leader* (*rukovoditel*). In one of his rare passages where the term *holder of hegemony* (*gegemon*) appears, it is clearly used as a synonym for leader.[45] The term 'hegemony' and the words that have derived from it, appeared quite late in Gramsci's language too, in the two works of 1926 (in *Letter to the Central Committee of the Soviet*

Communist Party and in the unfinished essay 'Alcuni temi della Questione Meridionale'),[46] that is in his last works before the *Prison Notebooks*. On the contrary, it is used very seldom in the works which are directly inspired by Lenin, that is in the ones from 1917 to 1924.[47]

However, what we are mostly interested in is the conceptual problem and not the linguistic one. From the conceptual point of view, the same term 'hegemony' no longer has in the *Prison Notebooks* (and in the *Letters*) the same meaning as in the two works of 1926. In these the term is used – and conforms to the prevailing official meaning of the Soviet texts – to indicate the alliance between the workers and the peasants, that is with the meaning of *political leadership*,[48] while in the former texts it also generally acquires the meaning of 'cultural leadership'.[49] It is with this change of meaning that the originality of Gramsci's thought lies. This change has been generally and erroneously neglected, so that now, in spite of the homage paid by Gramsci to Lenin as the theorist of hegemony in the present day debate over marxism, it is not Lenin who is the pre-eminent theorist of hegemony, but it is Gramsci himself. Schematically, the change took place through an inadvertent and yet important distinction between a narrower meaning, where hegemony means *political leadership* (this is the meaning one finds in Gramsci's works of 1926, and it also prevailed in the tradition of Soviet marxism), as well as a wider meaning, according to which it also means *cultural leadership*. I have said 'also', because in the *Prison Notebooks* the second meaning does not exclude, but it includes and integrates the first one. In the opening pages, which are dedicated to the modern Prince (heading the *Notes on Machiavelli*), Gramsci proposes two fundamental themes for studying the modern party: one on the formation of the 'collective will' (which is the theme of political leadership), and the other on 'moral and intellectual reform' (which is the theme of cultural leadership).[50] I insist on these two different meanings of hegemony because, in my opinion, a comparison between Lenin and the official leninism on the one side, and of Gramsci on the other, can lead to a profitable result only if we understand that the concept of hegemony, in the passage from one author to the other, has become wider, so that it includes the moment of cultural leadership. And it is also necessary to recognise that by 'cultural leadership' Gramsci means the introduction of a 'reform', in the *strong* meaning which this term has when it refers to a transformation of customs and culture, in opposition to the *weak* meaning which the term has acquired in the political use (the same as the difference between 'reformer' and 'reformist').

We could say that in Lenin the meaning of political leadership prevails, while in Gramsci the one of cultural leadership does; but we should add that this prevalence has two different aspects:

a   For Gramsci, the moment of force is instrumental, and therefore subordinated to the moment of hegemony, while for Lenin, in the works he wrote during the Revolution, dictatorship and hegemony proceed together, and anyhow the moment of force is the primary and decisive one.

b   For Gramsci, the conquest of hegemony precedes the conquest of power, while for Lenin the former accompanies the latter, or at least follows it.[51]

But, even though these two differences are important and based on their texts, they are not essential. They can both be explained by the great diversity of the historical situations in which the two theories were elaborated: Lenin's theory, during the struggle; and Gramsci's theory, during the retreat after the defeat. The essential difference, in my opinion, is another: it is not a difference of more or less, before or after, but it is a qualitative difference. I mean that the difference does not lie in the relation between the moments of hegemony and dictatorship, but – independently from the different conception of this relation, which can be explained historically – it lies in the *extension*, and therefore in the *function* of this concept in the two systems respectively. As regards the extension, Gramsci's hegemony includes, as we have seen, both the moment of political leadership and the moment of cultural leadership. Therefore it embraces, as its own bearers, not only the party, but all the other institutions of civil society (in Gramsci's meaning of the term) which have some connection with the elaboration and diffusion of culture.[52] As regards the function, hegemony not only aims at the formation of a collective will, capable of creating a new state apparatus and of transforming society, but it also aims at elaborating and propagating a new conception of the world. In short, Gramsci's theory of hegemony is not only connected to a theory of the party and of the state, or to a new conception of the party and of the state, and it not only aims at political education, but it also includes, in all its forms, the new and wider conception of civil society understood as a superstructural primary moment.

This clarifies the importance of civil society in Gramsci's system. The resolutive function which Gramsci sees in hegemony *vis-à-vis* mere domination, reveals the pre-eminent position of civil society, which is the mediating moment between the structure and the secondary superstructural moment. Hegemony is the moment of junction between determinate objective conditions and the actual domination of a leading group: this junction comes about *in* civil society. As we have seen, in Gramsci only, and not in Marx, this moment of junction has an autonomous space in the system, for it is placed in civil society. So, in the same way, in Gramsci only, and not in Lenin, the moment of hegemony, which is widened to occupy the autonomous space of civil society, acquires a new dimension and a broader content.[53]

7 Civil society and the end of the state

The end of the state is the last of Gramsci's themes where the concept of civil society has a primary role. The withering away of the state in a society without class divisions is a constant theme in the works which Lenin wrote during the Revolution and, at the same time, it is an ideal borderline of orthodox marxism. In the *Prison Notebooks*, which were written when the new state had already been solidly founded, this theme does appear, but only in a marginal way. In most of the rare passages which mention the end of the state, it is conceived as a 'reabsorption of political society in civil society'.[54] The society without a state, which Gramsci calls 'regulated society', comes from the enlarging of civil society and, therefore, of the moment of hegemony, until it eliminates all the space which is occupied by political society. The states which have existed until now are a dialectical unity of civil society and political society, of hegemony and dominion. The social class, which will succeed in making its own hegemony so universal that the moment of coercion will become superfluous, will have achieved the conditions for the transition to a regulated society. In one of the passages mentioned, 'regulated society' is even used as synonymous of civil society (and also of ethical state),[55] that is as civil society freed from political society. Even if it is only a matter of a different *stress* and not of *contrast*, we could say that in the theory of Marx and Engels, which was received and divulged by Lenin, the movement which leads to the withering away of the state is essentially a structural one (supersession of the antagonism between classes until the classes themselves are suppressed), while in Gramsci it is principally a superstructural process (enlargement of civil society until its universalisation). In Marx and Engels, the two terms of the antithesis are: society *with* classes/society *without* classes; in Gramsci they are civil society *with* political society/civil society *without* political society.

The fact (which I have often repeated) that civil society is a mediating element between the structure and the negative moment of the superstructure, brings an important consequence as regards the dialectical process which leads to the withering away of the state: where the terms are only two, that is civil society-state, the final moment (that is the society without classes) is the third term of the dialectical process i.e. the negation of the negation; where the terms are already three, the final moment is attained by a strengthening of the intermediate term. It is significant that Gramsci does not speak of *supersession* (or of suppression), but of *reabsorption*.

At the beginning of the nineteenth century, as I have already said, the first thoughts about the Industrial Revolution led to an inverted conception of the relation between society and state. It is a cliché that, in the works of the philosophers of natural law, the theory of the state is directly influenced by a pessimistic or optimistic conception of the state of nature; whoever considers the state of nature as evil, sees the state as an innovation; whoever considers the state of nature as fundamentally good, sees the state more as a restoration. This interpretative scheme can be applied to the political writers of the nineteenth century, who invert the relation society-state by seeing, concretely, the pre-state society in the industrial (bourgeois) society. There are some, like Saint-Simon, who move from an optimistic conception of industrial (bourgeois) society; and others like Marx, who move from a pessimistic conception. For the first group, the withering away of the state will be a natural and peaceful consequence of the development of the society of producers; for the others, an absolute reversal will be necessary, and society without the state will be the effect of a true and real qualitative change. Saint-Simon's scheme of evolution foresees the transition from a military society to an industrial one; Marx's scheme, on the other hand, foresees the transition from capitalistic (industrial) society to socialist (industrial) society.

Gramsci's scheme is undoubtedly the second one of the two mentioned above. But, in Gramsci's scheme, civil society comes in as a third term, after its identification, no longer with the state of nature, nor with industrial society, nor generally with pre-state society, but with the moment of hegemony, that is with one of the two moments of the superstructure (the moment of consent as opposed to the moment of force). This introduction seems to draw Gramsci's scheme nearer to the first of the two mentioned above, because in the first scheme the state disappears following the withering away of civil society, that is through a process which is of reabsorption rather than of supersession. Yet, the different meaning which Gramsci gives to civil society prevents us from interpreting it rather too simply. Against the tradition which expressed the old antithesis state of nature–civil state into the antithesis civil society–state, Gramsci expresses another great historical antithesis, that is the one between the church (broadly speaking, the modern church is the party) and the state, into the antithesis civil society–political society. So when Gramsci speaks of the absorption of political society in civil society, he does not intend to refer to the whole historical process, but only to the process which takes place within the superstructure, which, in turn and in the last instance is conditioned by changes in the structure. So, it is absorption of political society in civil society, but also at the same time, transformation of the economic structure, which is dialectically connected to the transformation of civil society.

In this case too, for an articulated interpretation of Gramsci's conceptual system, it is necessary to understand that 'civil society' is one of the two terms, not of only one antithesis, but of two different antitheses, which are interwoven and which only partially overlap. If we look at civil society as the close of the structure–superstructure antithesis, the end of the state is the overcoming of the superstructural moment in which civil society and political society are in reciprocal equilibrium; if we look at civil society as a moment of the superstructure, the end of the state is a reabsorption of political society in civil society. The apparent ambiguity is due to the real complexity of the historical bloc, as Gramsci conceived it. That is, it is due to the fact that civil society is a constitutive moment of two different processes, which happen interdependently but without overlapping: the process which moves from the structure to the superstructure, and the one which takes place within the superstructure itself. The new historical bloc will be the one where this ambiguity as well will be resolved by the elimination of dualism in the superstructural sphere. In Gramsci's thought, the end of the state consists precisely in this elimination.

Notes

This chapter was originally published in *Gramsci e la cultura contemporarea; Atti del Convegno Internazionale Qi Studi Gramsciani*, Editori Riuniti, Rome, 1968. It was translated into English by Carroll Mortera. The text which is now being published only differs from the one presented at the Congress of Cagliari in that it has had a few formal corrections. I particularly wanted to clarify or strengthen several sentences from which some critics, especially Jacques Texier, had understood that my intention was to see Gramsci as an anti-Marx. I stress, however, that the content has remained the same.

1 For more details refer to my essay, 'Hegel e il giusnaturalismo', *Rivista di filosofia*, 57, 1966, p. 397.

2 'Critique of Hegel's Philosophy of Right', *Marx and Engels, Collected Works*, Moscow, Progress Publishers, London, Lawrence & Wishart, 1975, vol. 3, p. 63.

3 See for example the chapter 'L'Organisateur' in *Oeuvres de Claude-Henri de Saint-Simon*, Paris, Editions Anthropos, 1966, vol. 2, pp. 17 ff. English translation in *The Political Thought of Saint-Simon*, ed. G. Ionescu, Oxford University Press, 1976, pp. 138–42.

4 Karl Marx, *Capital*, London, Lawrence & Wishart, 1970, vol. 1, p. 703.

5 *Manifesto of the Communist Party* in K. Marx and F. Engels, *Selected Works* (3 vols.), Moscow, Progress Publishers, 1973, vol. 1, pp. 110–11.

6 F. Engels, 'On the History of the Communist League', *Selected Works*, vol. 3, p. 178.

7 K. Marx, *Preface to a Contribution to the Critique of Political Economy*, *Selected Works*, vol. 1, p. 503.

8 In *Metaphysik der Sitten, bürgerliche Gesellschaft* stands for *status civilis*, that is for state in the traditional meaning of the word. English translation in I. Kant, *The Metaphysical Elements of Justice*, trans. J. Ladd, New York, Bobbs-Merrill, 1964, p. 75.

9 Ibid., pp. 75–7.

10 A. Smith, *An Inquiry into the Nature and Causes of the Wealth of Nations*, London, 1920, p. 249.

11 G. W. F. Hegel, *Hegel's Philosophy of Right*, trans. Knox, Oxford University Press, 1965, pp. 123–4.

12 'The perfected political state is by its nature the *species-life* of man in *opposition* to his material life. All the presuppositions of this egoistic life continue to exist *outside* the sphere of the state in *civil* society, but as qualities of civil society.' (K. Marx, *Early Writings*, trans. R. Livingstone and G. Benton, Harmondsworth, Penguin Books in association with *New Left Review*, 1975, p. 220.) See also 'Economic and Philosophical Manuscripts (1844)', *Early Writings*, p. 369, '*Society*, as it appears to the political economist, is *civil society*.'

13 F. Engels, 'Ludwig Feuerbach and the End of Classical German Philosophy', Marx and Engels, *Selected Works*, vol. 3, p. 369.

14 'The sum total of these relations of production constitutes the economic structure of society, the real foundation, on which rises a legal and political superstructure and to which correspond definite forms of social consciousness.' (*Selected Works*, vol. 1, p. 503.)

15 *The German Ideology*, *Selected Works*, vol. 1, pp. 38, 76.

16 For more detailed indications see my article 'Sulla nozione di societa civile', *De homine*, nos. 24–5, pp. 19–36.

17 In particular, to my knowledge, G. Tamburrano, *Antonio Gramsci*, Manduria, 1963, pp. 220, 223–4.

18 *Quarderni del Carcere*, ed. V. Gerratana, Turin, Einaudi, 1975, p. 9. English translation in *Selections from the Prison Notebooks*, ed. and trans. Hoare and Nowell Smith, London, Lawrence & Wishart, 1971, p. 12. There

are even some extracts where, as is well known, civil society is considered, broadly speaking, as a moment of the state. See also *Lettere dal Carcere*, Turin, Einaudi, 1948, p. 481; *Note sul Machiavelli*, Turin, Einaudi, 1966, p. 130, *Prison Notebooks*, p. 261; *Passato e Presente*, Turin, Einaudi, 1966, p. 72, *Prison Notebooks*, p. 239.

19 *Machiavelli*, p. 121, *Prison Notebooks*, p. 170 n.

20 *Passato e Presente*, p. 164.

21 *Machiavelli*, p. 128, *Prison Notebooks*, p. 259.

22 Ibid.

23 For a biased interpretation of Hegel, which has already been pointed out by Sichirollo, see the passage on the importance of the intellectuals in Hegel's philosophy (*Quarderni del Carcere*, pp. 46–7).

24 G. W. F. Hegel, *Philosophie des Rechts*, para. 308, English translation *Hegel's Philosophy of Right*, op. cit.

25 *Passato e Presente*, p. 164.

26 Hegel, op. cit., para. 255.

27 Ibid., para. 265.

28 Ibid., para. 256, which states that it is through the corporation that 'the transit from the sphere of civil society into the State takes place'.

29 K. Marx, *Preface to a Contribution to the Critique of Political Economy*, *Selected Works*, vol. 1, p. 503.

30 *Studi Gramsciani*, Editori Riuniti, Rome, Instituto Gramsci, 1958, pp. 280–1.

31 Ibid., p. 281.

32 *Il Materialismo Storico e la filosofia di Benedetto Cròce*, Turin, Einaudi, 1948, p. 40, *Prison Notebooks*, p. 366.

33 'The structure is actually the real past, because it is the testimony, the indisputable document of what has been done and continues to exist as a condition of the present and of what is to come' (*Il Materialismo Storico*, p. 222).

34 Ibid., p. 40, *Prison Notebooks*, p. 367.

35 For an interpretation and a criticism of fatalism, see *Passato e Presente*, p. 203.

36 Tamburrano has pointed out to me that, as regards the relation between civil society and state, it is more a matter of distinction, rather than of antithesis. This remark is a sharp one. But I am tempted to answer that it is a characteristic of dialectic thought to resolve the distinctions into antitheses, so that one can then proceed to overcome them.

37 *Machiavelli*, p. 121, *Prison Notebooks*, p. 170 n.

38 *Lettere dal Carcere*, Turin, Einaudi, 1948, p. 481.

39 'The ideas of the ruling class are in every epoch the ruling ideas: i.e., the class which is the ruling *material* force of society, is at the same time its ruling *intellectual* force.' Immediately afterwards he gives the example of the doctrine of the division of powers as an ideological reflection of a society where power is truly, that is in reality, divided (see *The German Ideology*, *Selected Works*, p. 47).

40 A. Labriola, *Saggi sul materialismo storico*, Rome, 1964, pp. 136–7.

41   *Passato e Presente*, p. 38, *Prison Notebooks*, p. 276.

42   *Machiavelli*, pp. 150–1.

43   *Passato e Presente*, p. 38, *Prison Notebooks*, p. 268.

44   *Il Materialismo Storico*, pp. 32, 39, 75, 189, 201, *Prison Notebooks*, pp. 55–6 n, 357, 365, 381–2, 381 n; *Lettere dal Carcere*, p. 616.

45   'As the only completely revolutionary class of contemporary society, it (the proletariat) must be the leader (*rukovoditolem*), the holder of hegemony (*gegemonon*) in the struggle of all workers and all the exploited against the oppressors and the exploiters. The proletariat is revolutionary inasmuch as it is conscious of this idea of hegemony (*etu ideu gegemonii*) and inasmuch as it puts it into practice' (11, p. 349). I am grateful for this and other linguistic information in the paragraph, to the kindness of Vittorio Strada. The only extract from Lenin which, to my knowledge, has been quoted by the scholars of Gramsci and where the term 'holder of hegemony' should appear is *Due tattiche della social-democrazia nella rivoluzione democratica*, in *Opere Scelte*, Rome, 1965, p. 319; see the Preface to *Duemila pagine di Gramsci*, ed. G. Perrata and N. Gallo, Milan, Il Saggiatore, 1964, vol. 1, p. 96, the term which Lenin actually used is not 'holder of hegemony' but 'leader' (*rukovoditel*). For Stalin's language, see *Dal colloquio con la prima delegazione operaia americana*, where, when enumerating the themes upon which Lenin had developed Marx's doctrine, he says: 'In the fourth place, the theme of the hegemony of the proletariat in the revolution, etc.' (J. U. Stalin, *Opere Scelte*, Moscow, 1947, vol. 1, p. 35).

46   *Deumila pagine di Gramsci*, vol. 1, p. 799 and pp. 824–5.

47   Ferrata recalls the article 'La Russia Potenza Mondiale', 14 August 1920, where we can find the expression 'hegemonic capitalism' (*L'Ordine Nuovo (1919–20)*, Turin, Einaudi, 1954, pp. 145–6). Ragionieri pointed out that the term 'hegemony' is used also in one of Gramsci's works written in 1924.

48   'It is the principle and practice of hegemony of the proletariat that are brought into question; the fundamental relations of the alliance between workers and peasants that are disturbed and placed in danger' (*Duemila pagine di Gramsci*, vol. 1, p. 824); 'The proletariat can become the leading and dominant class to the extent that it succeeds in creating a system of class alliances, etc.' (*Duemila pagine di Gramsci*, vol. 1, p. 799). English translations in Antonio Gramsci, *Selections from Political Writings 1921–26*, trans. and ed. Q. Hoare, London, Lawrence & Wishart, 1978, pp. 431, 443 respectively.

49   *Lettere dal Carcere*, p. 616: 'The moment of hegemony or of cultural leadership'. Also 'intellectual and moral leadership' (*Il Risorgimento*, Turin, Einaudi, 1949, p. 70, *Prison Notebooks*, p. 59).

50   *Machiavelli*, pp. 6–8.

51   I am referring to the well-known extracts where Gramsci explains the success of the politics of the moderates during the Risorgimento (*Il Risorgimento*, pp. 70–2). For Lenin, the passage from the *Political Report* at the Eleventh Congress of the Party (1922) is very important, the one where he complains about the inferiority of communist culture compared to that of the opponents: 'If the conquerors have a higher cultural level than that of

the defeated, they impose their own culture on them; if the contrary is true, the defeated ones impose their own culture onto the conquerors' (Lenin, *Collected Works*, vol. 33, London, Lawrence & Wishart, 1966, p. 262).

52 *Lettere dal Carcere*, p. 481, where he speaks of 'hegemony of a social group over the whole of national society, which is carried out through the so-called private organisms, such as the church, the trade unions, the schools, etc.'

53 We can find two decisive proofs of this new dimension and of this broader subject in the way in which Gramsci deals with the problem of the active subjects of hegemony (the intellectuals), and in the way he understands the content of the new hegemony (the theme of the 'nation-popular'). But because these are two very broad subjects, I will keep to these two observations only:

a) Gramsci is certainly inspired by Lenin in his reflections on the new intellectual, who must be identified with the leader of the party. Still, as regards the problem of the intellectuals, his thought cannot be understood if we miss its connection with the discussion on the function of the intellectuals, which began very dramatically in about the 1930s, during the years of the great political and economic crisis (Benda, 1927; Mannheim, 1929; Ortega, 1930), even if Gramsci's constant interlocutor is Benedetto Croce alone.

b) With the reflection on the 'nation-popular', a characteristic subject of the historiography of opposition of the anti-history of Italy, Gramsci connects the problem of social revolution with the problem of Italian revolution. The problem of the intellectual and moral reform accompanies the reflections on the history of Italy, from the Renaissance to the Risorgimento, and it has as its first interlocutors mainly Machiavelli, as regards the first problem, and Gioberti (the importance of whose research on Gramsci's sources has only been stressed by Asor Rosa) as regards the second problem.

54 *Machiavelli*, pp. 94, 130, *Prison Notebooks*, pp. 253, 261. In *Il Materialismo Storico*, p. 75, he only speaks of the 'disappearance of political society' and of the 'coming of a regulated society'. In a different way, in *Lettere dal Carcere*, p. 160, the party is described as 'the instrument for the transition from civil-political society to "regulated society"', because it absorbs both in order to overcome them.

55 *Machiavelli*, p. 132, *Prison Notebooks*, p. 263.

2 Gramsci, theoretician of the superstructures
On the concept of civil society [1]

Jacques Texier

Three fundamental requirements

It is usually maintained that Gramsci made an original contribution to the development of historical materialism through his elaboration of the concept of the relations between infrastructure and superstructures. Such a view would appear to be quite justified.

To be more specific about the direction in which development occurred, it can be added that the conception of the relations between infrastructure and superstructures enables Gramsci to form a concrete idea of historical dialectics through an analysis of the origin and development of superstructural historical activities in given infrastructural conditions up to the decisive moment of the 'overthrow of praxis' or revolution in social relations.[2]

The development of historical materialism, therefore, took the shape of an eradication of all residues of historical determinism and all economic determinism in particular.[3]

Gramsci attributed a precise meaning to Marx's phrase that it is men who make history in specific conditions, by analysing all the moments and phases of the process by which men become aware in the ideological sphere of the historical tasks they must solve and at the same time develop, in the sphere of organisation, the institutions which will enable them to pursue these struggles 'to the end'.[4]

It can therefore be said that Gramsci was the theoretician of the superstructures, in other words, of political science, of the relations between civil society and the state, of the struggle for hegemony and the seizure of power, of the moments of consensus and force, of the relations between ethico-political and economico-political history, and lastly, that he was the theoretician of the function of the 'intellectuals' and the political party.[5]

This development which engendered the theory of superstructures was achieved by Gramsci on the basis on the leninist theory and practice of revolution,[6] as well as his own experience as a revolutionary leader,[7] but also through a critical reflexion on the crocean theory that history is ethico-political.[8]

The concepts of *hegemony* and *civil society*, therefore, appear to be important moments in the theory of superstructures and it is essential to attempt a precise definition of their theoretical content which is not easy to grasp. But if we are to have some chance of succeeding, it would appear opportune to remind ourselves at the outset of certain elementary facts which are readily apparent in the *Prison Notebooks*.[9]

First, the concepts which denote a moment or an aspect of historical reality are inseparable from the concepts which designate the opposite but complementary aspect of that reality. In contrast to the state, understood in the narrow sense of government apparatus, stands *civil society*, in the sense of hegemonic apparatus of the ruling class; in contrast to the moment of force and dictatorship there is the moment of persuasion and consent, and in contrast to the moment of economico-political struggle which transforms the infrastructure, stands the moment of cultural or ethico-political expansion, etc. ... In the theory of superstructures, *civil society* cannot be separated from *political society* or *state* in the narrow sense: the state in its 'integral sense' is, says Gramsci, 'dictatorship plus hegemony'[10] or again, '... by "State" should be understood not only the apparatus of government, but also the "private" apparatus of "hegemony" or civil society.'[11]

On the other hand, the theory of superstructures is itself part of a wider complex which aims to take account of the living dialectic of history in its totality (the 'integral' and not the partial history, says Gramsci, of economic forces alone or the moment of ethico-political expansion alone). The theory of superstructures is, therefore, also a theory of the relations between infrastructure and superstructures, the theory of their unity, and of the 'historical bloc' which they comprise.[12]

Without the theory of the 'historical bloc' and the unity of economy and culture and culture and politics which results from it, the gramscian theory of superstructures would not be marxist. His 'historicism' would go no further than the historicism of Croce. If, in his attempt to think the moment of historical initiative, Gramsci had neglected the infrastructural conditions from which the tasks to be solved stem and on the basis of which the 'historical movement' arises, he would simply have been reiterating Croce, and his conception of historical dialectics would consequently have remained speculative or 'disembodied'.[13]

We shall, therefore, posit that if the authentic ideas of Gramsci on the concepts of *hegemony* and *civil society* are to be reinstated, a certain number of fundamental requirements which are inherent to his methodology must be respected.

The first consists in starting out from the basis of the concept of the 'historical bloc' to reach an understanding of the dialectical unity of infrastructure and superstructures, the passage from the economic to the political moment and therefore, the birth of the 'historical movement' and its development up to the moment of the 'overthrow of praxis' and ethico-political expansion. This principle holds good for all moments of superstructural activity and is, therefore, applicable to the concepts of hegemony and civil society. In gramscian terms we would say that it is theoretical nonsense to separate quality from quantity, liberty from necessity, ideology from economy.[14]

Failure to observe this requirement will result in upsetting 'the unity of the real process of history', and in separating in the most absurd way the 'form' and the 'content' of historical dialectics. It will, therefore, lead to a 'de-realisation' of the superstructures and the ideologies which would in fact be nothing more than 'appearances' or 'individual whims' if their economico-social content did not give them the 'organicity' which forms the basis of their 'historical rationality' and consequently of their efficacity.[15]

Failure to observe this fundamental requirement leads, according to the general direction prevailing, to two erroneous conceptions, namely 'economism' and 'ideologism': in the one case the mechanical causes are overestimated and in the other the voluntarist and individual element is given excessive importance.[16]

At the political level we shall, therefore, be faced either with the opportunism and political subordination which go hand in hand with 'economism' or with the inconsistent programmes and political adventurism which accompany 'ideologism', or else with an amalgam of the two tendencies.[17]

The second fundamental requirement concerns not the relation between superstructures and infrastructure within the 'historical bloc', but the relationship between the different aspects or moments of superstructural activity. This superstructural historical activity comprises two contrary aspects which may be designated by various terms: coercion and persuasion, force and consensus, domination and leadership, dictatorship and hegemony, political society and civil society, etc. ... There can be no doubt that it is possible, useful and necessary to establish this *distinction* between the two moments, aspects or phases of superstructural activity; the essential point is to agree on the nature of this *distinction*. Gramsci himself formulated what we shall pose as the second fundamental requirement by very clearly indicating that a 'methodological distinction' should not be confused with an 'organic distinction'. The *distinction* between the moment of force (political society) and of consensus (civil society) is a practical canon of research, an instrument permitting a better analysis of an organic reality in which it is radically impossible to separate these two moments. 'In actual reality', says Gramsci, 'civil society and state are identified.'[18]

In terms Gramsci borrows from Croce, the second fundamental requirement can also be formulated by posing the unity of the ethico-political and economico-political moments and by refusing to separate 'the ethico-political aspect of politics' (the theory of hegemony and consensus) from the 'aspect of force and the economy'.[19]

Though it is useful to distinguish between these two facets *of politics* (force and consensus) or of the state in the integral sense (political society and civil society) either in the sphere of historiographical research or in that of action, we should not lose sight of the fact that in reality Gramsci integrates them within the superior term of politics or the state *in the integral sense.*

It is perhaps useful to indicate that we come face to face with the cause of a good many misunderstandings in the dual meaning of such terms as *politics* or *state* in Gramsci's texts. There is the narrow everyday sense in which the state signifies apparatus of government and politics signifies violence and force and then there is the wider sense proposed by Gramsci in which the state is the apparatus of government *and* apparatus of hegemony and in which politics is coercion and persuasion. This is the source of the surprise occasioned by Gramsci's identification of politics and philosophy wherein one fears a pretext may be found for all the unfortunate instrumentalisations of the theory. Such fears are unjustified, yet it is no more legitimate to present a diametrical opposition between 'culture' (intellectual and moral activity) and 'politics' (relations between the forces present) as the essence of Gramsci's thought. For, in fact, what we find in Gramsci is an attempt to grasp the underlying unity of these two moments and thus to arrive at a new concept of politics. An opposition of such a kind, with the mistrust of all political organisations it implies, would lead to a curious way of conceiving the struggle of the working class to win hegemony in civil society. It would not be surprising if it led to the following formula: to win hegemony, the proletariat must transform the revolutionary party into a House of Culture!

Before going on to formulate the third general principle that we shall need for an examination of Gramsci's notion of civil society and of the interpretation of Gramsci's ideas that Professor Bobbio believes can be deduced from it, it will be useful to consider for a moment the organic relationship which exists between the two principles we have already pinpointed. Is it not possible to assert that the unity of force and consensus, of dictatorship and hegemony at the level of superstructural activities (second principle) flows from the unity of superstructures and infrastructure within the 'historical bloc' (first principle)? To show this, one need only recall that the social relations of production which comprise the infrastructure imply a confrontation between fundamental classes whose interests are opposed and that, as a result of the superstructural activities which take place in the historical movement to resolve the contradictions of the social mode of material production, can only represent an element of radical struggle to conquer the adversary (the moment of dictatorship). This will be the case so long as humanity remains embedded in its prehistory.

As for our third principle, it can be introduced by recalling that the *unity* of superstructures and infrastructure can only be a *process* in which the sole agent is human activity in its various forms. This process is historical dialectics considered as a whole and which Gramsci describes in philosophical terms as the passage from the objective to the subjective, from quantity to quality, from necessity to liberty. It results, periodically, in an 'overthrow of praxis' and in a novel historical synthesis when the development of social productive forces and the political initiative of men have created all the conditions which in fact make the 'possible' real. The infrastructure, objective base and point of departure of men's political initiative, and the origin of the contradictions which have to be resolved, is itself the result, at a given historical moment, of the creativity of social work, but its 'efficacity' would be non-existent without the elaboration that these 'mechanical' forces experienced at the levels of ideology and organisation.[20]

This conception of historical dialectics throws a new light on the thesis of the unity of infrastructure and superstructure which destroys all epiphenomenalist reduction and all voluntarist inflation of ideology. It shows us on what conditions the superstructural moments of force and persuasion base their historical validity and rationality in order to become effective.

On the part of the historian or philosopher who deals with it, it demands an aptitude for dialectical thought which, clearly, is not a natural gift. It introduces into knowledge a new principle of intelligibility which Hegel expressed in his way, but which Marx conceptualises in the *Theses on Feuerbach*. It can be summarised, as Gramsci frequently does, by saying that the 'person educated' educates the 'educator' or that the 'educator' needs 'to be educated'.

Basically, it needs to be understood that man is the product of the history which he produces as much by his work as by his political initiative, or, in marxist language, that the change in circumstances and the change in human activity 'coincide' and that this coincidence is a self-change which can only be rationally understood as revolutionary practice.[21]

We shall have to consider the question of whether the theoretical deductions of Professor Bobbio as regards Gramsci's conception of civil society conform at all to this third principle.

The relation between infrastructure and superstructures in Marx and Gramsci

It is Professor Bobbio's aim to highlight the originality of Gramsci's conception of history and society, starting from an analysis of the notion of 'Civil Society' in the *Prison Notebooks*. The central question is, therefore, the relations between Gramsci and Marx and it can be summed up simply by asking whether Gramsci is a marxist or else whether his 'originality' does not lie, on the contrary, in what separates him from Marx.

It is, therefore, not simply a matter of terminology but of basic principles. The fact, for instance, that Gramsci does not use the expression 'civil society' in the same way as Marx does is not decisive in itself. What has to be discovered is whether this difference in usage reveals a substantial difference.[22] We shall see in fact that, according to Bobbio, the difference in terminology does indeed betoken a substantial difference between Marx and Gramsci.

It is in fact possible, according to him, to identify two 'inversions' in Gramsci with respect to the usual reading of Marx and Engels:[23] '... the first consists in the prevalence of the superstructure over the structure;

whereas the second consists in the prevalence, within the superstructure itself, of the ideological moment over the institutional moment' (Bobbio p. 36). We shall deal with the 'second inversion' in the third part of this article in which we shall examine Gramsci's notion of 'Civil Society'. Let us now look at the first 'inversion', which has a bearing upon the relation between infrastructure and superstructures.

'Of the two moments ... in Marx the former is the primary subordinating one, while the latter is the secondary and subordinate one. ... In Gramsci, it is precisely the opposite' (ibid., p. 33). For Gramsci, in fact – and this is what would appear to constitute its theoretical originality – the infrastructure, from being originally a conditioning moment of history, is transformed into a conditioned moment (ibid., p. 34). In order to express his idea of Gramsci's 'inversion' of infrastructure–superstructure relations and the privileged status of the latter with respect to the former ('*privilegiamento della sovrastruttura rispetto alla struttura*'), Professor Bobbio resorts to a series of opposites: 'primary'/'secondary', 'conditioning'/'conditioned', '*subordinante*'/ '*subordinato*', whose precise meaning is indicated by the adjectives 'active' and 'positive'. This is the case in the following assertion: 'In Marx this active and positive moment is a structural moment; in Gramsci it is superstructural' (ibid., p. 31).

One could, of course, ask what exactly these quotations *mean*. Is this really an argument on Gramsci's conception of history or is it rather a way of saying – in an inadequate way – that Marx devoted the essential portion of his intellectual power to studying the economico-social formation and Gramsci his powers to the study of superstructural formations? To which it might be added that by elaborating his theory of superstructures Gramsci elucidated their active character in historical dialectics more than all the marxists who preceded him.

In fact this hypothesis will have to be abandoned. The author links together his propositions with great logical rigour; it is theses which are at issue here and not divergences in terminology. And the various theses are perfectly coherent. Take for instance the assertion that in Gramsci a theoretical condition of the active character of the superstructures is an inversion of the relation established by Marx between infrastructure and superstructures, and supposes a mechanistic interpretation of Marx himself. It clearly calls for a certain 'boldness' to put forward an interpretation of this kind nowadays. Knowledge of marxism has progressed. Yet it is this kind of reading which the author – very 'logically' – suggests. According to him the concept of 'reflection' and ideological 'justification' of what is, represents the sole content that Marx and the marxist tradition would ascribe to the notion of superstructure.[24]

The thesis becomes clear when, having stated, with the text in front of him, that for Gramsci 'civil society' is not, as it is for Marx, the complex of relations of production and exchange, but a moment of the superstructural activities, the author poses the question: 'Does this displacement of meaning not ... immediately raise the question whether [Gramsci] situated "the real home", "the real theatre of all history" elsewhere?'[25]

The author replies simply that Gramsci 'inverted' the fundamental thesis of historical materialism, since the expression Marx sometimes uses to designate the economic base of a society, in Gramsci's case serves to designate a moment in the superstructure. In Marx the infrastructure is the 'primary', 'conditioning', 'positive', 'active' moment and therefore the 'real home' of history; in Gramsci it is not even the complex of the superstructures, but, within the latter − 'the whole of ideologico-cultural relations', 'the whole of spiritual and intellectual life' (ibid., p. 31), which is the 'primary', 'conditioning', 'positive', ¦active' moment and thus the 'real home' of all history.[26]

Before proceeding to analyse the validity of this interpretation of Gramsci, it would seem instructive to deduce from it a certain number of 'logical' consequences which will provide food for thought for no small number of Gramsci's readers. First, this thesis implies a reading of the marxism of Marx which is nothing but a reduction of Marx to economism and mechanicism.

But it so happens that this 'economistic' interpretation of marxism is precisely the reading Croce makes, and Gramsci takes him severely to task on account of the irresponsibility and lack of scientific objectivity this attitude exhibits; he also denounces its practical origin. Logically it should, therefore, be maintained that it is Croce's view of marxism not Gramsci's which is correct and that it is the young Gramsci who is still 'tendentially crocean' and the author of *The Revolution against 'Capital'* who is the true Gramsci.[27]

Similarly, it would have to be maintained that Gramsci − contrary to what he himself supposed − is not the continuer of Marx and Lenin and the critic of the crocean concept of history as ethico-political, but the unconscious critic of Marx and the brilliant disciple of Croce. In other words, his view of his own relationship to Marx and Croce was completely mistaken. And in conclusion, that his theoretical originality must be understood on the basis of his points of rupture with historical materialism.

In fact there is nothing strange about the idea that a theoretician should have *produced* original knowledge and theoretical principles which do not correspond to his own idea of them. But even then an examination of the texts would have to justify the hypothesis. In Gramsci's case the proof seems difficult.

The formal repudiation of Professor Bobbio's theses should begin with a critique of the mechanistic interpretation of Marx which, implicitly and explicitly, they contain. But it so happens that the best refutation of such an interpretation is to be found in the *Prison Notebooks* themselves. Gramsci's notes on historical materialism are, in fact, a running commentary on Marx's texts and this is particularly the case of the *Preface* of 1859 and the *Contribution*.

It would not be difficult to assemble several dozen of Gramsci's texts in a small volume in which the content of the *Preface* is minutely analysed and in which Gramsci's essential propositions are transformed into methodological criteria of interpretation. An anthology of this kind would make it possible to show that Gramsci's conception of historical dialectics bases itself directly on two passages from the *Preface*.

The first of these, which defines the infrastructural conditions of the 'historical movement' is summarised by Gramsci as follows: 'Evolution must proceed within the limits of two principles':

First principle: that a society should not set itself any task for which necessary and sufficient conditions do not already exist, or conditions which are at least in the process of appearing and developing.

Second principle: that no society can wither away and be replaced until it has developed all the forms of life which are implicit in its relations.[28]

The second passage from the *Preface* of 1859 on which Gramsci bases himself is the one in which Marx speaks of 'juridical, political, religious, artistic or philosophical forms', 'in short, ideological forms in which men become aware of this conflict [the conflict of productive forces and relations of production] and pursue it to its conclusion'.[29]

Gramsci comments on this by stating that to understand the relation between infrastructure and superstructures it is necessary to recall[30]

> Engels' assertion that economy is only in the final analysis the
> driving force of history ... which assertion should be directly linked
> with the passage from the Preface to the *Critique of Political Economy*

in which it is stated that it is on the terrain of ideologies that men become aware of the conflicts which occur in the economic sphere.

Speaking elsewhere of 'historically organic ideologies ... which are necessary to a given structure', he specifies that 'To the extent that they are historically necessary, they have a validity which is "psychological"; they "organize" human masses, create the terrain on which men move, acquire consciousness of their position, struggle, etc. ...'.[31]

It does not, therefore, seem possible, in our view, to go along with the author's interpretation of the 1859 *Preface*. Similarly, it seems erroneous to assert that in *The German Ideology* Marx and Engels view ideology as a 'reflection' which 'always comes after' to justify what already exists. This attributes scant importance to the theory of communist revolution the text contains. Without communist awareness ('conscience'), there can be no communist revolution, Marx explains. This communist awareness is 'the awareness of the necessity for a radical revolution' and 'a massive transformation of men shows itself to be necessary for the creation of communist awareness on a mass scale and also to carry the thing itself through.'[32] One might say of communist awareness that 'it is not found only in *pure theory* but also in *practical awareness*, in other words in awareness which is self-liberating and which has come into conflict with the existing mode of production, *which does not simply form religions and philosophies, but states also'*.[33]

It is evident that this is the thesis Marx upholds in the 1859 *Preface* when he maintains that it is on the terrain of ideology that men become aware of economic conflicts and that they 'pursue them to their conclusion'. It can quite legitimately be maintained that Gramsci developed the theory of the role of superstructures, but not that he introduces it into the marxist tradition and even less so that he breaks with it on this point. To oppose Gramsci and Marx in respect of the 'active' and 'positive' character of the superstructures is, therefore, pointless.

It might be added that it seems incorrect, in our view, to assert as does Bobbio, that for Marx social relations of production are the 'active' and 'positive' moment of the historical process. For him they are the basis of the historical movement, the centre and the scene of all history, not *the* motive principle. For Marx, in fact, 'the form of social relations' – the infrastructure – results from the development of the productive force of social work and reciprocally conditions this development positively or negatively as the case may be. It is, therefore, conditioned and conditioning and in a position of *general* dependence with regard to the development of productive forces. It is the place where social and political contradictions arise, the historical struggles by means of which men strive to resolve the conflict between the social relations of production and the productive forces.

Let us now examine Bobbio's thesis in the light of the principles formulated in the first part of this article and more specifically in the combined light of the first and third principles. The first forbids the separation of infrastructure and superstructures whose organic unity is theoretically contained in the concept of the 'historical bloc'. The third is the very principle of dialectics itself, the principle which poses the re-education of the educator by the person educated, the principle, then, which enables us to grasp the *unity* of the historical bloc as a creative *process* wherein the superstructural activities of men ultimately transform the infrastructure.

If this is really so, is there any meaning in saying that Gramsci gives pre-eminence to the superstructures as against the infrastructure? Isn't this assertion contrary to the concept of the historical bloc in which, Gramsci specifically tells us,[34]

material forces are the content and ideologies the form, though this distinction between form and content has purely 'didactic' value, since the material forces would be inconceivable historically without form and the ideologies would be individual fancies without the material forces.

Does this mean to say that Gramsci thinks the moment of historical initiative, which he calls the 'passage from economy to general history'[35] or the birth of the historical movement, on the basis of the infrastructure? Must one deduce from this that for him it is consequently not the infrastructure which is 'primary' or 'conditioning'? Is this the dialectical 'nexus' of liberty and necessity? Must necessity cease to exist for there to be liberty? In order to maintain that it is men who make their own history is it necessary to reject the idea that the conditions in which they make history are imposed upon them and condition all their acts and all their thoughts? If the question is posed in such a way then we are departing from the principle of dialectical intelligibility which we posited as our third general principle.

In fact, for Gramsci, the infrastructure is indeed 'primary' and 'conditioning' ('*subordinante*') and in this he is a marxist. But this in no way means that the superstructures are not active at all times, nor even that men's superstructural activity does not become 'determinant' (*'subordinante'*) in relation to the infrastructure when a period of 'social revolution' commences that is, when relations of production have become irrational.[36]

The texts in the *Prison Notebooks* in which Gramsci discusses the crocean concept of history enable us to establish beyond any possible doubt that this is indeed Gramsci's view. To undertake a serious criticism of Croce is no small matter. On the one hand Gramsci has to refute Croce's thesis that marxism transforms the infrastructure into a metaphysical force which controls men's activity from without, like an 'unknown God'. And on the other hand he must undertake a critique of the *unrealistic* character of Croce's concept of history as ethico-political, while proving that it formulates methodological requirements which marxism can integrate and found.

Rejecting the economistic and metaphysical caricature of the 'structure − Unknown God', Gramsci writes:[37]

Is structure therefore viewed as something immovable and absolute and not, on the contrary, as reality itself in motion and doesn't the assertion put forward in the *Theses on Feuerbach* that 'the educator must be educated' pose a necessary relation of active reaction by man on the structure, which is an affirmation of the unity of the process of reality?

Marxism, writes Gramsci, does not detach the superstructures from the structure and upset the unity of historical reality by transforming the economy into a metaphysical cause. Does this mean that by posing the unity of the different moments of the historical process of becoming and highlighting the importance of the superstructural moment, Gramsci is led to a rejection of the marxist thesis of the determinant character of the economy? And is it necessary, for a recognition of the place and importance of the ethico-political moment in the 'historical movement', to reject the idea of tracing the history of the 'economico-political moment'? In fact Croce distinguishes a phase of 'violence, misery, and bitter struggle whose ethico-political history [in the restricted sense in which he understands it] is impossible to trace, and a phase of 'cultural expansion which would be "true history" '.

So in his historical works on Italy and Europe, he disregards the 'moments of force, struggle and misery' and begins his account only in 1870 for Italy and 1815 for Europe. Marx's superiority resides in the fact that in his work one finds 'not only the aspect of force and economy but also, in embryonic form, the ethico-political aspect of politics, that is to say, the theory of hegemony and consent'.

The necessary development of political science requires that politics be thought in an *integral* way and therefore that a theory of superstructures be elaborated which will resolve the question of the relations which exist between 'the economico-political moment and other historical activities'. The crocean solution of this problem remains purely speculative. The relation of implication of the 'distincts' in the unity of the mind, posed by Croce, is at the most a suggestion for the real solution which must be produced by a realistic historicism. The point of departure must be the concept of the 'historical bloc' Gramsci stipulates. What does this mean? To think the unity of the distinct aspects or moments of superstructural activity, the moment of force and consent, of dictatorship and hegemony and the economico-political and ethico-political moment one must begin from the basis of the organic unity of the superstructures and infrastructure in the historical bloc and recognise the ultimately determinant character of economic conditions. Furthermore, since Croce refrains from studying the economico-political moment in his history of Europe and Italy, it can be maintained, says Gramsci, that he implicitly recognises *the primacy of the economic fact*, in other words, of the structure as a point of reference and dialectical impulse for the superstructures.[38]

One wonders how Bobbio can reconcile his thesis of the 'inversion' of infra-superstructure relations in Gramsci with his affirmation of the 'primacy of the economic fact', and the conclusion one draws is that it is not necessary to break with the fundamental principles of historical materialism in order to be the theoretician of the creativity of men, as Gramsci is. This is a crucial point, given the theoretical debates which have come to light recently. Any rupture or 'inversion' of this order would destroy Gramsci's thesis of 'the man who walks on his legs' and take us back to the idea of 'the man who walks on his head' and therefore to a disembodied conception of creativity and historical dialectics.

Man's creativity, furthermore, should not be understood merely on the 'political' or superstructural level. It occurs – and should first of all be thought – in the development of the productive forces of social work. This is the point of departure for Gramsci and marxism.[39]

We thus encounter once again with the concrete embedding of historical dialectics in production and with a concept of man which could withstand many a criticism, namely what: 'man is to be conceived as an historical bloc of purely individual and subjective elements and of mass and objective or material elements with which the individual is in an active relationship.'[40]

Gramsci's view of civil society

Let us now turn to the second basic thesis put forward by Bobbio and his analysis of Gramsci's concept of 'Civil Society'.

We have seen that, according to him, Gramsci's concept of history is characterised by two inversions as against the usual reading of Marx and Engels. We have examined the first, now let us look at the second. It consists in 'the prevalence, within the superstructure itself, of the ideological over the institutional moment' (Bobbio, p. 36).

As with the relations between infrastructure and superstructures, it is the 'primary' and 'secondary' moments which we are seeking to discover. In Gramsci, the author tells us, 'ideologies become the primary moment of history and institutions the secondary one' (ibid., p. 36). In fact, what is at issue here is the problem of the relations between political society and civil society. The author points out in fact that the dichotomy 'force and consent' corresponds to the 'dichotomy between institution and ideology' (ibid., p. 36). We therefore arrive at a further formulation of the author's second thesis:

> Gramsci adds to the principle antithesis between structure and superstructure a secondary one, which develops within the sphere of the superstructure between the moment of civil society and the moment of the State. Of these two terms the first is always the positive moment and the second is always the negative one (ibid., p. 35).

Or, to use another pair of adjectives we have already encountered, it can be said that, according to Gramsci, civil society must be considered 'as superstructural primary moment' and political society as 'secondary superstructural moment' (ibid., p. 35). Some examples will allow us to grasp the full meaning of the two pairs of adjectives used.

Why is the moment of force only the secondary moment in Gramsci? This, the author tells us, is because in the *Prison Notebooks* 'the stable conquest of power by the subordinate classes is always considered as a function of the transformation which must *first* be operated in Civil Society' (ibid., p. 37). And how is one to understand that the 'secondary' moment of force and dictatorship is 'always' the negative moment? The answer to this lies in learning that one can 'distinguish the phases of ascent and the phases of decline along the process of history, according to the prevalence of the positive or the negative one (ibid., p. 37). This raises the problem of revolution, the passage to socialism and also Gramsci's relation to Lenin: 'For Gramsci, the conquest of hegemony precedes the conquest of power; while for Lenin, the former accompanies the latter or even follows it' (ibid., p. 40). The question posed by the analysis of Gramsci's concept of 'civil society' is, therefore, whether, as Bobbio constantly asserts, Gramsci is a continuation of Lenin in the domain of political science or whether he is not rather a theorist of 'democratic socialism'.

Finally let us see what, according to the author, is the content of Gramsci's concept of 'civil society'. He determines it by opposing it to the infrastructural content Marx gives this expression:[41] 'Paraphrasing the passage from Marx quoted above, one could say that civil society comprises for Gramsci not "the complex of material relations", but rather the whole of ideologico-cultural relations, not the "complex of commercial and industrial life", but rather the whole of spiritual and intellectual life' (ibid., p. 31).

From this definition of the concept, Bobbio goes on to assert that it is 'the keystone' of Gramsci's conceptual system. And this assertion, when it is linked to the thesis of Gramsci's two 'inversions' – the primary and conditioning character of the superstructures and the primary and positive power of civil society within the superstructures – takes on a very precise philosophical and political meaning. It makes Gramsci into a disciple of the hegelian left and a theoretician of an 'ideological' concept of history, for whom it is the intellectuals, the protagonists of 'civil society', who are the motive force of history in the making. There is no need to undertake a critique of such a conception for it is to be found in *The German Ideology*, written in 1845–46, although a chapter on 'Italian ideology' would have to be added. It will be our task to show that it is a quite different conception which is found in the *Prison Notebooks*.

To begin with, it can be said that Gramsci's concept of 'civil society' is part of his theory of superstructures which we have interpreted in quite a different way from Bobbio. Our approach will also, therefore, be quite different from his. His aim was, in fact, to start with the 'central' concept of 'civil society' in order to show that its existence in Gramsci signified a reversal of the marxist conception of relations between infrastructure and superstructures. It has been our intention to establish, by close examination of the texts, that this was by no means the case and we have maintained that on the contrary, the unity of infrastructure and superstructures in the 'historical bloc' must be the point of departure for a correct analysis of Gramsci's concept of 'civil society' (first fundamental requirement).

On the other hand, the concept of 'civil society' is an aspect of a theory of the state taken in its *integral* sense which includes not only the governmental apparatus of coercion (or political society) but also the hegemonic apparatus (or civil society), by means of which the class in power rules society as a whole with its consent (second fundamental requirement). The state, in the limited sense of governmental apparatus, represents only one aspect of superstructural activities; the integral state in Gramsci's sense (political and civil society) incorporates the whole body of superstructural activities.[42]

This way of posing the problem makes it possible to grasp immediately *the historical class character* of all superstructural activities and, in particular, intellectual and moral activities whose relation to political government is frequently very indirect. This is the sense of Gramsci's theory of the intellectuals. The distinction of two levels within the superstructure – political society and civil society – enables Gramsci to think the more or less indirect tie which links the intellectuals to the fundamental social groups and thus to the sphere of production.[43]

The class character of superstructural activities seems, in our view, to be the first point that should be highlighted, for it brings one back to the existence of fundamental social groups and thus to their function in the sphere of production, and leads one to think the content and function of the superstructural activities in conjunction with the general direction given to economic activity by a class. It is the new direction ('orientation') of economic activity, rendered possible by the overthrow of earlier social relations of production and by the establishment of new relations, which the social class coming to power must be able to impose and make acceptable. 'The hegemonic apparatus' comprising 'private' organisms, like the 'governmental apparatus' run by 'functionaries', are each a class 'apparatus' by which a new social group, that undertakes to give 'the productive apparatus' a new direction, rules and dominates society as a whole.

It is because all superstructural activities have a class character or because the state, taken as an integral whole is in an organic relationship with the sphere of the economy, that the distinct moments of the superstructure must not be separated.

It is a 'theoretical error', Gramsci asserts, to transform this 'methodological distinction' into an 'organic distinction'; 'in actual reality civil society and state are identified.'[44]

This identification clearly does not mean that the state is reduced to political society alone. It serves in effect to pinpoint the economico-political or class character of all superstructural activities and to indicate that it is impossible to oppose them *absolutely* or dissociate them. From this point of view – that of the identity of opposites – some of Gramsci's formulae are valuable precisely because they stress the unity of consensus and dictatorship. This is the case with the definition of the integral state as follows: 'State = political society + civil society, in other words, hegemony protected by the armour of coercion.'[45]

It is the 'identity' of political society and civil society, that is, the economico-political character of all superstructural activities, that we shall atempt to establish by analysing the complex content of Gramsci's concept of hegemony.

A social group exercises its hegemony over subordinate social groups which accept its rule so long as it exercises its dictatorship over the hostile social groups which reject it. In what conditions and in what forms is this hegemony achieved? For a social group to obtain the consent of other subordinate social groups, the group must first of all be an essential force in society, in other words it must, basically, occupy a place and fulfil a decisive function in the sphere of production.[46] We thus encounter once again the priority of the economic factor. The new social group must be revolutionary in economic terms, that is, it must be capable of transforming the economic base and establishing such production relations as will permit the new development of productive forces. Its political hegemony will therefore have an economic base and content.[47]

What does this hegemony mean in economic terms? That the new social class has found and is able to maintain a just equilibrium between its own fundamental interests, which must prevail, and those of secondary social groups which must not be sacrificed.[48] Thus economic 'compromise' or economic alliance is the condition for the creation of a system of alliances which, in political terms, unites the 'subordinate' groups and the 'dominant' group under the rule of the latter. This political hegemony will, furthermore, have to be exercised on the intellectual and moral plane, which presupposes that the new social group holds a conception of the world which will be able to impose its 'superiority' and engender a new type of civilisation. These three aspects of hegemony, the political, the economic and the ideological, are perceived in their unity when Gramsci describes the moment of the 'struggle for hegemony' which precedes the foundation of a new type of state.

This decisive moment occurs when a social class in the course of its superstructural development[49]

> becomes aware that one's own corporate interests in their present and future development, transcend the corporate limits of the purely economic class, and can and must become the interests of other subordinate groups too. This is the most purely political phase, and marks the decisive passage from the structure to the sphere of the complex superstructures: it is the phase in which previously germinated ideologies become 'party', come into confrontation and conflict, until only one of them, or at least a single combination of them, tends to prevail, to gain the upper hand, to propagate itself throughout society – bringing about not only a unison of economic and political aims, but also intellectual and moral unity, posing all the questions around which the struggle rages not on a corporate but on a 'universal' plane, and thus creating the hegemony of a fundamental social group over a series of subordinate groups.

The objective of this 'struggle for hegemony' during the period which precedes accession to power, is on the one hand to isolate the dominant class politically and ideologically by securing the alliance of other groups, and on the other hand to secure the 'control' of the new political bloc thereby constituted. The struggle takes place in 'Civil Society', Gramsci states, through the 'private' organisms of which the most important are the political parties and the unions, but which also reveal a multitude of ideologico-cultural forms (newspapers, reviews, literature, churches, and associations of all kinds) which will have to be listed. The solidity of a state (apparatus of government) depends, in fact, on the consistency of the 'civil society' which serves as its basis.[50]

If this is, indeed, the content of the concept of hegemony, it would seem quite impossible, as we maintained, to separate the concepts of civil and political society on the one hand, and the concept of infrastructure on the other. The form of the superstructural activities, of which 'civil society' is the place, may well be ideological, but their content is economic and social and the struggle to win hegemony is a struggle for power. This is why civil and political society are identified in actual reality.

It would seem that even this preliminary analysis permits us to conclude that the opposition established by Bobbio between the so-called 'primary' character of the ideologies and civil society and the 'secondary' character of the institutions and Political Society, is not very opportune. To begin with, it is quite clear that ideological creation is necessary to political society, just as the creation of institutions is vital in civil society: parties, unions, churches and schools are 'organisms' or 'associations', or institutions in other words and the juridical and governmental apparatus of the 'state-force' does not function without intellectual activity. It is hard to see how and why the 'dichotomy institution/ ideology' would correspond to the 'dichotomy political society/civil society'. We can therefore abandon this 'correspondence' and restrict ourselves to examining the relations between the moment of force and the moment of consensus in Gramsci's conception of historical dialectics.

Can it be asserted, as Bobbio has done, that for Gramsci the moment of ethico-political hegemony, of cultural rule, is the primary moment of historical development? It is plain to see what, in the *Prison Notebooks*, leads Bobbio to such a conclusion, namely certain texts to which reference has already been made,[51] in which Gramsci examines the specific conditions for communist revolution in the 'socially' developed Western countries. The existence in such countries of a compact 'civil society' which serves as a base for the 'state-government' leads him to propose a new revolutionary strategy which corresponds, in the art of politics, to the passage from the war of movement to the war of position in military art. Since there is every chance that a revolutionary offensive aiming to overthrow the governmental apparatus will fail and come to grief on the 'trenches' and 'fortifications' of civil society, the working class must gain control of 'civil society' before the offensive and exercise its hegemony over it:[52]

> A social group can, and indeed must, already exercise 'leadership'
> before winning governmental power (this indeed is one of the
> principal conditions for the winning of such power); it subsequently
> becomes dominant when it exercises power, but even if it holds it
> firmly in its grasp, it must continue to 'lead' as well.

The question is whether these texts justify the attribution to Gramsci of *a conception of history* which 'inverts' the marxist relation between infrastructure and superstructures and which 'gives pre-eminence', in the realm of the superstructures, to the ideologico-cultural moment. The first point has already been satisfactorily explained. As for the second point, the matter in question is the very nature of the struggle for hegemony. We have shown in fact that if the struggle assumes an ideologico-cultural form, by virtue of the fact that it takes place in the realm of the superstructures, it is economico-political in content. The crucial question is not when to resort to 'violence' – or even whether violence will be resorted to or not – but it is to understand that the winning of hegemony is a social *struggle* which aims to transform the *relation of forces* in a given situation. An historico-political bloc has to be dismantled and a new one constructed so as to permit the transformation of the relations of production. This is why it can truly be said that dictatorship and hegemony are identified. The modalities differ, but the essence is the same, for this is a social struggle. If we say that Gramsci is marxist or leninist we are not chanting a kind of litany but reinstating the very essence of Gramsci's conception of history and politics.

We would also contest the purely analytical approach Professor Bobbio adopts when faced with the task of determining the content of civil society. He achieves this in fact by a dual radical opposition. The relations and activities of civil society *are not* synonymous with those of the economic structure and they *are not* synonymous with those of political society.

There is nothing questionable about this negative determination as such; it is characteristic of the activity of analytical understanding and produces 'distinctions' that dialectical reason can perfectly well subject to the process of dialectics ('dialectiser') by grasping their relativity and thinking their unity and their identification in a living and developing totality. It is unfortunate that this integrating task of dialectical reason which perceives links and discerns processes is not part of the author's approach.

Thus, since civil society in Gramsci does not belong to the moment of the infrastructure as is the case in Marx, but to the moment of the superstructure, its content is defined by stating that it comprises 'not "the complex of material relations", but rather the whole of ideologico-cultural relations, not the "complex of commercial and industrial life," but the whole of spiritual and intellectual life' (Bobbio, p. 31).

It is true that in Gramsci civil society is not the infrastructure; but this does not mean that its content is not 'economic', even profoundly 'economic'. One might well have suspected this in so far as Gramsci includes the unions among the 'private organisms' of civil society[53] and refers elsewhere to 'the changes brought about by the birth of the *Trade Unions* in the power situation which exists in Civil Society'.[54]

But in actual fact it is not a matter of a few scattered allusions which might well escape one's attention. For Gramsci specifically determines the relations between infrastructure and civil society and those between civil society and state-government in numerous texts where the meaning is quite explicit. It is surprising that the author never once alludes to them. A serious reflexion on their content would have enabled him to go beyond the absolute oppositions and 'abstract' definitions he offers the reader. It should, moreover, be added that one encounters in these texts a definition of civil society which is very different from that we have been dealing with so far and the reader cannot but be perplexed when the two definitions are placed side by side. What do we find in these texts? We find the idea that, after a revolution in the social relations of production, the new state has an essential task to carry out which consists in transforming the economic behaviour of man so as to adapt it to the needs of the new infrastructure. This economic behaviour is on the one hand his method of working and his productive capacity, and on the other his method of consumption and more generally his mode of life in so far as it reflects upon his manner of participating in production. In short, it is not sufficient to radically transform the infrastructure; *homo oeconomicus* must also be adapted to these new structures. *Homo oeconomicus* is not, therefore, an immutable reality, but on the contrary an historical reality: '*Homo oeconomicus*,' says Gramsci, 'is the abstraction of the needs and of the economic operations of a particular society and of a particular structure. Each social form has its own *homo oeconomicus*, which is to say a type of economic activity particular to it.'[55]

When the infrastructure is transformed, it therefore becomes necessary to change the economic behaviour ('il modo di operare economico') to conform to the new structure. The state, with its juridical and coercive apparatus, is precisely the power which can and must effect this transformation:[56]

> If each State tends to create and maintain a certain type of civilization
> and a certain type of citizen (and therefore a type of communal life
> and individual relationships), to eradicate certain customs and
> attitudes and to develop others, the Law will have to be the
> instrument (as well as school and other institutions and activities) by
> which this aim is achieved.

The transformation of *moeurs* (morals) is first and foremost a transformation of the needs and patterns of behaviour of *homo oeconomicus.* It would be a grave error on the part of the new ruling class to consider that, since the essential task is the transformation of the economic infrastructure and development of the apparatus of production, 'the superstructural facts' can be ignored, 'left to themselves' and 'to develop spontaneously'. The needs and patterns of behaviour of *homo oeconomicus* are the most important of the superstructural facts and 'the State, in this field too, is an instrument of "rationalisation," of acceleration and of taylorisation. ... The Law is the repressive and negative aspect of the entire positive, civilising activity undertaken by the State.'[57]

We know, therefore, that it is man's behaviour and economic needs that must be transformed in order that he become adapted to the new infrastructure. We know that it is the state with its legal and coercive apparatus which is the essential instrument of this adaptation. We have still to discover that these customs and attitudes, which are first and foremost those of *homo oeconomicus* and which we have seen are 'superstructural facts', constitute the fundamental content of 'civil society':[58]

> Midway between the economic structure and the state stands civil society, which must be radically transformed in a concrete manner and not only in legal documents and science books. ... The State is the instrument for adapting civil society to the economic structure, but the State has to 'wish' to do this and, consequently, it must be the representative of the change which has occurred in the economic structure which rules the State. Waiting for civil society to adapt to the new structure by means of propaganda and persuasion, and for the old *homo oeconomicus* to disappear without burying him with all the honours he deserves, is a new form of empty and inconsistent economic moralism, a new form of economic rhetoric.

We referred above to the perplexity that this apparently rather novel definition of 'civil society' could cause. In the texts examined above (the letter to Tatiana and the notes on *The Formation of the Intellectuals*), civil society and political society appear as two aspects of the activity of the state, understood in its integral sense, and 'civil society' is the place of an ideologico-cultural or ethico-political activity aiming to obtain the consensus of the whole of society. Without being, properly speaking, the infrastructure, 'civil society' would now appear to have a directly economic content (*homo oeconomicus*) and to be the *object* of an essential activity of the juridical and governmental apparatus. The question is therefore whether these are two completely different uses of the same expression or whether, despite a certain difference in usage, it is not possible to integrate these texts into a coherent whole and to derive from them a more detailed view of Gramsci's conception of the relation between infrastructure and superstructures. It is this second hypothesis which seems to be correct.

It will perhaps be useful if we begin by recalling Gramsci's conception of 'human nature'.[59] Man, says Gramsci, is the 'complex of social relations'. These relations, of which the individual is the focal point, are not simple. On the one hand, in fact, 'the individual does not form relationships with other men by juxtaposition, but organically, that is to say, to the extent that he is part of the organisms, from the simplest to the most complex'; on the other hand, such social relations are either 'necessary' and independent of the will as are relations of production, or else they are voluntary such as those which I form by belonging to a political party. Lastly, these 'relations are not mechanical. They are active and conscious' and, consequently, one must beware of viewing the 'super-individual organisms' in a mechanistic, deterministic way. 'A doctrine must be elaborated in which all these relations are active and in motion, by clearly establishing that the seat of this activity is the conscience of the individual. ...'

To state that man is the complex of his social relations and that these 'organic' relations are active and conscious, is to state that man is 'history' and that he is his own history, for it can be said 'that each of us changes himself to the extent that he changes and modifies the whole complex of relations of which he is the focal point.' Of course, this does not mean to say that all changes are possible nor that I can change a great deal by dint of my own power alone. But it is true that 'the individual can associate with all those who desire the same change and, if this change is rational, the individual can multiply himself ('se multiplier') an impressive number of times and obtain a much more radical change than might at first sight have seemed possible'.[60] It can therefore be said that man is passive and active at the same time. He is the complex of the above relations and he is the activity which transforms them. As regards individuals, they are more or less active according to the degree of autonomy and initiative which they attain.

It seemed useful to recall these ideas so as not to lose sight of the fact that it is the social relations of individuals and the 'organisms' of which they form part that we mean when we speak of 'infrastructure' and 'superstructures', of 'civil society' and 'political society' and also the conscious activity by means of which they transform the different types of social relations.

Can we now proceed to reintegrate the various processes indicated by the term 'civil society' in an overall view of historical dialectics?

The point of departure is a complex of infrastructural conditions, determined by a certain development of productive forces. Corresponding to this infrastructural situation is a whole complex of superstructural activities, by means of which the ruling class *maintains* the economic system (juridical consecration of a régime of property, and protection of this régime by coercion), *impels* and *controls* the development of the productive apparatus (creation of a type of *homo oeconomicus* consistent with the type of production and relations of production at a given moment by means of juridical coercion and education), guarantees its power by developing a system of political and social alliances and an ethico-political system which permits it to exercise its hegemony and rule over society as a whole.

When society enters a period of social revolution, a new social group strives to overturn this political and ethico-political system in order to seize power and found a new state. This signifies the founding of a new system of relations of production and consequently the need to adapt *homo oeconomicus* to new requirements, etc.

In other words, what does civil society represent for Gramsci? It is the complex of practical and ideological social relations (the whole infinitely varied social fabric, the whole human content of a given society) which is established and grows up on the base of determined relations of production. It includes the types of behaviour of *homo oeconomicus* as well as of *homo ethico-politicus*. It is therefore the *object*, the *subject* and the *locality* of the superstructural activities which are carried out in ways which differ according to the levels and moments by means of the 'hegemonic apparatuses' on the one hand and of the 'coercive apparatuses' on the other.[61]

The reading which we are proposing would need to be supported by a precise analysis of numerous texts from the *Prison Notebooks*, and in particular the notes devoted to law, educational theory, americanism and fordism, etc. It is our view that such a reading is corroborated by a text in which Gramsci attempts to outline the essence of his views and which he entitles 'Unity in the constitutive elements of Marxism'[62]

Unity is provided by the dialectical development of contradictions between man and matter (nature—material forces of production). In the economy, the unitary centre is value, which is to say the relation between the worker and the industrial forces of production; in philosophy – praxis – which is the relation between human will (superstructure) and the economic structure; in politics – the relation between the state and civil society, which is to say the intervention of the state (centralised will) to educate the educator, the social milieu in general – (Develop and state in more exact terms).

It remains for us to examine a final point to complete this critique of the theses of Bobbio on Gramsci's conception of civil society. It has to be discovered what sort of activity the 'ethical' character of a historical period is linked with, in other words, what the activities are which have the power to promote the human being, to liberate man's creative capacities, to develop 'human richness'. We have seen in fact that, according to Bobbio, the moment of force and dictatorship always has a 'negative' connotation; the prevalence of this coercive moment over the opposite moment of consensus signifies that a period of decadence and regression is being undergone; the ethical character of history is exclusively linked to the deployment of intellectual and moral activities in 'civil society'. The question of the basis of the 'ethical' or 'universal' character of a historical period brings us back, as do the preceding questions, to the unity of infrastructure and superstructures on the one hand and to the question of the identification of civil society and political society on the other, that is to say, to a view which is quite contrary to that of Professor Bobbio.

In fact, one can indeed judge the 'ethical' character or the 'universal' scope of a historical movement by taking as criterion the 'qualitative' richness of the spiritual forms of civilisation it is capable of engendering. There is nevertheless the risk, with regard to popular historical movements, of adopting the blinkered attitude of 'Renaissance man', who is incapable of grasping the immense possibilities for cultural expansion which the Renaissance contains. On the other hand, if the ultimate justification of an historical movement is indeed this 'qualitative' expansion, the question facing each revolutionary is the economic or 'quantitative' conditions of that expansion. A 'quantitative' or economic approach to the problem of quality is the only serious, realistic and, one might say, authentically humanistic method.[63]

Thus we come face to face once more with 'the primacy of the economic factor' when the question of the 'ethical', 'universal' or 'human' character of history is raised. And this theme of the organic unity of the economy and culture runs like a leitmotive through those sections of the *Prison Notebooks* devoted to cultural problems.[64]

But the question Bobbio raises directly amounts to asking whether the moment of coercion and dictatorship can have an 'ethical' connotation; he replies in the negative. Gramsci's reply is quite different. In fact, his position with regard to 'the extreme forms of political society' (dictatorship in current political terminology) does indeed introduce an historical criterion, which does not appear in Bobbio, and from which judgment as to the progressive or regressive character of that dictatorship stems: 'It is an extreme form of political society,' writes Gramsci, 'either to struggle against the new and conserve what is already crumbling by consolidating it through coercion, or as an expression of the new to break down the resistance it encounters as it develops, etc.'[65]

Similarly, he writes that caesarism does not always have the same political significance: 'There can be both progressive and reactionary forms of Caesarism; the exact significance of each form can, in the last analysis, be reconstructed only through concrete history, and not by means of any sociological rule of thumb.'[66]

If we now take the example of a state which has succeeded in realising 'the equilibrium between political society and civil society', we shall also see that its ethical character is not manifest only in the realm of 'civil society'. What, in fact, is the essential function of the coercive apparatus? It is to 'make the popular masses conform to the type of production and the economy of a given moment.'[67] This, says Gramsci, is 'an educative, formative task of the state'.[68] And in this sense, one can say that '... every state is ethical in as much as one of its most important functions is to raise the great mass of the population to a particular cultural and moral level, a level (or type) which corresponds to the needs of the productive forces for development, and hence to the interests of the ruling classes.'[69]

The ruling class achieves this by using coercion as much as persuasion. There is thus no absolute opposition between these two modes of action. Moreover in all domains of human activity – whether it be educational theory or politics – a type of conduct which is initially imposed by force, may subsequently be freely accepted by the subject himself. Discipline becomes self-discipline, coercion becomes self-government. This is one aspect of the dialectics of 'necessity' and liberty. We hope to have shown that it is the very essence of Gramsci's conception of history.

Notes

This chapter was originally published in *La Pensée*, June 1968 and was translated into English by Hal Sutcliffe.

1 The following pages are a discussion of the paper presented by Professor Norberto Bobbio at the International Congress of Gramscian Studies, Cagliari, 23–7 April 1967, 'Gramsci and the conception of civil society', in this volume pp. 21–47. The theses put forward by Professor Bobbio were discussed at length during the first working day. This article develops the criticisms the author made of the paper at the Congress.

2 Analysing N. Bukharin's *Theory of Historical Materialism: A Popular Manual of Marxist Sociology*, Gramsci writes:
> This fundamental point is not dealt with: how does the historical movement arise on the structural base? ... This is ... the crux of all the questions that have arisen around the philosophy of praxis. ... Only on this basis can all mechanism and every trace of the superstitiously 'miraculous' be eliminated, and it is on this basis that the problem of the formation of active political groups ... must be posed (*Selections from the Prison Notebooks*, ed. and trans. Hoare and Nowell Smith, London, Lawrence & Wishart, 1971, pp. 431, 432).

3 'Determinism' is a concept which makes possible an understanding of *historical dialectics*. In the passage of the *Prison Notebooks* devoted to N. Bukharin, Gramsci writes:
> The historical dialectic is replaced by the law of causality and the search for regularity, normality and uniformity. But how can one derive from this way of seeing things the overcoming, the 'overthrow' of praxis? In mechanical terms, the effect can never transcend the cause or the system of causes, and therefore can have no development other than the flat vulgar development of evolutionism (*Prison Notebooks*, p. 437).

4 On this analysis of the different moments of the relation between forces, cf. Antonio Gramsci, *Prison Notebooks*, p. 185. Gramsci writes, for instance:
> If this process of development from one moment to the next is missing – and it is essentially a process which has as its actors men and their will and capacity – the situation is not taken advantage of, and contradictory outcomes are possible: either the old society resists and ensures itself a breathing-space by physically exterminating the elite of the rival class and terrorising its mass reserves; or a reciprocal destruction of the conflicting forces occurs, and a peace of the graveyard is established, perhaps even under the surveillance of a foreign guard.

5 See in the *Letters from Prison* particularly that of 7 September 1931 (*Letters from Prison*, trans. and ed. Lynne Lawner, London, Jonathan Cape, 1975, p. 204). Cf. also *Il Materialismo Storico e la Filosofia di Benedetto Croce*, Turin, Einaudi, 1949, p. 192.

6 The greatest modern theoretician of the philosophy of praxis, in the field of struggle and political organisation, in opposition to the various economistic tendencies and in political terminology, 're-evaluated' the front of cultural struggle and built the doctrine of hegemony as a

complement to the theory of the state-power (Gramsci, *Il Materialismo Storico*, p. 201).

7   In 1926, on the eve of his arrest, Gramsci, drawing positive conclusions from the Factory Council and the *Ordine Nuovo* movement behind which he was the moving force, writes:

> The Turin communists posed concretely the question of the 'hegemony of the proletariat': i.e. of the social basis of the proletarian dictatorship and the worker's State. The proletariat can become the leading (*dirigente*) and the dominant class to the extent that it succeeds in creating a system of class alliance which allows it to mobilise the majority of the working population against capitalism and the bourgeois State. In Italy ... this means to the extent that it succeeds in gaining the consent of the broad peasant masses (Antonio Gramsci, *Selections from Political Writings 1921–26*, trans. and ed. Quintin Hoare, London, Lawrence & Wishart, 1978, p. 443).

8   For Croce's conception of philosophy the same reduction has to be made as the first theoreticians of the philosophy of praxis made for the Hegelian conception. ... It would be worthwhile a whole group of men devoting ten year's work to ... such a task (*Il Materialismo Storico*, p. 200).

9   Let us freely admit, at the outset, that Gramsci's use of the expression 'civil society' in the *Prison Notebooks* causes the reader some confusion at first; we shall explain why this is.

10   Cf. *Passato e Presente*, Turin, Einaudi, 1952, p. 72, *Prison Notebooks*, p. 239.

11   *Note sul Machiavelli, sulla politica et sullo stato moderno*, Turin, Einaudi, 1949, p. 130, *Prison Notebooks*, p. 261.

12   'Ethico-political history, inasmuch as it neglects the concept of the historical bloc in which economico-social content and ethico-political form are concretely identified ... is not history' (*Il Materialismo Storico*, p. 204).

13   The level of development of the material forces of production provides a basis for the emergence of the various social classes, each one of which represents a function and has a specific position within production itself. ... By studying these fundamental data it is possible to discover whether in a particular society there exist the necessary and sufficient conditions for its transformation – in other words, to check the degree of realism and practicability of the various ideologies which have been born on its own terrain (Gramsci, *Prison Notebooks*, pp. 180–1).

14   'Since there cannot exist quantity without quality or quality without quantity (economy without culture, practical activity without the intelligence and vice versa), any opposition of the two terms is, rationally, a nonsense' (*Prison Notebooks*, p. 363).

15   For the origin of the epiphenomenalist conception of the superstructures, cf. Gramsci's analysis in *Prison Notebooks*, pp. 137–8.

16   Ibid., p. 178.

17   Cf. Gramsci's very pertinent text on the combination of historical fatalism and the 'tendency when no criteria exist, to blindly trust to the regulating virtue of arms to provide a solution' (*Oeuvres choisies*, Editions sociales, p. 231).

18 *Prison Notebooks*, p. 160; cf. P. Togliatti's comments in *Gramsci*, Editori Riuniti, 1967, p. 154.

19 *Il Materialismo Storico*, p. 240.

20 Necessity exists when there exists an efficient and active *premiss*, consciousness of which in people's minds has become operative, proposing concrete goals to the collective consciousness and constituting a complex of convictions and beliefs which acts powerfully in the form of 'popular beliefs'. In the *premiss* must be contained, already developed or in the process of development, the necessary and sufficient material conditions for the realisation of the impulse of collective will; but it is also clear that one cannot separate from this 'material' premiss, which can be quantified, a certain level of culture, by which we mean a complex of intellectual acts and, as a product and consequence of these, a certain complex of overriding passions and feelings, overriding in the sense that they have the power to lead men on to action 'at any price' (Gramsci, *Prison Notebooks*, pp. 412–13).

21 Thesis III on Feuerbach in Marx and Engels, *Selected Works*, 3 vols, Moscow, Progress Publishers, vol. 1, p. 13.

22 Let us recall certain texts to indicate these different usages. First Marx:

> My investigation led to the result that legal relations as well as forms of state are to be grasped neither from themselves nor from the so-called general development of the human mind, but rather have their roots in the material conditions of life, the sum total of which Hegel, following the example of the Englishmen and Frenchmen of the eighteenth century, combines under the name of 'civil society' (*Preface to A Contribution to the Critique of Political Economy*, ibid., p. 503).

Similarly, Marx and Engels write:

> Civil society embraces the whole material intercourse of individuals within a definite stage of the development of productive forces. It embraces the whole commercial and industrial life of a given stage. ... It is thus quite clear that civil society is the true centre and the true scene of all history (*The German Ideology*, ibid., p. 76).

In the *Prison Notebooks*, on the other hand, Gramsci uses the expression 'civil society' to indicate an aspect of superstructural activity.

> What we can do, for the moment, is to fix two major superstructural 'levels': the one that can be called 'civil society', that is the ensemble of organisms commonly called 'private', and that of 'political society' or 'the State'. These two levels correspond on the one hand to the function of 'hegemony' which the dominant group exercises throughout society and on the other hand to that of 'direct domination' or command exercised through the State and 'juridical' government. The functions in question are precisely organisational and connective. The intellectuals are the dominant group's 'deputies', exercising the subaltern functions of social hegemony and political government. These comprise:
> 1. The 'spontaneous' consent given by the great masses of the population to the general direction imposed on social life by the dominant fundamental group ...

2. The apparatus of state coercive power which 'legally' enforces discipline on those groups who do not 'consent' either actively or passively (*Prison Notebooks*, p. 12).

Let us recall that for Gramsci, the state in the restricted sense is the coercive apparatus or political society, but that in the integral sense, the state is political society and civil society.

23 Norberto Bobbio, 'Gramsci and the conception of civil society', in this volume pp. 21–47.

24 In the *Preface to A Contribution to the Critique of Political Economy*, as in *The German Ideology*, he explains that 'ideologies *always* come *after* the institutions, as a sort of reflexion … by virtue of the fact that they are considered from the point of view of their being posthumous, mystified-mystifying justifications of class domination' (Marx and Engels, *Selected Works*, p. 504).

25 Bobbio, in this volume p. 31. The words between inverted commas in the quotation are from Marx, for whom 'civil society', or the infrastructure, is the base of all history, cf. note 22.

26 In the third part of this article we shall have to consider the question of the suitability of Gramsci's definition of 'civil society'.

27 The influence of Croce's judgment on Marx is very apparent in this article dating from 1918, in which Gramsci praises the Russian Revolution and the authentic marxism of the Bolsheviks: 'They [the Bolsheviks] are living Marxist thought; which is eternal, which represents the continuation of Italian and German idealism, which in Marx was contaminated by positivist and naturalist encrustations' (*Scritti giovanili*, 1914–1918, Turin, Einaudi, 1958, p. 149; English translation in Antonio Gramsci, *Selections from Political Writings*, ed. Quintin Hoare, London, Lawrence & Wishart, 1977, p. 34).

28 Gramsci, *Prison Notebooks*, p. 177.

29 Marx and Engels, *Selected Works*, p. 503.

30 Gramsci, *Prison Notebooks*, p. 162.

31 Ibid., p. 377.

32 Marx and Engels, *The German Ideology*.

33 My italics in ibid.

34 Gramsci, *Prison Notebooks*, p. 377. Compare this text with note 20.

35 'In the passage from economy to general history, the concept of quantity is completed by the concept of quality and by the concept of dialectical quantity which becomes quality', and the following explanatory note: 'Quantity = necessity; quality = liberty. The dialectic (the dialectical nexus) of quantity–quality is identical to the dialectic necessity–liberty' (*Oeuvres choisies*, p. 93).

36 To say that *in certain conditions* political activity becomes the determining moment in no way contradicts the fundamental marxist thesis, according to which 'the mode of production of material life *in general dominates* the process of social, political and intellectual life.' This *general domination*, in particular conditions, implies the decisive role of political praxis.

37 *Il Materialismo Storico*, p. 231.

38 Ibid., pp. 240–1. Let us add two texts which will make Gramsci's conception of the unity of infrastructure and superstructures clear. The first is as follows:
   The ensemble of material forces of production is at the same time a crystallisation of all past history and the basis of present and future history; it is both a document and an active and actual propulsive force. But the concept of activity applied to forces of this kind must not be confused or even compared with activity in either the physical or metaphysical sense (*Prison Notebooks*, p. 466).
   The second text reads:
   The economistic attitude with regard to expressions of will, action and political and intellectual initiative which looks upon them as though they were not in fact an organic emanation of economic necessities and even the only effective expression of the economy is strange to say the least (*Oeuvres choisies*, p. 22).
   Compare texts cited in notes 20 and 34.
39 'Unity [in the constituent elements of marxism] is provided by the dialectical development of contradictions between man and matter (nature-material forces of production)' (*Oeuvres choisies*, p. 97).
40 *Il Materialismo Storico*, p. 35, *Prison Notebooks*, p. 360.
41 Cf. the quotation from *The German Ideology* in note 22.
42 In the 1859 *Preface*, Marx distinguishes these two moments of superstructural activity and at the same time affirms their unity: 'The sum total of these relations of production constitutes the economic structure of society, the real foundation, on which rises a legal and political superstructure and to which correspond definite forms of social consciousness' (Marx and Engels, *Selected Works*, p. 503).
43 Gramsci, *Prison Notebooks*, p. 12. This is also the sense of the unity Gramsci affirms between philosophy and politics.
44 Ibid., p. 160.
45 Ibid., p. 263.
46 Ibid., p. 161.
47 The content of the political hegemony of the new social group which has founded the new type of State must be predominantly of an economic order: what is involved is the reorganisation of the structure and the real relations between men on the one hand and the world of the economy or of production on the other' (ibid., p. 263).
48 Undoubtedly the fact of hegemony presupposes that account be taken of the interests and the tendencies of the groups over which hegemony is to be exercised and that a certain compromise equilibrium should be formed – in other words, that the leading group should make sacrifices of an economic-corporate kind. But there is also no doubt that such sacrifices and such a compromise cannot touch the essential; for though hegemony is ethical-political, it must also be economic, must necessarily be based on the decisive function exercised by the leading group in the decisive nucleus of economic activity (*Prison Notebooks*, p. 161).
49 Ibid., p. 181.

50 In a socially developed country where the elements of civil society are numerous and very articulate, it is not enough to state that political society is in a state of crisis, to ensure that a revolutionary offensive will lead to victory. Political strategy must be adapted and the 'war of movement' replaced by the 'war of position'. The massive structure of modern democracies, whether one is talking about the organisations of the state or the complex of the associations of civil life, represents for political art the equivalent of the 'trenches' and the permanent fortifications of the front in the 'war of position' (ibid., p. 235). '[In Russia in 1917] the state was everything, civil society was primordial and gelatinous; in the West there was a proper relation between State and civil society, and when the State trembled a sturdy structure of civil society was at once revealed' (ibid., p. 238).

51 Ibid.

52 Ibid., pp. 57–8.

53 Gramsci, *Letters from Prison*, p. 204.

54 *Il Materialismo Storico*, p. 266, *Prison Notebooks*, p. 400 n.

55 Ibid., p. 266.

56 *Machiavelli*, p. 88, *Prison Notebooks*, p. 247.

57 Ibid., p. 88.

58 *Il Materialismo Storico*, p. 267. On the necessity for creating a new type of man, adapted to the working methods of modern industrial production, see the sections in the *Prison Notebooks* entitled 'Americanism and Fordism'.

59 Ibid.

60 *Oeuvres choisies*, p. 97.

61 In the texts we examined first (letter to Tatiana, *Formation of the Intellectuals*), 'civil society' is at one and the same time the apparatus of hegemony and the locality in which this ethico-political hegemony is exercised. For greater clarity the expression should only be used to indicate the locality. Civil society would comprise, on the one hand, the complex of needs and modes of behaviour of *homo oeconomicus*, and on the other the complex of ethico-political needs and types of behaviour. Coercive and hegemonic superstructural activities strive to transform these.

62 *Oeuvres choisies*, p. 97.

63 *Prison Notebooks*, pp. 363–4.

64 Cf. for example the notes on the problem of school in *Prison Notebooks*, 'The Intellectuals' and 'On Education', pp. 3–43.

65 *Machiavelli*, p. 161.

66 *Prison Notebooks*, p. 219.

67 Letter to Tatiana of 7 September 1931, *Letters from Prison*, p. 204.

68 *Oeuvres choisies*, p. 251.

69 *Machiavelli*, p. 128. *Prison Notebooks*, p. 258.

3   Gramsci and the problem of the revolution

Nicola Badaloni

1   In order to understand the significance of Gramsci's contribution to the development of marxism, one should use as a starting-point (as Leonardo Paggi has done[1]) the crisis in socialism and, in a more general way, the crisis in theoretical marxism. For that reason we should first take a look at Antonio Labriola's thought. His third essay, *Discorrendo di socialismo e di filosofia*, defined three fundamental factors of historical materialism. The first was its 'philosophically-inclined character in its general outlook on life and the world', the second was represented by that criticism of the economy, 'the modes of development of which cannot be reduced to laws except in that they represent a given historical phase', the third, finally, referred to that interpretation of politics 'as being necessary and useful in order to lead the working-class movement towards socialism'.[2]

Labriola's personal contribution concentrated on shifting the first and second concepts towards the third, in the sense that those two concepts were in fact defined as an awareness directly concerning the proletarian class. This was the theorisation of a new *social pedagogy*, the premises of which were, on the one hand, that the actual conditions of the working class had to be taken into account (the 'direction of the possible is given by the condition of the proletariat',[3] i.e. by its 'psychological capacity to receive scientific theory'), and on the other hand the need to employ the instruments of orientation offered by teaching (therefore the first two points) as 'true' theory, capable of interpreting the social facts without forcing them as such into rigid schemes, and to maintain the general orientation of life and the world in perpetual dialogue with the development of the sciences. Although Labriola linked his 'pedagogy' with a theory of experimentation[4] (thus avoiding the danger of indoctrination), yet he interpreted the traditional dichotomy between philosophy and science[5] as a trend of the times. The overall result, although it certainly did not diminish science from the point of view of the working class (since science maintained its autonomy and its independence), nevertheless revealed that in the working class a new social force existed capable of elaborating, on the basis of science, its own general outlook on the world. Thus socialism, of necessity objective, tended to transform itself into a subjective point of view of the working-class struggle and, through this means, to weld the objective laws of historical development to the subjective awareness of the new progressive class.

It is in fact on this point in Labriola's thought that the divergence emerges from the 'critics of Marxism' (Bernstein, Sorel and Croce), i.e. with regard to the bond which Labriola – here following Engels – continued to assume between the objective assessment of historical development and socialist consciousness. In his view, the contradictions of civilisation necessitated the erection of a new order of human society (socialism), even though this necessity still needed to mature psychologically. If we pass from Labriola to Bernstein and Sorel, we see that it is precisely this general principle of dialectics which is placed in question. Historical development can take place in new legal and social orders, the form of which need not necessarily be the socialist form. The analysis of such non-dialectical transitions had been suggested by Bernstein (for example by altering the pattern of increasing poverty and that of the concentration of capital) and had been taken up by Sorel – an analysis which denied *in toto* the link between historical development and dialectical rhythm.

Sorel appreciated the philosophy of action in Labriola's thought, understanding by that term the effort 'to clear the way theoretically which the proletariat follows in practice'.[6] On the psychology and teaching side he was essentially in agreement with Labriola. On the other hand, it was on the side of dialectics (i.e. objective processes) that his conception differed radically. In fact, for Sorel socialist morphology was beyond our powers of experimentation and correlatively our capacity to foresee.[7] What was still for Labriola the general law of historical development had for Sorel the additional value of 'common sense' rules.[8] The logic of history, instead of being situated in dialectical development, was concretised in the coexistence of higher and lower forms of production,[9] i.e. in a combination in which the principle of simultaneity replaced that of succession.[10] The model for such a historical movement was no longer Hegelian dialectics but, on the contrary, Vico's philosophy of history, amended in such a manner that the ages (and the corresponding 'states of mind' which engender myth and reason) coexist in time.

To this theoretical revision of marxism (in which a combinatory is substituted for dialectics) there corresponds a different interpretation of Marx's thought. In fact Sorel distinguishes an initial phase in Marx's thought (which culminates in *The Poverty of Philosophy*, in the *Manifesto* and in his historico-analytical writings on the events of the 1848 Revolution), a phase in which the *productive forces* are central to his thinking, and which confer a dialectical order on their tensions. It is from the moment of the *Preface* to the *Critique of Political Economy* of 1859 that Sorel detects in Marx the consolidation of a problematic of juridical forms. Dating from that moment, the different epochs are no longer characterised by the productive forces, but by a socio-economic complex or bloc which indicates in fact (according to Sorel) a return to the hegelian concept of civil society, since the relations of production are identified with the relations of ownership. In this (definitive) form of Marx's thought the relations of ownership, inherent in civil society, contain and retain the dynamics of the forces of production,[11] which has the effect of restricting its importance considerably. No longer having this dynamic impulse (which signifies a reduction of the economy to a generic pre-eminence of fact or, as it was to be subsequently termed, to an overdetermination), the *historical bloc – the interpenetration of the juridical and the economic, within the limits of civil society –* no longer moves in a linear way in the direction of expected historical progress (socialism), but can generate various combinations even though they might not necessarily be similar to it.

Sorel then arrived at a theoretical result signifying the abandoning of the theme of the necessity of socialism and its replacement by a combinatory of various possibilities, connected with the co-penetration of the juridical and the economic. He presented this result (in a way which does not differ from that which, fifty years later, the structuralist school of French marxism was to arrive at) as the authentic thought of Marx and, what is more, as a result of Engels' vulgarisations, as a return to Marx. The historical bloc (in the sense of a permanent symbiosis of the economic and the juridico-political) realises its possibilities in spite of man's intellectual consciousness. This is the meaning of Sorel's polemic against democracy, and the climax of his discussion with Renan on the role of intellectuals. For Sorel intellectuals are a social group which, owing to the force of circumstances, have interests different from those of the producers and which, by this very fact, of necessity reinforce 'the defence of the bourgeois form *vis-à-vis* the proletarian revolution'.[12] On the other hand, the idea of 'party' is foreign to marxism, which has better defined the idea of 'class' (precisely as class of producers), as also the idea of political struggle is foreign to it, in the sense that it consists of substituting intellectuals for other intellectuals,[13] the political struggle thus being a movement which only concerns the superficial stratum of society.

Thus we have managed to reveal a superficial dimension and a profound dimension of social existence. The first dominated by consciousness (nevertheless false and powerless), the second, on the contrary, having the classes as protagonists. The task of issuing from the ideological viscosity imposed by the historical bloc fell to myth, in so far as it is the expression of a spontaneity directly connected with the class (of producers). It is at this level that practice is re-established and, to a certain degree, dialectics itself. In fact Sorel, who re-examines the famous rapprochement suggested by Bernstein between hegelianism and blanquism, claimed that in the blanquist conception the absolute revolution becomes – as for all parties and intellectual groups – an ability to conform to the fluctuations of political interests. In contrast, in hegelian dialectics as adopted by Marx, the revolution remains in its mythical form. Overthrow is expressed for Hegel and Marx meta-phorically; for blanquism it is led 'by the circumstances that arise'.[14] The negation of the negation against which Sorel polemicised during the first stage of his thought is now a social myth which returns to its beginnings in the form which Sorel found in Machiavelli and in Vico. The same laws, expressed by Marx in the *Preface* of 1859, are now reinterpreted in the compass of this (practical-mythical-prophetic) concretisation of the demand of the producing class and become, for revolutionaries, the guidelines for action.

2   And so, as we can see, for Sorel the restoration of Hegel takes place in a different way from that of Croce. In fact the latter had not only his eyes turned towards the working class, but also towards the bourgeoisie. And whereas in the case of the working class, by substituting the dialectic of distincts for the dialectic of opposites, he accepted fully Sorel's conclusions (progressively reducing the conceptual value of Marx's criticism of political economy to practical interest and myth; more concretely still, by denying that socialism is the necessary method for allowing the contradictions of bourgeois society to be overcome),

where the bourgeois class is concerned, he restored all its value to the use and possession of reason. In other words, and more simply, *Croce withdrew from the proletariat its instruments of intellectual leadership, on the one hand by attacking the philosophy of history* (even in the consciously critical form we find in Labriola) *and on the other hand by ridiculing the eclectic positivist-reformist game.* Furthermore, whereas the utility of the hegelian–marxist myth should have been, according to Sorel's aim, that of inciting the 'producers' to escape from the viscosity of the historical bloc, for Croce, the myth remained subject to this rational control which only the intellectuals of the already hegemonic class were capable of exercising. At a polemical level it is, therefore, not completely wrong to say that in Croce's thought we find the characteristics of a primitive (*indigeno*) platonism tinged with humanism. And yet, the whole of Croce's construction indicates a design of remarkable clarity. *The ruling class reaffirms its hegemony through the mediation of culture, controls practical tensions and social 'myths'.* To free oneself from the tedious marxist and positivist claim to interpret history scientifically, means precisely offering again to intellectuals their traditional function of humanist mediation, to the exclusive advantage of the already hegemonic class, but within the framework of an overall plan in which the eternal structure of forms of the spirit deprives the subordinate classes both of the possibility of overturning the system of values and of infiltrating it with new ones via the complex hierarchy it engenders.

But to turn to Gramsci. There is no doubt, it appears, that he was formed in this matrix of cultural, political and moral problems. *He did not accept all the consequences of sorelism, but certainly he evolved within its perspective of a problematic of anti-reformist and anti-positivist struggle.* When Gramsci began to write, sorelism, as philosophy of the revolution, had already experienced a significant defeat. So caustic was he in his polemics against the mediation of intellectuals, that he proved incapable of protecting himself from anti-democratic interpretations of bourgeois philosophy. Sorelism was one of the matrices of nationalism and irrationalism, and it was for this reason that Gramsci felt the need to emphasise its hegelian–marxist aspects. His work entitled *Il sillabo ed Hegel* is in fact a hegelian presentation of this Hegel–Marx relationship, the re-evaluation of which we saw in Sorel. The famous article 'La rivoluzione contro il "Capitale"' was written from the same viewpoint:[15]

if the Bolsheviks reject some of the statements in *Capital*, they do not reject its invigorating, immanent thought. These people are not 'Marxists', that is all: they have not used the works of the Master to compile a rigid doctrine of dogmatic utterances never to be questioned. They live Marxist thought – that thought which is eternal, which represents the continuation of German and Italian idealism, and which in the case of Marx was contaminated by positivist and naturalist encrustations. This thought sees as the dominant factor in history, not raw economic facts, but man, man in societies, men in relation to one another, reaching agreements with one another, developing through these contacts (civilisation) a collective, social will; men coming to understand economic facts, judging them and adapting them to their will until this becomes the driving force of the economy and moulds objective reality, which lives and moves and comes to resemble a current of volcanic lava that can be channelled wherever and in whatever way men's will determines.

The opposition between the Constituent Assembly and the Soviet is formed in an analogous way (with reference to the Russian Revolution). The Constituent Assembly is the 'vague and confused myth of the revolutionary period, an intellectual myth ... '; the Soviet results from the clarification of these forces which 'are in process of elaborating spontaneously, freely, according to their intrinsic nature, the representative forms via which the sovereignty of the proletariat will have to be exercised ... the Russian proletariat has offered us an initial model of direct representation of the producers: the soviets.'[16]

The theoretical framework within which Gramsci evolved is therefore that offered by Sorel – by his theory of spontaneity, by the interest he concentrated on the producer class, by the fact that it is foreign to the democracy of the intellectuals. And yet Paggi is right to note also quite a new attitude, i.e. that, contrary to Sorel's predictions, the 'extraneity' (*estraneità*) of the consciousness of the producers was affirmed historically with a suddenness which imposed on the new political groups tasks of political leadership. The Russian Revolution not only overturned the revisionists of the right, to whom it presented a political realisation not mediated by the necessary moments of its development, but it also overturned the revisionists of the left for whom, in place of the myth, *the tasks of political construction arose*. The traces of this new way of posing the problem were already evident in the criticism of *socialism* and *reformism* voiced by Gramsci in his article 'La reazione italiana'.[17] From this, at the theoretical level, an emphasis emerged of the hegelian theme i.e. of that hegelian–marxism[18] which had in fact been upheld by Sorel, but which now took on the particular meaning of re-establishment – in the field of the liaison between economics and politics (i.e. of the historical bloc) – of these very dynamic tensions, the importance of which sorelian revisionism had denied. In fact, during the closing years of the century, Sorel had rejected the trend manifested by the economy, in its reified version, to develop in a socialist direction and on the contrary had accepted the bernsteinian analysis of the retentive capacity of the historical bloc (i.e. of the existing relations of production and ownership). Later, by connecting his theory of the myth of the general strike to the producer class, he had, to a certain degree, reopened to historical tensions the possibility of a socialist outcome, making it depend on the fact that the new social groups are extraneous (*estraneità*) to politics. Now, thanks to the victory in Russia, that extraneity emerged as full of unsuspected implications and practical possibilities, which determined a new, necessary course for history, according to which ideas lost their arbitrary character by materialising in the economy. The idea (i.e. the new possible course of history as it emerged from the producer class) *found in the economy* (that is in the knowledge *of objective reality and objective class relationships) the means for its realisation.* The party acted not at the level of the reified laws of economics (which expressed the attitudes made necessary by adaptation to the environment), but at the level of the 'idea' i.e. of the possible mastery of the reified forces.[19] The hegelian scheme of quantity–quality became the scheme of fundamental interpretation in which the economic structure corresponded to quantity and human actions to quality.[20] The consequence of all this was not only a *new dimension given to the idea of the party,*[21] but there was also a reactivation of the idea of historical development, now entrusted to the ideal force of the proletariat and guaranteed, not by the conformist motivation of economic realities but on the contrary by that revolutionary freedom of choice, in relation to which the economy had only the function of indicating the depth of reified relations which should be repudiated. From the theoretical point of view the solution seems to be pure idealist inspiration.[22] From the political point of view the outcome is the opposite, compared to the various humanist solutions which suggest again the idea of evolution. In fact, it is not on evolution that Gramsci placed the emphasis, but on rupture or substitution.[23] The 'revisionist' negation of the importance of historical laws and of the socialist outcome towards which their hidden movement leads, is thus accepted as a whole. In their stead is placed an 'extraneity' identified, according to Sorel, with the producer class, and which takes on, as for Sorel, very distinctly idealist characteristics. With the difference that, for Sorel, this 'extraneous' component has not the function of self-preservation (even in providing for the future), but of bringing about a substitution of power (within the framework of civil society). On the basis of this 'extraneity' *Gramsci's hegelian marxism therefore tends to re-establish the scope of a historical dynamic, i.e. at the political level to promote the extraneity of the proletariat, and at the theoretical level to place at its disposal those same instruments which Croce had placed at the disposal of the bourgeois class.* This undertaking of society which Croce had entrusted to the mediation of education can, via the discipline of the party, become a proletarian instrument. It was an idea which, as far back as 1918, began to make headway within the Italian Socialist Party (PSI), in particular in the polemics on party discipline imposed on the parliamentary groups and the trade union organisations.

3   Furthermore, it must be said that this process was anything but linear. In the writings of 1919–22, there are in fact two conflicting trends. One still under Sorel's influence, which considered that the essential point was the conservation of the idea of extraneity and its concretisation in the instruments of proletarian democracy (*the idea of councils*); the other influenced by bolshevism (which, in that period, was not uninfluenced by *Bordiga*) which felt the necessity of achieving, thanks to the party, a more organised overall outlook. At the historical level, Gramsci was convinced that, with regard to the choice between *syndicalism* and *reformism*, it was the latter which had triumphed, since at the very least[24]

> the syndicalists worked outside of reality. ... On the other hand, the parliamentary socialists worked in close contact with events and while they could make mistakes ... they made no mistake in the direction their activity took and so they triumphed in the 'competition'.

The reformists had made mistakes because they had lost their antithetical position,[25] they had believed in the perpetuation of the parliamentary state. The 'stupidly parliamentary' tactics had to be changed into the act of the conquest of the state.

Gramsci's point of view during these last years was therefore no longer that of extraneity, which had taken on the limited aspect of purity and simplicity in opposition to the conception of the existing historical bloc, but on the contrary it was the plan to construct, on the basis of antithesis, an articulation just as complex with a view to constructing a totality – the proletarian state. The new representative institutions of the producers had leadership functions involving the whole of Italian social life, and more particularly the peasants. The transformation of the rural economy, which was still semi-feudal, into a technically developed economy, could be realised both under the leadership of bourgeois institutions and under that of proletarian institutions. But in the former case it led to 'a disaster'. Only a proletarian state could bring about the industrial transformation of agriculture 'with the agreement of the poor peasants, via a dictatorship of the proletariat that is embodied in Councils of industrial workers and poor peasants'.[26]

The conditions for all this lay in creating in the worker the 'psychology of the producer, of the creator of history'.[27] To accusations of *syndicalism* Gramsci replied in his article 'Sindacalismo e consigli' with a theory, in great part still influenced by Sorel, which set up against the figure of the wage-earner that of the producer, that is of a figure who intentionally dominates the sphere of production and the market. The trade union is reduced to a form of capitalist society which organises the workers as wage-earners. The producer therefore does not feel he is a component of the process of trade, but its creator. Private property (starting from the factory) is therefore conceived as alien, precisely because it 'is not a function of productivity' and the worker 'becomes revolutionary, because he sees the capitalist, the private property owner, as a dead hand, an encumbrance on the productive process which must be done away with'.[28] Gramsci reached this conclusion that 'Syndicalism has never once expressed such a conception of the producer, nor of the process of historical development of the producer society; it has never once indicated that this leadership, this line, should be impressed upon the workers' organisation.'[29]

The new awareness of the *overall situation* which he connects with the figure of the producer therefore simply demands this conclusion. Moreover, it is in this opposition between the *producer* and the *wage-earner* that the kernel of Gramsci's marxism resides. It sums up the essential elements of Marx's analysis of bourgeois capitalist society. Thanks to the mediation of Sorel, Gramsci was not confronted with the opposition between the producer's class (workers and technicians) and that of the owners. It is to this opposition that he integrates the new ideological and political totality, and it is precisely through it that it takes on a new meaning. Sorel had remained faithful to the need to withdraw the working class from an integration which (according to Bernstein) was identified with a historical movement which still had bourgeois institutions as its protagonists. *Gramsci himself continued firmly to believe that it was not historical laws which automatically oriented progress towards socialism, but the movement of 'withdrawal' which, having become a 'rising', re-established the possibility of leading the movement of history.* Viewed in this light, Bordiga's objections were somewhat weak, when he asserted that it was 'foolish to talk of worker-*control* as long as political power was not in the hands of the worker state'.[30] The assumption of political power, in fact, could not be an instantaneous and impromptu fact either, but had to rely on class consciousness completed by a new consciousness: that of promoting, by antithesis, the development of civilisation. Hence the way in which Gramsci formulated the problem of power. It was no longer a question of giving it to a group of intellectuals who would be replacing another group of intellectuals, but of 'how to organise the whole mass of Italian workers into a hierarchy that reaches its apex in the Party', and of confronting the problem of 'constructing a State apparatus which internally will function democratically, i.e. will guarantee freedom to all anti-capitalist tendencies and offer them the possibility of forming a proletarian government ... '.[31]

During this period, Gramsci's wariness with regard to the limitations of the trade union was far from having disappeared. Moreover, not even the party 'incarnated' the revolutionary process and could embrace 'the whole spectrum of teeming revolutionary forces that capitalism throws up in the course of its implacable development as a machine of exploitation and oppression.'[32] But what was new, on the other hand, was a double point of reference. The first was presented by the re-establishment of the 'process' dimension of history;[33] the second, closely connected with the first, was the original representation of the dimension of the productive forces. In Gramsci's mind, the 'councils' are the 'spontaneous response of the working class to the new situation imposed by capitalist development'.[34] The relationship with the councils is the equivalent of the relationship with the economy. Economic development is reflected in the factory where it provokes movements of revolt which the 'councils' render visible. Thus the councils liberate the productive forces.[35] The future of the party is defined, on the basis of this encounter, with the productive forces, in the sense that it offers them, by creating a sure and durable economic basis of political power in the hands of the proletariat, a subsequent development and expansion. This encounter with the productive forces led Gramsci to keep the councils as a new historical form of organisation. The soviet is a universal institution, precisely because it establishes a link between the productive forces and political organisation.[36]

It is this link with the productive forces which represents a new element, but also continuity, in relation to Sorel. The new aspect with regard to the hegelian concept of civil society is the discovery of its strong point. On this point, the reduction of marxist dialectics to their hegelian form was continuous with Sorel's adherence to Bernstein's theses, i.e. to the idea that the historical process no longer developed according to the problematic of the transition from one social structure to another, but on the contrary via a development of the institutions of the old social structure. The fact that the *idea of freedom* (i.e. the possibility to jump from one institutional type to another) which for Gramsci had a distinctly idealistic tone – hegelian and crocian, in the sense of the overturning of this trend on behalf of the proletariat – finds concrete shape in the rediscovery of the productive forces, is a characteristic fact of this new point of view. In fact, the councils do not present a 'voluntary' dimension (that is, of statutory protection) of the worker-state, but on the contrary are an expression of the figure of the producer, that is, a totalising point of view of the problem of civilisation. *Ordine Nuovo*, Gramsci stated, 'was developed around a concept – the concept of liberty (and concretely developed, on the level of the actual making of history, around the hypothesis of autonomous revolutionary action by the working class)'; the factory Council 'is an institution of a "public" character while the Party and the trade unions are associations of a "private" nature'.[37] In essence, Gramsci means here that *the councils are the organ representing the liaison between the two socio-economic groups and between the two organisations*. It is only on these conditions that political life can be regained, identifying itself with the work of a headquarters which makes decisions on the basis of the analysis of real class relations.

The aspect of continuity in relation to Sorel rests in the maintenance of total extraneity in relation to present social organisation and hence in relation to the compromises and adjustments which the replacement of one group of intellectuals by another may involve. Political life is not a self-sustained field, but on the contrary is only the concretisation of a hypothesis which already finds, *in the councils*, its field of experimentation; this hypothesis means in fact that at the time of imperialism, of the domination of finance capital, of the subjection of production to the demands of capital profit, the factory council, as a home of liberty, constituted the momentum through which it became possible to set in motion a society of revolutionaries and a society of free producers, capable of organising, together with production, a new era of development of economic civilisation.

4   In a reading of the writings of the period 1921–2 (when open reaction was already raging), and those of subsequent periods, it can be seen that the problem of 'councils' had not disappeared. The latter was still considered as the instrument of response – valid on a universal scale – to the new faces of capitalism. The subject of the councils becomes incomprehensible if we do not take into account the interpretation given at the time to the concept of imperialism. For Gramsci the concentration of the forces of production and the crisis of overproduction foreseen by Marx materialised in 'economic imperialism'.[38] The fact that the orientation of production was abruptly shifted towards financial monopoly, in such a way that it provoked 'an organisation and massive concentration of the material means of production and trade, obtained in particular via the monopoly of credit and, on the other hand, via a crushing and massive-scale disorganisation of the most important instrument of production, the working class',[39] confirmed Gramsci in the belief that the struggle must be presented globally, as defence of the productive forces, as an attempt to withdraw them from subjection to the market (in particular from financial monopoly). The working class, as main productive force, was to realise its own autonomy by reversing 'this hierarchical scale', by eliminating 'from the industrial camp the figure of the capitalist owner' and by producing 'according to established work-programmes, not through the monopolistic organisation of private property, but through world-wide industrial power of the working class'.[40]

As we can see it, the idea of 'councils' became, in Gramsci's mind, a world-wide strategy – the working-class reply to the imperialist development of capitalism towards the pre-eminence of financial capital. This was not yet socialism in Gramsci's thinking: it was a matter of the response of the (international) proletariat to the problems raised by the period of transition. Even the Russian experience could, in fact, be defined as a bourgeois process without the bourgeoisie. The communists,

Gramsci recalled, have always seen in the Russian state not communism but a period of transition between capitalism and communism (it is in this sense that the gramscian concept of dictatorship of the proletariat must be explained). In this way Marx's prophecy is fulfilled:[41]

> Capitalism, at a certain point in its development, can no longer manage to dominate and organise the productive forces which it itself has created. The historical phase which follows economic imperialism is communism: either economic development finds in the revolutionary working class the necessary political force to determine this transition, or, it is the regression, the destruction of the productive forces, *chaos*, the death of the surplus population. Of course the capitalists want to return to individualism, want to destroy the social organisation born of the imperialist phase, in so far as it contains the vital impulse towards communism.

It is therefore surprising to find that, confronted with this explicit confirmation of the experiment of the 'councils' and its extension to a world scale, Gramsci's analyses were developed essentially on the theme of the alliance (working and peasant classes) and of the analysis of such phenomena via the prism of the intellectuals. In order to understand this apparent contradiction, however, the peculiar nature of the Italian situation should be recalled, which at the time imposed on the political party the function of 'representation' of these complex class relationships a direct verification of which was hindered by fascism. This assessment is corroborated by what Gramsci asserted in the report to the Central Committee of 2–3 August 1926, a report in which, after having distinguished between a situation of advanced capitalism and a situation of more 'backward' capitalism (in Italy), he maintained that[42]

> one of the most important problems arising, especially in the big capitalist countries, *is that of factory councils and of workers' control*, as the basis for a new rallying of the working class, fitted to promote a more efficient struggle against syndical bureaucracy and to encompass the great masses, who are disorganised not only in France, but also in Germany and England.

It was the councils, therefore, which constituted for Gramsci the best way to facilitate the creation of a universal awareness of the proletariat, where the struggle is more directly engaged against social democracy. On the other hand, when the struggle is engaged against fascism, then the affirmation of the link with the demands of the working class must be elaborated, as it were, in the party. The conditions for realising such

an elaboration are various. We can try to sum them up as follows:
1   The class/party relationship remains such that the party is a part of the working class and not an organ of the latter, as the bordigans held, who saw in the function of the party with regard to the working class, a relationship of substantial superiority, affirming the fact, therefore, that the intellectuals (and not the workers themselves) are the true organisers of the working class.[43]
2   The party is inserted in an international dimension of problems, i.e. it is a 'detachment' of the International. Gramsci did not immediately reach this conviction. What decided it explicitly was the realisation that the party had to present itself to the masses not only as a mere instrument of elaboration and debate, but armed with an analysis of objective problems, of rational tactics and strategy. It is by this transformation of the party (which became the vehicle for an analysis of class, already formed, so to speak), that Gramsci defined the leninist stabilisation of the party. He acquired the conviction, he wrote, in a letter to Scoccimarro, 'that the main force which holds the party together is the prestige and ideals of the International, not the bonds which the specific action of the party has succeeded in creating'.[44] Hence the consequences which Gramsci drew from this: the analysis of the Italian situation had to be effected with reference to the specific characteristics of a situation which, furthermore, revealed contracts and contradictions at world level.

In order to understand the exact meaning of this conclusion, it is necessary to read the very significant letter written to Togliatti on behalf of the Political Bureau of the PCI in October 1926. The setting up of a permanent opposition within the Bolshevik party between majority and minority meant in effect for Gramsci the admission of the impossibility of effective oppostion to the social-democratic and syndicalist tendencies of the working class, directed towards the triumph of corporative trends and those of class interests at a non-hegemonic level. What Gramsci criticised in Trotsky's attitude was that, basing himself on the theory of American superimperialism and of the dwindling of prospects of world revolution, it was certainly possible to improve the economic conditions of the Russian working class, but on condition of renouncing its hegemonic ambitions on a world scale and, in particular, the specific task of the construction of socialism.[45] The problem which Gramsci emphasised, on the other hand, as at present essential, was precisely that of the political hegemony of the proletariat and it was the terms of such a problematic that he expressed in his criticism with regard to the 'corruption' brought in by the intellectuals. Now the working class, via the party, took up the struggle against social-democracy and syndicalism, on the basis of the awareness of its universality, which also justified its capacity to sacrifice its own immediate interests.[46]

3 The final fundamental point of this new vision of the political struggle of the proletariat is connected with the peculiar nature of Italian problems, that is, with the analysis of the conditions of the revolution in Italy. Here the political struggle could develop from the basis of an analysis of class analogous to the Russian analysis, since in Italy the motive forces of the revolution were also the workers and the peasants. Yet the 'peculiar nature' of Italy was constituted by the intertwining of the Vatican question and the 'Southern' question. The former was linked to the fact that the Catholic powers controlled a large section of the peasant class of the North and this consequently posed the problem of the liberation of those masses. The latter, for its part, was linked to the question of the intellectuals. In fact, during these years Gramsci had come to interpret what was called 'Italian revolutionary syndicalism' as a version of anti-giolittism culminating in Salvemini's radical liberalism. Salveminism and syndicalist-revolutionary rigour (including that ideology of intransigence which had dominated the socialist party and which Gramsci recognised as an expression of the peasant world of the Po Valley) constituted the effect of the peasant hegemony on the working-class movement. Salvemini's liberalist and anti-parasitic intransigence illustrates in its turn the way in which the peasant world reacted to the 'sucking' (*'succhiona'*) economy of big industry. In return, working-class hegemony over the peasant world would not be realised via the reformist advantages of giolittism, but via a proposal of alliance which also implied for the working class a realisation that they would have to face certain sacrifices. It was not a matter of a 'moralist' conclusion but of the transfer onto the working class of the analysis of class carried out by Salvemini on behalf of the peasant on the basis of an anti-reformist and anti-giolittian polemic, which fascism had partially instrumentalised.[47] This complex transfer of the idea of petit-bourgeois radicalism to that of the working class (but in a subordinate position in relation to the fundamental themes of workers' control over the economy and society) could still have appeared groundless, if the model of the New Economic Policy had not been present in the memory. In Russia in fact the working class (through the sacrifice of its corporative interests, but also in connection with objective conditioning), realised, according to Gramsci, proletarian leadership over the peasant world,

giving it the necessary concessions which could not be deferred (which did not mean, it should be noted, a lessening of working-class hegemony but, quite the contrary, its realisation). Where Italy in particular was concerned, such a class strategy implied on the one hand the leninist stabilisation of the party and on the other, as a correlative of effective workers' control, the immediate introduction of socialist objectives. Gramsci replied to Piero Sraffa, who was encouraging him to give pride of place to democratic objectives, that[48]

> if our party did not find, *even for today*, its own autonomous solutions to general Italian problems, the classes which form its natural base would shift *in toto* towards the political currents which offer some kind of solution to those problems, which would be the fascist solution.

Leninist stabilisation, and the contribution of salveminism (and sorelism) now allied themselves to the view that fascism was a violent domination of class, realised precisely at a historical moment in which the subsequent development of science itself had become impossible 'unless the proletariat assumes power, constitutes itself into a ruling class, by impressing on all society its specific class characteristics'.[49] Fascism was still for Gramsci the obvious sign that there could be no progress except through the forms of power of the proletariat and the creation of this democracy of producers in the councils, which still remained, in his mind, the prime condition for a renewal of the development of the productive forces.

5   The problem of the intellectuals had furthermore assumed a new aspect in Gramsci's thought. In order to understand the meaning of this 'transition' the sorelian presentation of the problem should be recalled. To give credit to the intellectuals meant for Sorel, as we know, opening oneself to positivist culture and to reformism; it meant shifting the problem of the revolution to the field of a compensation internal to the existing social structure. The point of departure of this analysis was still *bernsteinism*. In fact, if the shifting of social development had results having nothing to do with socialism, then the possibility of the revolution was bound to a dimension of overthrow (modelled on Christianity and its various revivals)[50] which assumed the character of a reconstruction *ab imo* conditioned not by the use of reason but by that of the myth.

Gramsci escaped from this antithesis by returning to a valorisation of intellectuals, and going on from there to discovering the validity of certain ideas of Sorel's antagonist, Renan.[51] But this turn-about is less shocking than it appears at first sight, for two reasons. The first emphasises, among the Italian intellectuals of the first quarter of this century, that current which ran from Salvemini to Gobetti and which encountered on its course the fringes of reformism (Modigliani, for example, when he drew closer to Salvemini) as well as syndicalism. This current held that free trade was the condition for the maintenance and development of the democratic structure and was logically opposed to protectionism (with its imperialist components), towards which, in the end, Giolitti himself was drawn and which constituted the landing stage of fascism. To recall the question of the intellectuals was, therefore, equivalent for Gramsci to presenting the demands of social groups whose requirements were antithetical to those of fascism; this was basically the political conclusion resulting from the famous testimony of Athos Lisa.[52] In fact, the theme of the Constituent Assembly meant the awareness of the fact that the battle against fascism demanded intermediate stages between the present state of social relations and the dictatorship of the proletariat. As is now clear, it was this awareness which caused Gramsci's isolation within the party during the last years of his life.

The second reason concerns the new position attributed to those intellectual groups in relation to the proletariat. When Sorel lamented the fact that the political struggle emerged as a clash between groups of intellectuals, and that in such clashes the interests of the masses were not included, he had in mind the typical situation of the socialist parties at the beginning of the century, whose doors were open to intellectuals and to the ideologies which the latter conveyed. But Gramsci had a different conception of the party as a section of the working class. To re-examine the question of the intellectuals no longer meant in this context to subordinate the party to those ideologies of which the latter were the bearers but, on the contrary, meant utilising them, not in order to isolate the working class but to widen the scope of class confrontation. The hegemonic capacity of the proletariat constituted, as we have emphasised, the condition of this alliance. The party, by its severity and discipline, interrupted the connection between the parliamentary action of the 'intellectuals' and sectional and corporative claims. Such a break indicated the capacity of the working class to become aware (via the party) of its historic mission and no longer solely of its own daily difficulties and problems.

These, then, were the famous themes which Gramsci developed, when he raised the problem of the 'creation of a new intellectual class'.[53] By freeing himself of the concept – which he considered mistaken – according to which the intellectual is generally defined in relation to his activity and not in relation to the 'whole general complex of social relations within which these activities (and hence the groups which personify them) are to be found',[54] Gramsci no longer thought of the question of intellectuals as an abstract and indeterminate problem; on the contrary he discovered the concrete ties existing between the type of work of intellectuals and particular social groups. Sorel's polemic against intellectuals no longer had a *raison d'être, since the intellectual was no longer regarded as an indeterminate figure but as a specific bond with a class or special group.* The problem of the construction of a new type of intellect bound to the working class was identified therefore with the possibility of developing and guiding from below a new cultural demand: in concrete terms, to create a new culture which was not subordinate, which would be dominant and not let itself be dominated by the traditional cultures.

According to Bobbio, such a problem is symptomatic of the transition from a thematic of marxist type to a thematic of hegelian type, and thus of a retreat to the idea of the hegelian civil society. But we have seen what civil society meant for Sorel and in what sense it is an alternative to the development represented by the dynamic capacities of the productive forces. In the period in which he was almost exclusively under the influence of Bernstein, Sorel had accepted this alternative in the framework of a conception aimed at denying the historical law of the transition from a capitalist socio-economic formation to a socialist formation. To fall back on civil society meant, in this context, to accept that historical movement was realised as an internal movement of groups and social forces within the old formation. Sorel himself, in one of his original (if somewhat questionable) formulations, had managed to correct this overtly revisionist conclusion and to present the *myth* as an instrument of autonomous formulation of the working class. Gramsci, who accepted leninism (in the sense outlined above), was far from returning to Sorel's starting-point. In reality, for him the problem of the education of *organic intellectuals* (technical and political) constituted precisely a means of leading the working class into the field of history rather than into that of the internal workings of civil society. The proletariat can construct its *hegemony*, because its power is now affirmed on an international scale and because the experiences and the effects of that power are interdependent and cannot be isolated. The upsetting of power relationships (understood as liberation from subordination and on the other hand as capacity to subordinate to oneself the other conceptions of the world) occurred in the field of ideologies. But this reflects the capacity the producers have to cause the development of the productive forces to progress in a more coherent and complete manner than that in which the bourgeois and petit-bourgeois classes are now capable of, obliged as they were to subject the development of the productive forces to that of the valorisation of capital at the time of imperialism. On the other hand, Poulantzas is wrong too to reduce the question merely to a clash of ideologies in defining the latter as a real relationship of men with their conditions of existence invested in an imaginary relationship.[55] The relationship with ideology – even if it is of necessity imaginary – possesses in fact very different characteristics if the ideology remains within the social relationships existing in a given national society or if it reflects the most advanced relationships on a world scale. It was not only a question, for the Italian working class, of filling an internal void, of national character, determined by the subordinate position in which, as a class, it had been placed. *It was a question, via this, of filling that more radical void created by the October Revolution.* The aim of the working class was no longer a reformist aim of greater social justice; it was now a matter of *taking over an economic and social process which had the importance of a historical transition*, a transition which, under present conditions (imposed by fascism), the party indicated as of prime importance. If the objective of the reformist policy was to fill the void of inferiority in which bourgeois domination had left the working class, the task which the 'communist' Gramsci gave himself was to fill the gap that the October Revolution had left between working-class consciousness and the whole complex of contemporary bourgeois institutions. From this angle, the national question was only the translation of a vaster problem; Gramsci's contribution must be viewed – if its specific nature is not to be lost – on this broader base. Poulantzas does not perceive this aspect of the question, since he does not understand that character of the working class in which it finds itself not only conditioned by the domination of the bourgeoisie of each country but as having experienced historically (even though in an ideological and mythical way) the new historic phase born of the October Revolution.

To conclude, could it be said that Gramsci returns to the problem of civil society in the same terms as those used by Bernstein and Sorel?

When Gramsci established his distinction between the two broad superstructural levels: 1 Civil society − 'all the organisations which are commonly called "private" '; and 2 ' "political society or the state" which corresponds to the function of "hegemony" which the ruling class exercises over the whole of society and to that of "direct rule" or of command which is expressed in the state and in "juridical" government',[56] when he saw in the state this reserve of domination constituted 'in anticipation of moments of crisis in command and direction when spontaneous consent diminishes',[57] Gramsci had in mind the weakness of the historical moment in which the bourgeois state fell which, in the case of fascism, had had to turn to the direct exercise of force. Gramsci's problem was precisely that of offering (as had emerged to a certain degree with the NEP) a guarantee of force and power (the dictatorship of the proletariat) which was capable of leaving room for those social groups (those for whom Salvemini had made himself the spokesman) who were in need of 'freedom' − needing to free themselves from parasitism and protectionism. The room left to these groups meant a great limitation of the spontaneous demands of the working class, a strong moral and ideological tension in the latter and consequently imposed a monolithic political leadership.

Hence the two ideas confronting Gramsci: on the one hand the theory of this monolithic party as condition of the historical bloc; on the other, the perspective of the fusion and unification of the forces of the bloc, prepared by a strong and ideal expansivity of the latent and peasant forces (a whole thematic linked with the utilisation of national literature).[58] Populism, for Gramsci, meant the tendential fusion of the classes/matrices of the revolution (working class and peasant) in the leninist presupposition of the dictatorship of the proletariat. It was a question of a bloc of social forces in which the 'consent' was made possible by the intellectual and moral hegemony of one group over another and by its capacity to prepare a new historic condition for the future.

6   There is no doubt that this was the state of affairs and that the national-popular elements were ways of concretising the hegemony of the international class.[59] And this is confirmed by the extremely radical criticism which Gramsci levelled at theoretical syndicalism, which in fact appeared to him now as the ideology of a subordinate group 'who were prevented, by this theory, from becoming dominant some day'.[60] Furthermore, if we want to remain faithful to Gramsci's texts, it should

be kept in mind that the political party does not constitute for him a mere reflection of civil society. To go beyond the reformist character of the intellectual condition should reflect, in its monolithic structures, the central problem arising for civil society, a problem which has in fact a historical and not merely a contingent dimension[61] or, to use Gramsci's phraseology, *which invests the structure* (i.e. the organic phenomena of society) *and not just the superstructure* (i.e. the occasional and contingent phenomena).[62]

Although this is the problem today (*the necessity of the modern prince, as revival of the historical problem*), the outcome of the process is nevertheless different. There has been a return to the link between civil society and the state. Hegel, who had viewed the link between consensus and force in an explicit way (and outside the liberalist ideology of spontaneity), was the theoretician for this. *Hegel was the theorist of the 'permanent hegemony of the urban class over the whole population'.* For him, the organisation of consent was left to private initiative; therefore it had a moral and ethical character.[63] The state, in its turn, 'has and demands consent, but also "educates" this consent'.[64] But this great Hegelian theory and the situation it interpreted had its day, in the post-war period, when the hegemonic apparatus disintegrated and the 'exercise of hegemony became permanently difficult and hazardous'.[65] *At that moment, the search for consent was replaced by the exercise of force.* Fascism was therefore for Gramsci the end of a historical epoch. The idea of freedom had now passed to the other side, but not in the sense of the subordination of 'liberalist' ideas (mentioned above) to working-class hegemony, *but in the sense of the global direction of the historical process,* since in the doctrine of the state-society[66]

> the transition will have to be made from a phase in which 'state' is equal to 'government' and identifies itself with a 'civil society', to a 'night-watch state', i.e. a coercive organisation which will protect the development of the elements of a society regulated in constant progress but nevertheless gradually reducing its authoritarian and coactive interventions. But this could never lead one to think of a new 'liberalism' although this is almost the beginning of an era of organic liberty.

The line of historic movement is thus indicated in Gramsci's thought by two events: the October Revolution, which marked the beginning of international power for the proletariat; *fascism, which marked on the part of the bourgeoisie the abandonment of the search for consent.*[67] At present the search for consent and the whole idea of freedom (in Salvemini's sense of liberation from exploitation and parasitism) had been taken over by the working class which, by passing through the monolithic phase of the party and of the dictatorship of the proletariat, again opened up the way for the historic development of an organically free society of co-operating producers.

We have emphasised these points as they demonstrate how the gramscian idea of intellectuals and the renewal of interest in a civil society resulting from this, are totally separate from the problem as viewed by Bernstein, and show that Gramsci was fundamentally interested in a reconquest of the historical dimension (either organic or structural) of the problems. Gramsci was not the theorist of an ingenious social machinery but a revolutionary thinker. I think that even the questions raised at the strictly philosophical level – in particular the discussion with Croce – must be evaluated in this perspective.

7 *'The materialism and the phosophy of Benedetto Croce'* represents a *return to Labriola,* nevertheless, defined as the philosopher who theorised the independence of philosophy from praxis, contrary to any other philosophical trend.[68] This definition is accompanied by another which defines the concept of *orthodoxy* in the field of marxism. Orthodoxy, said Gramsci,[69]

is not to be looked for in this or that adherent of the philosophy of praxis, or in this or that tendency connected with currents extraneous to the original doctrine, but in the fundamental concept that the philosophy of praxis is 'sufficient unto itself', that it contains in itself all the fundamental elements needed to construct a total and integral conception of the world, a total philosophy and theory of natural science, and not only that but everything that is needed to give life to an integral practical organisation of society, that is, to become a total integral civilisation.

The return to Labriola was therefore for Gramsci a return to orthodoxy, defined in the above sense. It should also be added that from the theoretical point of view this 'self-sufficiency' took the form of a resumption of the historical movement in the sense indicated by Marx and Engels;[70] that is, as a transition to a different and higher form of civilisation. In order to understand this transition, it is necessary to note certain theoretical tools Gramsci used. The first is constituted by *the relationship of the philosophy of praxis with materialism and with idealism*; the second, by the adoption of what we might call *the method of filling* (*riempimento*). Where the first point is concerned (as we said for the young Gramsci), Gramsci managed to free himself from the domain of mechanicism and from the territory of reification and passivity, by recovering a theoretical dimension which he defined as *creativity*.[71] Such an outcome posed him the problem of 'becoming true', of 'subjectivism'. This 'becoming true' lay, Gramsci thought, in the theory of super-structures. In other words, the course of history runs in the direction of a progressive liberation of partial and fallacious ideologies (as ex-pression of restricted and static situations), in order to arrive on the con-trary at a progressive unification of humanity in which subjectivity and objectivity are welded into a single unit. It is in this sense that Gramsci attributed to the concept of historical development, in the field of marxism, *a tension which invests both structures and superstructures* (i.e. the historical bloc). What Gramsci called the hegelian idea, the fact of a progressive historical tension, is reflected as much in the structure as in the superstructure. The possibility of the structure's being drawn in to history ('*coinvolta*'), is the development of the idea of councils, where in fact the main productive force becomes capable of talking in the first person. In these new conditions, the modern prince takes up in the same sense the problem of the historicisation of reality at the level of the economy.

The linear tension in the guiding of the historical process (which manifested itself, as we know, in the fact that fascism appeared to Gramsci as the negation of such a process and the eruption of an alien violence) must be integrated furthermore in the other dimension which we have defined as that of *filling* (*riempimento*). One manages to rediscover the possibility of progress only by exercising a strong pressure on the passive components of the social world. To get society to submit to a strong thrust from below is to put historical progress on the road again. Here we see the double aspect of Gramsci's theory of common sense. On the one hand it indicates a 'disintegrated, incoherent, inconsistent concept, conforming to the social and cultural position of the masses whose philosophy it is';[72] on the other, recalling (and, in part, distorting the sense of) the famous passage in *Capital*,[73] Gramsci theorises common sense as a determined historical fact. According to this fact, if will 'is initially represented by a single (remarkable) individual, its rationality is constituted by what is gathered by the great number, gathered in a permanent manner, i.e. become a culture, "good sense", a conception of the world, with an ethnic conforming to its structure'.[74]

Gramsci's idea was that historical tensions will arise, correspondingly, when this thrust from below has been set in motion. Contrary to what occurs in the institutional framework of struggles kept at trade-union level, here the working class, finding itself at the head of historical movement, *leads politically according to a historical perspective.* This latter concept is defined (as we know) in relation to the historical bloc, i.e. in relation to the possibility of taking over the development of the forces of production in new terms which arise from the capacities of the 'producers' to substitute themselves for the former social forces in leading development. *The sorelian concept of the historical bloc acquires new content* in relation to this 'filling' of social differences and relative cultures, marked off, as we know, not by the practice of reformism but by the point of outcome constituted (not just for the Russian workers) by the October Revolution. If the movement was represented from below, if such a demand was maintained at the level of internationalism, if the social demand recovered, a positive reply to such a demand would inevitably imply taking up the historical movement in the form conceived by Engels and Labriola, i.e. *as an organic structural movement and not just as a partial and reformist movement.* The retranslation of the theme of 'creativity' on the basis of its purely speculative meaning is connected for Gramsci with this filling of the internal void, giving rise finally to this new common sense of the producers. In this context, we can understand that Gramsci had felt the need to settle his account with Croce definitively. In the face of sorelism, Croce had presented the idea of hegemony as an ethical instance. Consequently, he opened a hegemonic outlet (in the bourgeois sense) to a situation which only offered the path of leninism as an outcome. All things considered, by presenting bourgeois hegemony, Croce actualised a great number of theoretical operations proposed by Sorel. Like Sorel's Vico, Croce's Vico suggested the installation of a synchronisation of types of thinking. The separation between morals and politics meant the speculative reception of another theme on which Sorel had so insisted: the link between the problems of the family and those of morals. Furthermore, *Croce also reduced politics to a myth* but afterwards offered to bourgeois hegemony a complex range of connections between myth and thought, between practical mythology and Olympian serenity, which in fact constituted civilisation. When he tackled the problem of Croce, Gramsci was deeply aware that it was a question of a version – a particularly significant one, on the strength of its links with the Italian situation on the one hand and with German idealism on the other – of *bernsteinism*, i.e. of that philosophy which had in fact theorised the formation of the complex articulations of civil society mediating historical development and reducing it little by little to something imperceptibly slow. For Croce, the workings of civil society were sublimated in eternal forms of the mind, but exercised the same function of interruption and arrest of historical development.

The speculative version of croceanism is, therefore, once more, a type of reformism.[75] This stems from the fact that the unification lacking between the pressure from below and the field of productive forces *reduces history again to the history of intellectuals*. Not only is there no modification of the 'popular thought' ('mummified popular culture'),[76] but furthermore efforts are made to divide what the philosophy of praxis had, to a certain degree, united. Hence the meaning of what Gramsci called 'absolute historicism'. Hegelian immanentism 'becomes historicism, but it is only absolute historicism with the philosophy of praxis, absolute historicism or absolute humanism'.[77] The identification philosophy/politics was not for Gramsci a mere categorical parallel. On the contrary, it aimed at taking into account this qualitative leap (the echo of which is also found in Sorel) indicating that the politics made by intellectuals alone is necessarily reformist ('a history of busybodies'), even though now that anti-sorelian awareness has been achieved it is possible to set the masses in motion *politically* and understand that intellectuals are necessary for such an end. The sorelian polemics against intellectuals, globally presented in the very term of *historical bloc*, continued thus to filter into the determination of the concept of *absolute historicism* (i.e. of a historicism which annuls these practical and theoretical intellectual mediations, tending to arrest praxis in so far as it emanates directly from the working masses). This means that a great historical objective is not reached by returning to the automatism of facts, or even by claiming to guide them from the basis of an intellectual situation of exteriority in relation to those same facts, but on the contrary by giving to ideas this character of mass and unity which turns them into historical forces.

If social automatism determines in a relative way (and only as a trend) the historical outcome, the difference between Gramsci and Bernstein will be found in the fact that the former restores historical laws on the basis of an interpretation (strongly influenced by Sorel but reinforced by a leninist conception of the party) of what the ideas and the practical confirmation of the producers and of the masses can realise to fill the historical void and determined by the October Revolution; while the second leaves to working-class corporative praxis the task of filling the social void produced by productive development.

The philosophy of *absolute historicism* (contrary to current interpretations) is precisely this humanist philosophy of the historical bloc, *as a unity of theory and praxis*. To reject the dichotomy between praxis and theory is to restore (in the only way possible to Gramsci), the historical, structural and organic dimensions of history and hence, to overcome the limits of revisionism.

Notes

This chapter was originally published in *Dialectiques*, No. 4 : 5, 1974, and was translated into English by Della Couling.

1 L. Paggi, *Gramsci e il moderno principe*, vol. 1, *Nella crisi del socialismo italiano*, Rome, 1970.
2 This distinction appeared in A. Labriola, *Saggi sul materialismo storico*, a cura di V. Gerratana e Augusto Guerra, Rome, 1964, p. 182.
3 Ibid., p. 195.
4 'Experimented on intentionally, things end up by becoming mere objects for us, created by our way of looking at them' (ibid).
5 Ibid., p. 217.
6 G. Sorel, *Saggi di critica del marxismo*, Palermo, 1903, p. 46, and again: 'Labriola arrives at ... *a psychological conception of history*' (ibid., p. 778).
7 In reading the works of the democratic socialists one remains surprised at the certainty with which they 'arrange' the future; they *know* that the world is moving toward an unavoidable revolution, the general results of which they discern. Indeed, some of them have such confidence in their theories that they end at quietism (ibid., p. 59).
8 Ibid., p. 69. Further on: 'to transform a doubtful point of common sense into a scientific problem is to ignore the true character of science' (ibid., p. 91).
9 Ibid., p. 167.
10 'Particularism, collectivism and communism, instead of characterising three successive epochs, can very well be notions which science ascertains simultaneously in the developed societies' (ibid., p. 168). The flaw in dialectics is precisely its discontinuity. It 'introduces into history a paradoxical discontinuity which hinders us from recognising the evolutionary mechanism' (ibid., p. 192).
11 'Contrary to what is encountered in the first system, the productive forces are placed in the second position; it is civil society which is considered here as the fundamental element' (ibid., p. 246).
12 Sorel, 'La decomposizione del marxismo', in *Nuova collana di economisti stranieri ed italiani*, ed. G. Bottai and C. Arena, Turin, 1936, p. 895.

13 Ibid., p. 909.
14 Ibid., p. 911.
   Marxism should not be confused with political parties because in fact the
   latter are forced to function as bourgeois parties, assuming a rigidified
   attitude according to the needs electoral circumstances impose and at
   times making compromises with other groups which have an electoral
   following similar to their own, while it remains steadfastly attached to the
   perspective of an absolute revolution (ibid., p. 914).
15 A. Gramsci, *Scritti giovanili 1914–1918*, Turin, 1958, p. 150; translation in
   Selections from Political Writings 1910–20, ed. Q. Hoare, London,
   Lawrence & Wishart, 1977, pp. 34–5.
16 Ibid., p. 160.
17 Ibid., p. 173.
18 Gramsci's expression is 'marxist hegelianism' (ibid., p. 233).
19 'Development is governed by the rhythm of freedom' (ibid., p. 285).
20 The quantity (economic structure) becomes quality since it becomes an
   instrument of action in the hands of men, men who are of value not only
   for their weight, their stature, the mechanical energy they might develop
   with their muscles and nerves but who are of value in that they are souls,
   in that they suffer, understand, play, desire and refuse. ... The success or
   defeat of the (Russian) revolution will be able to supply us with a credible
   document of the ... capacity (of the proletariat) to create history : for the
   moment we can only wait (ibid., p. 281).
21 The power of the working class, as an economic fact, as effect of an
   objective cause, is not a political asset. In order for it to become so, this
   power must organise itself, discipline itself with the aim of achieving a
   political goal (ibid., p. 259).
22 'Philosophical idealism is a doctrine of being and knowledge according to
   which these two concepts identify themselves, and reality is what is known
   theoretically, our ego' (ibid., pp. 327–8).
23 'An evolution ... a substitution, the conscious and disciplined force of which
   is the necessary means' (ibid., p. 328).
24 A. Gramsci, *L'Ordine Nuovo 1919–1920*, Turin, 1954, p. 15; *Political
   Writings 1910–20*, p. 75.
25 'The socialists forget that their role had to be essentially one of criticism, of
   antithesis. Instead of mastering reality, they allowed themselves to be
   absorbed by it' (ibid., p. 16, *Political Writings 1910–20*, p. 75).
26 Ibid., p. 25, *Political Writings 1910–20*, p. 36.
27 Ibid., p. 38.
28 Ibid., pp. 46–7, *Political Writings 1910–20*, p. 111.
29 Ibid., p. 48, *Political Writings 1910–20*, p. 112. To compare this with Sorel's
   theory of producers, cf. 'La morale dei produttori', the last chapter of
   Considerazioni sulla violenza, Italian trans., Bari, 1909, pp. 257 ff.
30 A. Bordiga, *Il Soviet, organe de la fraction communiste abstentionniste du
   parti socialist italien*, Naples, 8 February 1920. English translation in
   Political Writings 1910–20, p. 227.
31 *L'Ordine Nuovo*, pp. 59–60. And elsewhere, 'No workers' government can

exist unless the working class is capable of becoming, as a whole, the executive power of the workers' state' (ibid., p. 95, *Political Writings 1910–20*, p. 133).

32 Ibid., p. 124, *Political Writings 1910–20*, p. 261.

33 When we say that the historical process of the workers' revolution which is inherent in the capitalist social system ... that this ... had exploded into the light of day, does this mean that it can now be controlled and documented? ... We say it can be when the whole of the working class has become revolutionary (ibid.).

34 For Gramsci the concept of *council* is always connected with that of spontaneity: 'By virtue of its revolutionary spontaneity, the Factory Council tends to spark off the class war' (ibid., p. 133, *Political Writings 1910–20*, p. 266).

35 'The revolution is proletarian and communist only to the extent that it is a liberation of the proletarian and communist forces of production that were developing within the very heart of the society dominated by the capitalist class' (ibid., p. 136, *Political Writings 1910–20*, p. 305).

36 Furthermore this universal bond had been disrupted as a result of recent experience and leninist elaboration, but also if one thinks of Daniel De Leon. Cf. A. Ransome, 'Conversazioni con Lenin', *L'Ordine Nuovo*, vol. 1, no. 18, Editori Riuniti, Rome, 1973, p. 137.

37 Ibid., p. 150.

38 A. Gramsci, 'Socialismo e Fascismo', *L'Ordine Nuovo 1921–1922*, Turin, 1966, p. 126.

39 Ibid., p. 500.

40 Ibid., p. 517.

41 Ibid., p. 127.

42 A. Gramsci, *La construzione del partito communista 1923–26*, Turin, 1971. English translation in *Selections from Political Writings 1921–26*, ed. and trans. Q. Hoare, London, Lawrence & Wishart, 1978, pp. 134 ff.

43 For this aspect, see 'The Lyons Congress', *Political Writings 1921–26*, pp. 313–78.

44 Cf. the letter in P. Togliatti, *La formazione del gruppo dirigente del partito communista italiano*, Rome, 1962, p. 151, *Political Writings 1921–26*, p. 174.

45 For this reason he was to object to Togliatti:
Your whole argument is tainted by 'bureaucratism'. Today, at nine years distance from October 1917, it is no longer *the fact of the seizure of power* by the Bolsheviks which can revolutionise the Western masses, because this has already been allowed for and has produced its effects. What is active today, ideologically and politically, is the conviction (if it exists) that the proletariat, once power has been taken, *can construct socialism*. The authority of the party is bound up with this conviction ... ' (ibid., pp. 136–7, *Political Writings 1921–26*, pp. 439–40).

46 'The whole tradition of social democracy and syndicalism which has until now prevented the proletariat from organising itself into a ruling class,

appears in the ideology and practice of the opposition bloc' (ibid., p. 130).
Shortly before, the condition of the revolution in Italy demanded that the
proletariat was 'very rich in the spirit of sacrifice and completely freed of
any residue of reformist and syndicalist corporativism' (ibid., p. 129).

47 'What I find characteristic of the present phase of the capitalist crisis,' wrote
Gramsci in 1926, 'is the fact that, contrary to the years 1920–1, today the
political and military formations of the middle classes have a radical left
character, or at least present themselves to the masses as radical left' (ibid.,
p. 22).

48 Ibid., p. 177.

49 Ibid., p. 250.

50 For these aspects of Sorel's thought, cf. his *Essai sur l'Eglise et l'Etat*, Paris,
1901.

51 By Renan, cf. in particular *La réforme intellectuelle et morale*, 3rd edn.,
Paris, 1872, and by Sorel, *Le système historique de Renan*, Paris, 1906.

52 Cf. 'Discussione politica con Gramsci in carcere. Testo integrale del
rapporto inviato nel 1933 al Centro del Partito. La costituente e le
prospettive della lotta contro il fascismo', *Rinascità*, no. 21, 12 December,
1964. A. Lisa's report sums up the trend of Gramsci's thinking around
1930.

53 A. Gramsci, *Gli Intellettuale*, Rome 1971, p. 17; *Selections from the Prison
Notebooks*, ed. and trans. Q. Hoare and G. Nowell Smith, London,
Lawrence & Wishart, 1971, pp. 3–43.

54 *Gli Intellettuale*, p. 16. On this subject, cf. N. Bobbio, 'Gramsci e la
concezione della società civile', *Gramsci e la cultura contemporanea*,
Cagliari, 1969, pp. 75 ff.; also J. Texier's contribution (ibid., p. 152) and
J.-M. Piotte, *La pensée politique de Gramsci*, Paris, Editions Anthropos,
1970.

55 N. Poulantzas, *Pouvoir politique et classes sociales*, vol. 2, Paris, 1972, p. 27.
English translation, *Political Power and Social Classes*, London, New Left
Books, 1973.

56 *Gli Intellettuale*, p. 20, *Prison Notebooks*, p. 12.

57 Ibid., p. 21.

58 'In fact any innovatory force is repressive to its own adversaries, but in so
far as it unleashes latent forces, makes them more powerful, it is expansive,
and expansiveness constitutes by far its most distinctive characteristic' (A.
Gramsci, *Letteratura e vita nazionale*, Rome, 1971, p. 38).

59 A class that is international in character has – in as much as it guides
social strata which are narrowly national (intellectuals), and indeed
frequently even less than national; particularistic and municipalistic (the
peasants) – to 'nationalise' itself in a certain sense. Moreover this sense is
not a very narrow one either, since before the conditions can be created
for an economy that follows a world plan, it is necessary to pass through
multiple phases in which the regional combinations (of groups of nations)
may be of various kinds (A. Gramsci, *Note sul Machiavelli*, Rome, 1971,
p. 154, *Prison Notebooks*, p. 241).

60 Ibid., p. 50.

61 The theme is linked to the gramscian idea that each class has in fact only one party. The multiplicity of such organisms has a reformist character, i.e. solely concerns 'partial questions'; in a certain sense, 'a division of the political work (useful, within its limits)', but 'when the main questions are at stake, unity is achieved, the bloc realised. Hence the conclusion that in the construction of parties, they should be based on a "monolithic" character and not on secondary questions' (ibid., p. 48, *Prison Notebooks*, p. 184).

62 Ibid., pp. 64–5.

63 Ibid., p. 138, *Prison Notebooks*, p. 258.

64 Ibid., p. 178, *Prison Notebooks*, p. 259.

65 Ibid., p. 140, *Prison Notebooks*, p. 259.

66 Ibid., p. 175, *Prison Notebooks*, pp. 261–3.

67 Regarding this aspect of the question, it should be noted that Gramsci admits that a certain structural alteration is possible even in a fascist regime. This is a question of the legislative intervention of the state which accentuates the production-plan element and thus socialisation and cooperation: 'Within the concrete framework of Italian social relations, this could be the sole solution for developing the productive forces of industry under the leadership of the traditional ruling classes' (A. Gramsci, *Il Materialismo Storico e la Filosofia di B. Croce*, Rome, 1971, p. 230).

68 Ibid., p. 92.

69 Ibid., p. 185, *Prison Notebooks*, p. 462. .

70 'Engels' idea, that "the unity of the world consists in its proven materiality … through the long and laborious development of philosophy and the natural sciences", contains in fact the germ of the correct conception' (ibid., p. 168).

71 'Classical German philosophy introduced the concept of "creativity" of thought, but in an idealistic and speculative sense. It would seem that only the philosophy of praxis has made a step forward in thought, on the basis of the classical German philosophy, avoiding any tendency towards solipsism' (ibid., p. 26).

72 Ibid., p. 139.

73 'The mystery of the expression of value … can be deciphered only when the concept of human equality possesses the solidity of a popular prejudice' (K. Marx, *Capital*, London, Lawrence & Wishart, 1974, vol. 1, p. 80).

74 Gramsci, *Il Materialismo*, p. 26, *Prison Notebooks*, p. 231.

75 Croce's historicism would therefore be nothing but a form of political moderatism which presents as sole method of political action that in which progress, historical development, results from the dialectics of conservation and innovation. In modern language this concept is called reformism (ibid., p. 262).

76 Ibid., p. 122.

77 Ibid., p. 123, *Prison Notebooks*, p. 465.

Part two

Hegemony, philosophy and ideology

4 Gramsci's general theory of marxism

Leonardo Paggi

To speak of Gramsci's 'general theory' of marxism may seem inappropriate, even incorrect, given the originality of Gramsci's work. In emphasising his originality, however, the central role of Gramsci's relation to established interpretations of marxism is overlooked. Although his early formation took place outside of the Second International, this does not mean that Gramsci was not involved in a close confrontation with it, from 1924 on, when the Comintern sought to bolshevise all communist parties. Certain aspects of a 'general theory' of marxism in Gramsci must be dealt with since his writings contain attempts to formulate a theoretical alternative to this bolshevisation.

In 1958, Togliatti described Gramsci's thought as a 'new chapter in Leninism'.[1] Yet, this does not imply a linear development from Lenin, since Gramsci accepted Lenin's main break but also went beyond it. Bukharin's *Manual* provided Gramsci and other European thinkers with the occasion to point out a series of differences between the Bolsheviks' interpretation of marxist theory and the 'marxist-leninist' line which became increasingly more distinct from it. Of course, Plekhanov always loomed behind Bukharin. In his *Fundamental Problems of Marxism* (1908), Plekhanov had provided the most complete attempt at a marxist philosophical manual after Engels' *Anti-Dühring*, and what Gramsci called the most significant example of 'the pseudo-scientific pedantry of the German intellectual group that was so influential in Russia.'[2] This Second International 'classic' provided Gramsci with the main guidelines for the theoretical elaborations in the *Prison Notebooks*. One must begin here to plausibly order the many definitions of marxism contained in Gramsci's work.

The central propositions of Plekhanov's study are contained in its first pages.[3] They can be summarised in three main points: 1 the philosophy of Marx and Engels is dialectical materialism, i.e., a materialism integrated by the logic of the contradiction as the logic of movement; 2 the tendency to make historical materialism and economic analysis independent of philosophical materialism is rejected (dialectical and historical materialism are inseparable); and 3 only when this inseparable bond is overlooked does the attempt become possible to *complete* marxism with foreign philosophies under the pretext that Marx and Engels did not sufficiently elaborate some part of their thought.

Already in his early writings, Plekhanov identified materialism as the philosophical nucleus of marxism. Subsequent positions came to be gradually defined during the *Berstein-Debatte* and then against every attempt to read marxist philosophy in a different way. These theoretical solutions outlined within the defence-lines of 'orthodox' marxists are severely criticised and rejected in the *Prison Notebooks*. Gramsci offered a different, if not opposed, solution to Plekhanov's attempt to prevent the completion of marxism. His aim was to open the way to a 'revolutionary', i.e. political, use of historical materialism. Already in his first major articles on the October Revolution, the effort to identify the philosophical nucleus of marxism, expressed as the rejection of any conception which would make history into a 'natural organism', is tied to a critical evaluation of major contemporary social phenomena. The acceptance, but reformulation, of Plekhanov's view of an indissoluble link between dialectical materialism and historical materialism is articulated in Gramsci's mature thought through the criticism of materialism in philosophy and of economism (or determinism, or sociology) in the reading of historical materialism.

1 Absolute historicism and humanism

In September 1925, *l'Unità* published some notes on leninism from a lecture that Gramsci had delivered at a party school. They began with the following general definition:[4]

> Leninism is the political science of the proletariat which teaches us how to mobilize all the forces necessary to demolish bourgeois dictatorship and to set up the dictatorship of the proletariat. For some, there is no such thing as a leninism different from marxism. This is not true. Leninism contains a unique world view without which Marx today could not be understood.

Setting aside for the moment Gramsci's interpretation of the relation between Marx and Lenin (at the time an issue in the whole communist movement), we find that the first definition of the doctrine remains unchanged throughout the prison writings.

Political science or, as Gramsci later would say, the science of history and politics, cannot be considered a pure method of analysis. Lenin's practical and theoretical work cannot be considered as a restoration of the analytical capacity of some given cognitive instruments. To reach Lenin's conclusions (even if only, as Gramsci often indicated, on the level of political praxis), it is necessary to reconsider the entire problem of the relation between marxism and modern philosophy. In this sense, for Gramsci, marxism is also profoundly monistic. None of its parts can be changed without automatically upsetting the whole system. Leninist political science rests on a philosophical revolution which has placed marxism in a different and more congruent relation, not only with objective problems, but also with the forms of consciousness of the contemporary epoch. Through this interpretation of leninism, Gramsci put forth his general conception of marxism and indicated both his philosophical course as well as his arrival point. With Gramsci, the historical materialism of the Second International marxist tradition became political science, i.e. an interpretive instrument of the process of development of the proletarian revolution. A crucial break, however, is hidden behind this terminological continuity with Plekhanov's account.

To understand what Gramsci meant by marxism as a philosophy which is also a world view, it is important to recall his recurrent assertion that marxism marks an irreversible break with every preceding conception of philosophy, i.e. that marxism is not a new philosophy next to, or contraposed to others, but is the expression of the need to restructure all philosophical knowledge. The break does not take place within the history of philosophy. On the contrary, it is characteristic of marxism to indicate the abandonment of the most fundamental philosophical categories. The first error implicit in adhering to the old materialism consists in identifying the philosophical nucleus of marxism through traditional philosophical categories, thus eliminating the task of conceiving its original content in new terms. Gramsci maintains that 'the new philosophy cannot coincide with any past system, under whatever name. Identity of terms does not mean identity of concepts',[5] and that 'at the level of theory, the philosophy of praxis cannot be confused with or reduced to any other philosophy. Its originality lies not only in its transcending of previous philosophies but also and above all in that it opens up a completely new road, renewing from head to toe the whole way of conceiving philosophy itself'.[6] Plekhanov's materialist orthodoxy is not only based on an extremely simplistic interpretation of the origins of Marx's thought, but does not avoid that logic of completing marxism which it meant to oppose. From this perspective the choice of materialism constitutes an entirely interchangeable option with the neo-kantianism of his adversaries. In discussing Croce's attempt to incorporate marxism as the 'handmaiden of traditional culture', Gramsci asserts even more explicitly that orthodox thinkers 'fall into a trap' when they make marxism 'subordinate to a general (vulgar) materialist philosophy just as others are to idealism'.[7]

It is appropriate here to recall Gramsci's appreciation for Labriola's theoretical proposal which he saw in need of rescue from oblivion, i.e. that 'the philosophy of praxis is an independent and original philosophy which contains in itself the elements of a further development, so as to become, from an interpretation of history, a general philosophy'.[8] The lack of a clear understanding of the Gramsci–Labriola relation is due to a lack of analysis of Labriola's own thought in relation to marxism. His approach to the problem of the philosophy of marxism is a result of a tacit but profound dissatisfaction with Engels' thesis concerning the death of philosophy through its dissolution in the development of positive sciences. Since for Labriola, also, science and philosophy are part of a process of development and transformation inevitably leading to their mutual recomposition, he does not consider this process completed for two reasons. First, because the development and proliferation of the particular sciences requires a level of epistemological reflection grounding them and relating their methodologies. Second, because revolutions occurring in scientific research, if not adequately thought out and grounded, can become entangled in a series of squabbles inhibiting their free development on the more general level of culture and world view. To ground the philosophical autonomy of a science means to guarantee its correct functioning.

The first pages of Labriola's *Socialism and Philosophy* clearly show the connection between the unfolding of marxist philosophy and its capacity to develop in different and occasionally hostile cultural contexts. A scientific vision of history cannot manifest all of its innovative force regarding the structure of knowledge implicit in it unless the philosophy of this science is specified. The philosophical terrain is no longer the foundation upon which new systems can be constructed, but rather the battlefield of opposing cultural and political tendencies. Labriola argues that 'historical materialism may seem to be suspended in the air so long as it has for opponents other philosophies which do not harmonize with it and so long as it does not find the means to develop its own philosophy, such as is inherent and immanent in its fundamental facts and premises'.[9] To elaborate this philosophy does not mean to develop a speculative marxism, but to find the most suitable means for defending its scientific content. 'Some vulgar expounders of marxism,' Labriola adds, 'have robbed this theory of its immanent philosophy and reduced it to a simple way of deducing changes in the historical conditions from changes in the economic conditions.'[10] Consequently, the recovery and elaboration of marxist philosophy is an indispensable premise for avoiding economistic and mechanistic reductions of historical materialism. To study the philosophical content of marxism means to assign to philosophy a task entirely different from that indicated by Plekhanov. The problem is not to define once and for all the external perimeter of the doctrine as a defence against every possible assault. Marxism must be conceived in terms of an 'intellectual revolution', which will concern ever growing fields of knowledge to the extent that it will be able to sustain victoriously a series of confrontations dealing with cultural hegemony and world views.

Labriola identified this philosophical nucleus in historical materialism as the philosophy of praxis.[11] The concept of labour, or praxis, upon which Labriola, on the basis of the *Theses on Feuerbach*, grounds sociality as the constitutive trait of the historical and human world, can become a crucial element in transcending any dichotomising temptation which could be reproduced even within the very interpretation of historical materialism.[12]

Historical materialism will be enlarged, diffused, specialized, and will have its own history. It may vary in coloring and outline from country to country. But this will do no great harm, so long as it preserves that kernel which is, so to say, its whole *philosophy*. One of its fundamental theses is this: The nature of man, his historical making, is a practical process. And when I say *practical*, it implies the elimination of the vulgar distinction between theory and practice. For, in so many words, the history of man is the history of labor. And labor implies and includes on the one hand the relative, proportional, and proportioned development of both mental and manual activities, and on the other hand the concept of a history of labor implies even the social form of labor and its variations. Historical man is always human society, and the presumption of a presocial or supersocial man is a creature of imagination.

This concept of labour, upon which the marxist notion of history is based, also prescribes the outer limit of every discourse on the nature of man, becoming, progress, etc. Thus, for Labriola, 'practical relations' are the social relations of production. Praxis is the marxist foundation of the sociality of the human world. It is necessary to move in this direction in order to defend and reassert the scientific character of marxism in the face of the development of other ideological approaches to history. On the other hand, it is also clear why Labriola insists on the immanent character of marxist philosophy. He wishes to emphasise its different nature with respect to every preceding type of philosophy.

Already in relation to Hegel's systematic and synthetic claims, Engels had stressed that 'the task of philosophy thus stated means nothing but the task that a single philosopher should accomplish that which can only be accomplished by the entire human race in its progressive development.'[13] Here Labriola continues the theme of the end of the traditional philosopher by individuating in this concept of praxis the way in which 'individual thought' is recognised as a 'social function'. When the 'I' recognises itself as a part of the 'we' which predetermines its nature and possible scope, philosophy abandons the path of metaphysics along with every pretext of systematisation.

This brief excursus on Labriola helps us to understand Gramsci's account of the philosophy of marxism. It is necessary to turn to Labriola in order to appreciate that break in the history of philosophy represented by marxism, and on which Gramsci so often insists. But this raises the question of the marxist definition of 'absolute humanism' and 'absolute historicism'. These two themes have allowed the reinsertion of Gramsci's thought into the history of Italian philosophy. Yet, precisely these two expressions represented for Gramsci not the criticism of specific philosophies from a new philosophical 'viewpoint', but what made of marxism the irreversible arrival point of the previous ways of understanding philosophy. Can it be claimed that Gramsci's re-evaluation of the role of subjectivity passes through a philosophical conception which aims to make of man as such the subject of history?

Actually, for Gramsci, the very question 'what is man?' implies a metaphysical vice. The appropriate answer to this question can be found only by formulating it in a different way, following the fourth thesis on Feuerbach.[14]

That 'human nature' is the 'complex of social relations' is the most
satisfying answer because it includes the idea of becoming (man
'becomes,' he changes continuously with the changing of social
relations) and because it denies 'man in general.' Indeed social
relations are expressed by various groups of men which each
presupposes the others and whose unity is dialectical, not formal.
Man is aristocratic in so far as man is a serf, etc.

The advantage of this restatement of the fourth thesis is that it
transforms the question by introducing the new concept of social
relations of production. The historicity of man is linked to that of social
relations, which change with the changing of the position of the various
classes. It is impossible to deal with man if social class divisions are
ignored. The history of man is the history of this division. The true
subjects of history are conflicting social classes which acquire their
respective physiognomy in this antagonistic confrontation. Struggle is
the only possible form of unity in class society. The ideological character
of the question 'what is man?' consists in obliterating this by postulating
a sphere where such antagonism becomes insignificant. In marxism,
Gramsci adds, ' "man in general," in whatever form he presents himself,
is denied and all dogmatically "unitary" concepts are spurned and
destroyed as expressions of the concept "man in general" or of "human
nature" immanent in every man.'[15]
Even those philosophies asserting the identity between history and
man's nature do not escape this ideological flaw. In this case the problem
has to do with what is meant by 'history'. Crocean philosophy's
secularisation of the great metaphysical question concerning the nature
of man becomes real only on one condition, 'if one gives to history
precisely this significance of "becoming" which takes place in a
"*concordia discors*" [discordant concord] which does not start from
unity, but contains in itself the reasons for a possible unity.'[16] If it is
claimed that men and not classes are the subjects of history, no insistence
on the historicity of human nature can avoid an apology for the existing
social order. 'In each individual', Gramsci says, 'there are to be found
characteristics which are put in relief by being in contradiction with the
characteristics of others.' The very concept of man in general will
become meaningful only when society will have found a form of non-
antagonistic unity. Absolute humanism is possible only by renouncing
every philosophy of man, as well as every form of historicism which
does not lead to the double identification of the concept of 'history' with

the social relations of production and of 'becoming' with the antagonistic development of these relations.

It is crucial in reading Gramsci's philosophical writings to abandon any inadequately defined concept of history. Though a frequent source of ambiguities, the term 'historicism' has been used to indicate how marxism brings about a radical renewal of philosophy. Historicism reintroduces the theme of the death of philosophy – a thesis similar to Labriola's view that the philosophical nucleus of marxism must be sought within historical materialism and the revolution of the concept of history. Here, it is useful to momentarily set aside the 'compromised' language of the *Prison Notebooks* to see how in a 1926 writing, Gramsci prefigured the general lines of that criticism of philosophy which eventually became a recurrent leitmotive in the prison writings.

The occasion was provided by a philosophical convention which sought, in the jargon of traditional Italian philosophy, to proclaim its distance from fascism. Gramsci argues the impossibility and inanity of such a proposal.[17]

What is a philosopher? One must distinguish *philosopher* from professor of *philosophy*. As every man is an artist, so is every man a philosopher, in as much as he can think and express intellectual activity. Often the philosopher must be sought outside the professor of philosophy. The Milan convention, apart from certain exceptions, was more of a congress of philosophy professors than of philosophers. What practical results could come out of a congress of philosophy professors? There were no deliberations or regular business to be voted on. The only practical result could have been in the speeches of different speakers who, as philosophers, had the pretence of placing themselves above the various classes and social relations by announcing the independence of philosophy as a science of the spirit, as if the spirit can exist outside of historical reality, which is the reality of the class struggle. Philosophy is bourgeois or proletarian, just as the society in which man thinks and acts is bourgeois or proletarian. An independent philosophy does not exist, just as man does not exist apart from the social relations in which he lives. Of course, thought generates thought, but it does not come out of nothing just as one cannot nourish oneself with nothing.

Engels' theme on the end of the individual philosopher as the elaborator of systems dealing with problems resolvable only through the development of the human species forcefully returns here and in

Gramsci's later writings, but with an emphasis very different from Engels'. It is not a question of seeking in the development of the positive sciences the solution of problems that have traditionally confronted philosophy. Rather, it is the concept of social relations of production which provides philosophical reflection with a new intelligibility. To recognise its dependence on social relations means that philosophy must realise that there are limits to thought imposed by the existing world. Thus, it must develop into a theory of contradictions, whose supersession depends on the transformation of existing social relations. Gramsci's brutal assertion that philosophy is bourgeois or proletarian does not mean that there are two philosophies according to class perspectives, but that there are two ways of doing philosophy: one conservative and one revolutionary, depending on their acceptance or rejection of the symbiosis of philosophy and existing social conflicts. To use concepts apart from their objective social meaning amounts to doing bourgeois philosophy precisely to the extent that it is a refusal to enter the new ground of marxism.

In a well-known text from his youth, Marx stated that the history of philosophy shows that in moments of crisis when reflection is forced to consider the real world, there are always timid attempts at reconciling old habits and pressing new needs.[18]

> In such times, fearful souls take the reverse point of view of valiant commanders. They believe they are able to repair the damage by decreasing forces, by dispersal, by a peace treaty with real needs, while Themistocles, when Athens was threatened with devastation, persuaded the Athenians to leave it for good and found a new Athens on sea, on another element.

To the extent that it is permissible to use this image, which seems to prefigure the meaning of Marx's successive 'break' with philosophy, the definition of marxism as historicism, far from indicating Gramsci's wish to provide a new account of marxism, expresses the same need to proceed with founding 'a new Athens on another element'. The concept of absolute historicism indicates the new element on which it is necessary to base a new philosophy. Gramsci's task is not to prefigure the new Athens, but to point out the path that one must take.

With the notion of historicism, Gramsci is pursuing a double objective. First, he seeks to prevent the philosophical reabsorption of marxism, as happened with the rehabilitation of the old materialism. Here, the temptation to proceed bureaucratically to a positive elaboration of marxism has led to the interpretation of the critique of bourgeois philosophy as the confrontation of two systems, preserving the illusion of an impossible victory on a terrain which had to be abandoned. This has meant the avoidance of the specific task of a marxist philosophy: to indicate how to actually conceptualise the social relations of production. Second, Gramsci criticises the concept of history in crocean historicism, which represents the most complete and 'modern' vehicle to exorcise the element of class from philosophical discourse. Thus, the historicisation of philosophy and marxism means something quite different from the annihilation of theory into a form of 'historical knowledge', as it has been accused of doing.

'For Croce,' Gramsci writes, ' "history" is still a speculative concept.' One of the most recurrent arguments in the *Prison Notebooks* concerning the ambiguities of idealist historicism consists in the criticism of Croce's identification of philosophy and history. If this eliminates the old idea of philosophy as a system and emphasises problems gradually arising from real life, it still amounts to the abolition of the most archaic forms of philosophical knowledge and not its real supression. What differentiates between a speculative and a realistic historicism and decides the dissolution of philosophy into history is precisely the concept of history or, as Gramsci says, the possibility of an identification of history and politics.

'The criticism of the concept of history in Croce is essential: does it not have an origin that is purely erudite and bookish? Only the identification of history and politics takes this character away from history.'[19] The meaning of this famous gramscian claim hinges on how one deciphers this concept of politics. Here Gramsci puts forth two different accounts which ultimately converge. According to one, politics means 'what is realised, and not only the various and repeated attempts at realization, some of which fail'. The other, more organic account, whereby history and politics are identified, is contained in the *Theses on Feuerbach*. From 1920 on, Gramsci held that anything dealing with the development of the productive forces must be stripped of all technical appearances and evaluated in terms of its political meaning, as part of a larger organic unity constituted by the totality of social relations.[20] What leads to the vindication of the 'political character' of philosophy and, more generally, of every intellectual and creative activity, is the same argument which *L'Ordine Nuovo* has put forth in vindicating the 'political character' of the world of production. It is a matter of recognising a determinate form of human activity as a function of a social totality. The starting point of

Gramsci's thought is the rediscovery of the economic sphere 'not only as the production of goods, but also of social relations'.[21] The activity of the individual professional philosopher can be seen by Gramsci as a 'function of political leadership' only as a 'function of social unity', or as the 'active social relation seeking to modify the cultural milieu'.[22] Having relegated to the level of simple metaphors the two expressions through which the great scientific discovery of marxism has been transmitted – that the anatomy of society must be sought in 'economics' and that superstructures are 'appearances' – Gramsci reintroduces a concept of immanence designating 'the ensemble of social relations in which real men move and function' as the only one capable of grounding idealist subjectivity anew as the 'subjectivity of a social group'.[23]

2 The science of history and politics

The two definitions of marxism as absolute historicism and as a philosophy of praxis have two separate functions. The first challenges post-marxist philosophical discourse that continues to appeal to 'history' without clarifying what is meant. The second indicates how, following one of Marx's texts, only the concept of the social relations of production can ground the notion of politics as the subjectivity of a social group. In both cases Gramsci's intention is not to undertake a positive elaboration of a marxist philosophy, but to recover the basic concept by criticising the ambiguities of some post-marxist philosophies. While the definition of absolute historicism leads directly to the mystifications of crocean philosophy, that of the philosophy of praxis seeks to rejuvenate Marx's 'real conquest of the historical world'.[24] Its significance lies in its interpretation of historical materialism, while what is at stake in the identification of the philosophical nucleus of marxism is the possibility of understanding the real importance of the new concept of history.

Already in 1921, when polemicising against bergsonianism as a way of salvaging subjectivity which is foreign to marxism, Gramsci had argued that 'to find the main path one must go back to Karl Marx and Friedrich Engels who from philosophical thought have evolved a precise doctrine of historical and political interpretation.'[25] In order to take another real step in understanding the philosophy of praxis, it is necessary to examine those passages in Gramsci where the traditional notion of historical materialism is transformed into a science of history and politics. This change is not a purely terminological one.

Here, any affinity with Labriola's position breaks down, and what emerges is the bond between Lenin's political work and the *Theses on Feuerbach*: the key to the gramscian acceptance and reinterpretation of marxism-leninism. Lenin's contribution is understood not only as a restoration and application of the doctrine to new historical themes, but also as its general reconstitution, which is relevant in political science in so far as it leads to the rediscovery of its true philosophical nucleus. As a result of the relation that he established between philosophy and the science of marxism, Gramsci could define leninism as 'a unitary system of thought and practical action in which everything is held and demonstrated within reciprocal relations, from the general world view to the smallest problems of organisation.'[26]

In 1924, after the Fifth Congress of the Communist International had placed at the centre of ideological propaganda the new concept of 'marxism-leninism', *L'Ordine Nuovo* published an extensive essay by Longobardi. It is not difficult to discern in this essay Gramsci's entire subsequent interpretation of Lenin's thought as the historically most advanced interpretation of Marx able to provide a total theoretical reconsideration of the doctrine after the Second International.

In his essay, Longobardi identified the role of Lenin with an interpretation of historical materialism which restored marxist philosophy's concept of praxis. The thesis of the 'double revision' of the philosophical nucleus of marxism in the *Prison Notebooks* is anticipated here by that of a 'double deformation' of historical materialism by revisionists, who saw a phase of peaceful capitalist development as a structural tendency and by orthodox marxists defined as the 'theologians of a theory crystallised in a series of dogma'.[27]

They simply forgot that marxism is a doctrine of action and presupposes action – mass revolutionary action. Thus, while Marx's thought permeated the whole direction of historical and economic studies, in the last decades of the century, even in the orthodox camp, it became an instrument of research, a peaceful method of investigation, a desk doctrine. It was simply stripped of its soul.'

Gramsci fought primarily the 'orthodox' revision of marxism. If in the philosophical field it identified marxism with the old materialism, on the level of the comprehension of social phenomena it turned historical materialism into a canon for research since it was unable to make it into a tool to analyse on-going political processes.

Gramsci had already reached this conclusion in one of his early writings which dealt with a problem engaging his whole subsequent reflection: the evaluation of the Russian Revolution. Because of the disequilibrium between the levels of economic and political maturity, the revolution could be disavowed, as it in fact was by a part of the labour movement, by recourse to a certain interpretation of historical materialism.[28]

> 'Political constitutions necessarily depend on economic structures: the forms of production and exchange.' With the mere enunciation of this formula, many think that they have solved every historical and political problem. ... Lenin is a utopian and ... the poor Russian proletarians live in a completely utopian illusion while a terrible awakening implacably awaits them.

Thus, a determinate political position implies the solution of a great theoretical problem: how to provide an interpretation of political processes in terms of the marxist interpretation of history. 'The canons of historical materialism,' argued the young Gramsci, 'are only valuable *post factum* to study and understand past events and must not become a mortgage on the present and the future.'[29]

This explains Gramsci's double identification of the current interpretation of historical materialism and economism, and of economism and the reduction of historical materialism to an interpretative canon. Economism consists in confining historical materialism to historical reconstructions and thus preventing an evaluation of ongoing historical and political processes. The orthodox marxists' error has been that of having provided an interpretation of marxism similar to the one circulating in European culture at the end of the nineteenth century. Croce can be better understood as a revisionist if it is kept in mind that his definition of marxism formalised the predicament of the orthodox interpretation. In a letter dated May 1932, Gramsci says: 'As a revisionist [Croce] contributed to the formation of the school of economical-juridical history.'[30]

The solution to the impasse is found in the reintroduction of the concept of antagonistic social relations of production. This concept can ground a general theory of history in which all the problems of past philosophy are dissolved and reformulated. The possibility of shifting historical materialism from the past to the present is a result of the rediscovery of the subjectivity of struggling social groups, of 'mass revolutionary action' which provides the image of the present as a field of opposing forces. In the previously mentioned 1924 article, marxism 'is a theory of action, the theorisation of human doing, of praxis'. But this 'human doing' is the meeting of antagonistic forces within a given situation, which, given their degree of cohesion and consciousness, bring about a result initially only objectively possible. The re-absorption of historical materialism as a canon becomes impossible for Gramsci as soon as it is demonstrated that, in Croce's words, political programmes can be deduced from scientific propositions by seeing collective wills as expressions of scientifically analysable objective contradictions.

These concepts are very clearly expressed in the blunt rejection of Engels' thesis that Marx's scientific contribution can be found in historical materialism and in the theory of surplus value. As Gramsci in 1926 replies to Arturo Labriola, who had become the interpreter of this commonplace concerning the previous marxist tradition, the fundamental point is the 'demonstration of the historical necessity of the dictatorship of the proletariat'. The use of the political formula should not be deceptive, since it expresses the desire to break with the view of marxism as an abstractly objective theory.[31]

> Already in the *Theses on Feuerbach*, Marx said that the present task is not to explain the world, but to transform it. To emphasise only that part of marxism which explains the world and to hide the much more important parts seeking to organise revolutionary social forces, the proletariat, which must necessarily transform the world, means to reduce marxism to the level of an ordinary theology.

The terms 'theology' and 'speculation', characterising in these political texts an interpretation of marxism separated from its political implications, are the same ones used by Gramsci in prison to attack those conceptions of history which avoid coming to terms with the marxist scientific revolution. 'The philosophy of praxis is the historicist conception of reality freed from every residue of transcendence and theology, even in their latest speculative embodiment. Croce's idealist historicism still remains in the theologico-speculative phase.'[32] Marxism has shown how the notion of subjectivity of the entire idealist tradition is to be understood as the 'form of a concrete social content and the way to lead all of society to fashion itself into a moral unity'. If this social subjectivity and its concern for the outcome which it seeks are removed from marxism, then a relapse into traditional theory is inevitable.

Thus, historical materialism can become a science of politics to the extent that it rids itself of that caricatured concept of history deduced from it, according to which 'it was a kind of ledger, with one entry for "receipts" with a mathematically corresponding entry for "expenditures". Five *lire* of capitalism or economic interest under the entry "expenditures" determined exactly five *lire* of politics and socialism under the entry "receipts".' With these premises it is impossible to develop an analysis of the revolutionary process. To develop such an analysis, it is necessary to start from the premise that marxism, 'by studying relations among material things, wishes to explain relations among men and does not in the least wish to subordinate men to material things'. Thus, 'we focus on social relations among men which, if they are a function of relations among things, are not bound to these by means of a bookkeeping formula of "receipts" and "expenditures".'[33] Gramsci's problem becomes one of elaborating a 'conception of a marxist political method'.[34] Lenin's method, which consists 'in knowing how to do "natural history", i.e. how to carry out the most minute analysis of the factors in a situation in order to determine our tactic in relation to', is the new achievement Gramsci sets against the repetition of a scheme deriving the superstructure from the structure, which regularly leads to the dispersal of the 'concreteness of political and social contrasts'.[35]

Furthermore, the methodological inadequacy of the traditional interpretation of historical materialism is also evident in more strictly historical research, where its effects have been more diffuse and massive. It is worthwhile to recall Gramsci's distinction between 'the philosophy of praxis' and 'historical economism':[36]

what importance should be given to 'economism' in the development of the methods of historical research, granted that economism cannot be confused with the philosophy of praxis? It is clear that a group of financiers with interests in a given country can guide the politics of this country by instigating or preventing a war. But the vertification of this fact does not amount to the 'philosophy of praxis', but rather to 'historical economism,' the assertion that 'immediately', as by 'chance', the facts have been influenced by specific interest groups. That the 'odour of petroleum' can bring serious troubles to a country is also clear. But these controlled and demonstrated assertions still do not amount to the philosophy of praxis. On the contrary, they can be accepted and uttered by those who reject the philosophy of praxis *in toto*. It can be said that the economic factor (understood in the immediate and Judaic sense of historical economism) is only one of the many ways in which the more profound historical process presents itself (the race factor, religion, etc.), but it is this more

profound process which the philosophy of praxis wishes to explain
and this is why it is a philosophy, an 'anthropology', and not a simple
canon of historical research.

The philosophical 'dignity' of marxism, its completely autonomous
and independent nature, obtains for Gramsci only to the extent that it
succeeds in accounting for the totality of the historical process. This is
why marxist philosophy can also be defined as a 'methodology of
history'. This relation between philosophy and the science of history
characterising the limits of economism also constitutes the basis of the
critique of Bukharin's sociology. The latter is also an attempt to fix the
criteria of marxist social analysis by forgetting that marxism's
fundamental innovation, the concept of the social relations of
production, leads to a conception of philosophy as a theory of history. A
study of the scientific nature of marxism employing a concept of law
borrowed from the natural sciences is a result of that split between
dialectical materialism and historical materialism which has led the
doctrine to become subordinated to foreign forms of thought.

Gramsci had begun his discussion with Bukharin even before he was
imprisoned. Only fragments of this discussion remain, but they are still
quite significant since they anticipate the subsequent position elaborated
in the *Prison Notebooks*. During the Fifth Congress of the Communist
International, in a paper dealing with problems of the ideological
unification of the movement, Bukharin had denounced the existence of
forms of 'voluntarist idealism' in the Italian party as peculiar aspects of a
tendential re-birth of the 'old hegelianism'.[37] Bukharin's accusation was
related to the traditional charge of the bordigan left and posed problems
of a political nature within a very rigid climate characterised by the
bolshevisation of the communist parties which had begun in 1925. This
may explain why Gramsci decided to publish in two parts the
introduction and the first chapter of Bukharin's *Manual* for a party
school as a didactic exposition of some of the major aspects of marxist
doctrine. But a comparison of the published translation with the original
text reveals the presence of an interpolation in the concluding part of
Bukharin's introduction which appears as anything but casual or
theoretically neutral.

'Some comrades think,' Bukharin writes, 'that the theory of historical
materialism can in no way be considered a marxist sociology and that it
cannot be exposed systematically. These comrades think that it is only a
living *method* of historical knowledge and that its truths are

demonstrable only when dealing with concrete historical events.'[38] This passage and the definition that follows it of historical materialism as a 'general doctrine of society and of the laws of its development, i.e. sociology', which summarised the whole meaning of this introduction, was omitted in Gramsci's translation and substituted by another which, under close examination, contains in synthetic form his future response from prison to the interpretation of historical materialism as sociology.[39]

The doctrine and tactics of communism would be unintelligible without the theory of historical materialism. There are various bourgeois currents, some of which have even succeeded in influencing the proletarian camp, which by recognising some of the qualities of historical materialism seek to limit its importance and deprive it of its essential meaning, its revolutionary meaning. Thus, for example, the philosopher Benedetto Croce writes that historical materialism must be reduced to a pure canon of historical science, whose truths cannot be developed systematically into a general world view, but are only demonstrable concretely in so far as one uses them to write history books. ... One need only observe that historical materialism, in addition to having been a canon for historical research and having shown its worth in a series of concrete literary masterpieces, has also been concretely revealed in the Russian Revolution, in a living and actual historical phenomenon. It has been revealed in the world-wide labour movement which continuously develops according to marxist predictions, notwithstanding that, according to bourgeois philosophers, such predictions are to be considered phantasmagoric because historical materialism only serves for the writing of history books, and not for living and actively functioning in history.

Here Bukharin is criticised through Croce. The passage clearly distinguishes between the view of marxism as a historical methodology and its reduction to a canon. Second, the reply to Croce is found not by descending to the level of the systematic exposition of the doctrine (Bukharin's approach) but by upholding, although in a specifically political language, the validity of marxism as a philosophy by underlining its demonstrated capacity to function as the proletariat's political science. Coming back to this point in the *Prison Notebooks*, Gramsci writes that[40]

In the final section of the introduction the author is incapable of replying to those critics who maintain that the philosophy of praxis can live only in concrete works of history. He does not succeed in elaborating the concept of philosophy of praxis as 'historical methodology', and of that in turn as 'philosophy', as the only concrete philosophy. That is to say he does not succeed in posing and resolving, from the point of view of the real dialectic, the problem which Croce has posed and has attempted to resolve from the speculative point of view.

Once again, the problem is to identify history and philosophy and by means of the concept of social relations of production come to an identification of history and politics. Furthermore, Gramsci adds, to accept the thesis that marxism 'is realised in the concrete study of past history, and in the current activity of creating new history', does not amount to pulverising marxism's theoretical nucleus into a purely empirical casuistry, since 'even if the facts are always unique and changeable in the flux of the movement of history, the concepts can be theorised'.[41] Generalisations of a purely empirical casuistry are reached by substituting for the exposition of method the description of some possible uniformities, in which the material variety of concrete historical processes is preventively inserted. The criticism of Bukharin's concept of law is not an attack on the objectivity of the historical process, but reiterates the impossibility of confusing the theory with the method of the successive *generalisations*. At this point the problem becomes one of the logic of historical knowledge.[42]

> The historical dialectic is replaced by the law of causality and the search for regularity, normality, and uniformity. But how can one derive from this way of seeing things the overcoming, the 'overthrow' of praxis? In mechanical terms, the effect can never transcend the cause of the system of causes, and therefore can have no development other than the flat vulgar development of evolutionism.

3 The dialectic

In an anonymous note in *Rinascità* in 1945, Togliatti characterised the relation between Gramsci and Labriola as follows:[43]

> Marxist scholars recognise in Labriola a tendency towards a certain onesided, limited and ultimately fatalistic interpretation of the

doctrines of scientific socialism. It is this tendency which led Labriola to seriously err, for example, concerning Italian colonialism and, more generally, made his role as a socialist theorist in Italy rather impotent. Antonio Gramsci, who was an attentive student of Labriola in the finest sense of the word, corrected this erroneous tendency. A marxist does not and cannot reduce the analysis of historical and political facts to the explication of the simple relation of cause and effect between and economic and socio-political situation. This is how marxism had been understood by dilettantes unaware that for a marxist the very relation of causality is much more complex and implies action and reaction, interdependence and contrast. Thus (as Lenin put it), the historical process is *causa sui* and always contains, according to the unfolding of a dialectical development of real forces, not only its own justification, but positive and negative elements, contradiction and struggle.

Togliatti would return to the question of Labriola's 'fatalism', but never by so specifically indicating the reasons for a critique and summarising the methodological innovation introduced by Gramsci in the conception of historical materialism.

The dialectic, in fact, deals with the problem of causality in the concrete analysis of historical and political processes. Gramsci moves beyond the reduction of historical materialism to a canon to the extent that he provides a justification of events as well as a critical evaluation of these events as the outcome of struggles between conflicting social forces. There the victory of one part never means the definitive overcoming of the social antagonism. This antagonism remains, thus constituting its permanent contradiction. The dialectic does not introduce a weakening of the determination in the final instance, or provide a more complex representation. Notwithstanding frequent reference to Engels' letters on historical materialism to allow a greater space to the role played by the multiplicity of factors, Gramsci's theoretical perspective is substantially different. The dialectic relates the multiplicity of factors to the basic struggling forces and shows how a specific outcome is reached through the exclusion of other objectively possible alternatives.

Thus, historical analysis is no different from political analysis, particularly in the examination of historical processes whose constitutive elements are still operating, as when the form of the proletarian revolution is deduced from the form taken by the bourgeois revolution.

For this reason, there is a close relation between Labriola's historical methodology and his inability to provide concrete political indications for the development of the socialist movement. His interpretation of marxism is destined to remain a cultural fact which never penetrates to the level of political battles. Consequently, Labriola's interpretation and use of historical materialism tends to confirm the crocean theses concerning the impossibility of deducing political programmes from scientific propositions. Here again the gramscian criticism of economism corresponds with that of the crocean (and orthodox) revision of historical materialism.

Accordingly, Gramsci rejects the very formula of a 'materialist dialectic' and documents the specific meaning of the 'rational' marxist dialectic. The procedure is similar to the rejection of materialism as the content of marxist philosophy and the rejection of the consequent dichotomy between philosophy and the science of history. From these premises, the dialectic cannot be understood 'as a chapter of formal logic and not as a logic of its own, that is, a theory of knowledge'.[44] Gramsci rejects the presentation of the dialectic as a logic of movement contraposed to a logic of stasis. Rather, he defines it as 'the very marrow of historiography and the science of politics'.[45] The emphasis is on the double nature of the 'general theory' or of 'philosophy': its irreducibility to a preconstituted framework and its ability to provide the very possibility of a concrete, applied, scientific knowledge of historical processes.

In this conception of the dialectic as the mode of expression of marxist causality, Gramsci singles out two fundamental moments. First, there is the dialectic as the foundation of the marxist vision of social development, rooted in the anti-utopian polemics of *The Poverty of Philosophy*. Here, the dialectic is understood as *antagonism*. Against a dialectic of distincts, which is elsewhere regarded as a heuristic proposal, Gramsci carries out the same re-evaluation of hegelian dialectic that Marx did in relation to Proudhon. According to Marx, 'to find complete truth, the idea, in all its fullness, the synthetic formula that is to annihilate the contradiction, this is the problem of social genius'. And further on:[46]

> The *philanthropic* school is the humanitarian school carried to perfection. It denies the necessity of antagonism; it wants to turn all men bourgeois; it wants to realise theory in so far as it is distinguished from practice and contains no antagonism. It goes

without saying that, in theory, it is easy to make an abstraction of the contradictions that are met with at every moment in actual reality.

So far, then, the dialectic designates the existence of antagonisms between opposing social forces whose recognition constitutes the indispensable premise for every subsequent scientific analysis. To overlook this situation is not merely a theoretical error, but amounts to taking an ideological and political position. In this case, the problem is to restore the suppressed elements in the criticism of the apologetical position. But in addition to the objectively given form of social development, for Gramsci the dialectic is also the cognitive *method* necessary to gain a concrete and realistic representation of the antagonistic social unity. The dialectic is the tool needed to gain knowledge of the *unity*, *specificity*, and *concreteness* of social phenomena by organically relating the otherwise separate and juxtaposed individual constitutive elements. In this sense, the dialectic is the best way to re-introduce, and at the same time provide an empirical verification, of the structured marxist concept of history.

In the 'science of dialectics, the theory of knowledge', Gramsci says, 'the general concepts of history, politics, and economics are interwoven in an organic unity.' Once again, the peculiarity of marxism is seen in its ability to provide a theory of history where 'one cannot separate politics and economics from history.'[47] For this reason, the discussion concerning the three constitutive elements of marxism can only be understood as an account of the historical genesis of the doctrine, which leaves untouched the task of providing 'the synthetic unity' of its original parts. In the elaboration and concrete application of this second meaning of the dialectic, Gramsci has as his main reference point the theoretical patrimony accumulated by the leninist political elaboration.

In March 1925, during the Fourth Executive meeting of the Communist International in which Gramsci participated as head of the Italian delegation, the first issue of the theoretical journal *Bolshevik* was published containing the important chapter 'On the Question of Dialectics' excerpted from Lenin's still unpublished *Philosophical Notebooks*.[48] The journal's aim, as became all too clear in later years, was to completely restore Plekhanov's variety of dialectical materialism − a doctrine which had been eclipsed after the First World War by the western marxists' rediscovery of Hegel. Gramsci's appropriation of Lenin's elaboration of the dialectic was not only completely different from the way it was being presented by marxism–leninism, but it also differed from the interpretations provided by the left philosophers in the German Communist Party. Thus, in January 1926, by devoting a special column to an anthology of leninist texts, *l'Unità* exemplified Lenin's position on the dialectic by publishing the following account of the difference between the dialectic and eclecticism:[49]

A tumbler is assuredly both a glass cylinder and a drinking vessel. But there are more than these two properties, qualities or facets to it; there are an infinite number of them, an infinite number of 'mediacies' and interrelationships with the rest of the world. A tumbler is a heavy object which can be used as a missile; it can serve as a paperweight, a receptacle for a captive butterfly, or a valuable object with an artistic engraving or design, and this has nothing at all to do with whether or not it can be used for drinking, is made of glass, is cylindrical or not quite, and so on and so forth. Moreover, if I needed a tumbler just now for drinking, it would not in the least matter how cylindrical it was, and whether it was actually made of glass; what would matter though would be whether it had any holes in the bottom, or anything that would cut my lips when I drank, etc. But if I did not need a tumbler for drinking but for a purpose that could be served by any glass cylinder, a tumbler with a cracked bottom or without one at all would do just as well, etc. Formal logic, which is as far as schools go (and should go, with suitable abridgments for the lower forms), deals with formal definitions, draws on what is most common, or glaring, and stops there. When two or more different definitions are taken and combined at random (a glass cylinder and a drinking vessel), the result is an eclectic definition which is indicative of different facets of the object, and nothing more. Dialectical logic demands that we should go further. First, if we are to have a true knowledge of an object we must look at and examine all its facets, its connections and 'mediacies'. That is something we cannot ever hope to achieve completely, but the role of comprehensiveness is a safeguard against mistakes and rigidity. Second, dialectical logic requires that an object should be taken in development, in change, in 'self-movement' (as Hegel sometimes puts it). This is not immediately obvious in respect of such an object as a tumbler, but it, too, is in flux, and this holds especially true for its purpose, use and *connection* with the surrounding world. Third, a full 'definition' of an object must include the whole of human experience, both as a criterion of truth and a practical indicator of its connection with human wants. Fourth, dialectical logic holds that 'truth is always concrete, never abstract', as the late Plekhanov liked to say after Hegel.

The choice of this passage is extremely significant. Of the many illustrations of the dialectic found scattered in Lenin's political writings after 1915, this is certainly the most important both in terms of the quality of the exposition as well as in terms of the context within which it appears: an account of how to understand the relation between economics and politics at a time when the workers' state abandons wartime communism for a New Economic Policy. In these brief considerations, Lenin summarised what he considered the significance of hegelian logic.

In April 1924, Gramsci has published in *L'Ordine Nuovo* Lenin's writing on 'militant materialism',[50] which pointed once again to the 'systematic study of the hegelian dialectic' from a materialist perspective (which he had done between 1914 and 1915) as an irreplaceable tool in the movement's cultural battles. There Lenin called for the publication of extracts from Hegel's works with 'related commentary dealing with this dialectic in economic and political relations, readily available from history, especially after the recent imperialist war and revolution'. This is not the place to discuss the importance of this rediscovery of Hegel in terms of Lenin's political thought. It will suffice to say that, far from constituting a theoretical regression in relation to the first writings on *Capital* and on the development of capitalism in Russia, it develops the analysis to include international relations, the various components of the world-wide capitalist structure, and the rapid internal complication of its fundamental contradiction. These developments were no longer comprehensible on the basis of the capitalist model prevalent throughout the Second International. The imperialist war had not only brought about a political crisis within the organisation, but had also shown the inadequacy of an analysis that for more than a decade posed the problem of imperialism and its effects on the labour movement. In 1915 Lenin summarised his theoretical criticism of Kautsky as follows:[51]

There are no 'pure' phenomena, nor can there be, either in Nature or in society – that is what marxist dialectics teaches us for dialectics shows that the very concept of purity indicates a certain narrowness, a one-sidedness of human cognition which cannot embrace an object in all of its totality and complexity.

A year later, dealing with Luxemburg, Lenin reiterated this point: 'marxist dialectics require the concrete analysis of every specific historical situation',[52] as he did again in 1921, regarding Bukharin by pointing out that the 'dialectic includes historicity'.[53]

But what does Lenin mean by historicity as the essence of dialectical knowledge? What method could guarantee its possession? A quick excursus over Lenin's notes on Hegel's *Logic* might clarify the matter. Here Lenin emphasises the hegelian criticism of the concept of cause by claiming that its cognitive inadequacy must be sought in its inability to embrace the complexity of the elements characterising a given social phenomenon. 'The all-sidedness and all-embracing character of the interconnection of the world ... is only one-sidedly, fragmentarily and incompletely expressed by causality.'[54] But this is only the critical comprehension through which it is important to pass in order to grasp the importance of the knowledge of social processes guaranteed by dialectical logic. For Lenin, in fact, *objectivity* of knowledge is possible only by reconstituting the totality of the social phenomenon. In turn, only the totality can guarantee knowledge of the *specificity* of political analysis. By explicitly reasserting his rejection of triadic schemes[55] which make marxism into a generic philosophy of history, Lenin rediscovers in the dialectic the possibility to single out, at a new level of the development of political struggle, what he had called 'sociology' in his early writings.

The objectivity of dialectical knowledge consists in its ability to catch 'the *totality of all* sides of the phenomenon, of reality and their (reciprocal) *relations* ... as reflections of the objective world'.[56] The truth is reached to the extent that 'the effective connection between all the aspects, forces, tendencies, etc., of the given field of phenomena' is elucidated. But, given the very procedure through which one must pass to reach it, truth is by definition always *concrete*. This concreteness, however, is not a starting point, but tendentially the arrival point of an uninterrupted process of approach, constituting the very essence of of scientific knowledge. Truth, Lenin repeatedly writes, is a process. 'Man cannot comprehend, reflect, mirror nature *as a whole*, in its completeness, its "immediate totality", he can only *eternally* come closer to this, creating abstractions, concepts, laws, and a scientific picture of the world.'[57] Thus, human knowledge can be compared to a spiral, every segment of which 'can be transformed (unilaterally) in a straight line'. The unilateral extrapolation of one or more datum from the totality to which they are linked by a multiplicity of relations or mediations involves the reduction of dialectics to a sophism or an eclecticism. Lenin continuously characterises in this fashion the theoretical matrix of the political errors he constantly struggled against. Whatever their specific content, they both share a common matrix – the fragmentariness and thus the subjectivity of analysis.

The discussion could go on, but we already find its central nucleus in the long passage published by Gramsci in 1926. If Lenin's *Philosophical Notebooks* could have provided an important reference point for Gramsci's elaboration, he seems to have grasped in Lenin's political writings the immense separation between Lenin's concept of the dialectic and the way it had been presented as based on philosophical materialism. Lenin certainly realised that the discovery of this methodology would intimately transform the conception and praxis of historical materialism. In fact, the *Philosophical Notebooks* are punctuated with critical observations concerning Plekhanov. But it is also true that in writings meant for publication he consistently asserted to the very end, the importance of Plekhanov's theoretical contribution. On the other hand, Gramsci's task was to fully articulate the open break between Lenin's political analysis and the theoretical tradition of the Second International. For him, this conception of the dialectic was the most complete and mature weapon for attacking philosophical materialism *and* every economistic practice of historical materialism.

In the context of a certain interpretation of Ricardo's role in Marx's formation, Gramsci said that through the concepts of determinate market and tendential law 'the law of causality of the natural sciences has been cleansed of its mechanical aspect and has been synthetically identified with hegelian dialectical reasoning.'[58] Given that the dialectic is the logic of connections and mediations, Gramsci's problem is that of freeing himself from a linear derivation from a given economic base of the multiple aspects of historical and political processes. In prison conversations with his colleagues, in order[59]

> to break away from those who accused marxism of mechanicism, fatalism, economic determinism, and economism, he suggested that they no longer speak of economic 'structure' and 'superstructure,' but only of an historical process in which all the factors took part. Only the predominance of that process was economic.

Only by going beyond the limits of the reduction of materialism to an interpretative canon is it possible to grasp the specificity and historicity of the social phenomenon under examination. For Gramsci, the primacy of dialectical knowledge lies in going beyond both philosophy 'a method of scholarship for ascertaining particular facts', and sociology as an 'empirical compilation of practical observations which extend the sphere of philosophy as traditionally understood'.[60] Thus, to make the dialectic the cognitive instrument through which marxism becomes 'a general historical methodology' does not mean to reduce its range of effectiveness to descriptive history. On the contrary, it purifies historical materialism of some repetitive and abstract schemes and of its confinement to historiography as a result of its confrontation with other cultural traditions.

It is extremely significant for the whole subsequent gramscian elaboration that already in 1925 the marxist dialectic was employed in the polemic with Bordiga to defend a conception of the working-class political party that would incorporate its double nature as a voluntary association as well as an objective element of civil society. Some arguments of the young Togliatti, who carried out this polemic on behalf of the new gramscian leadership, provide the most significant documentation. In criticising the double error of removing the party from the working class and party activity from the objective situation within which it comes about and functions (this is the theme around which rotates all of Gramsci's battle for a change in the party's political and tactical direction), Togliatti wrote that[61]

one of the characteristics of the dialectical conception of reality is that of never isolating any of the elements of a situation from all others and from the situation considered in its totality and in its development, and to hold that only in this mutual, complete and continuous correlation and inter-dependence of elements in development can its meaning be grasped.

Furthermore, the 'marxist dialectic generates a coherent, solid, and indissoluble whole out of the various constitutive parts of the real world.'[62] Gramsci himself, in commenting on the results of the Lyons Congress, defined Bordiga's position concerning the tactical questions arising in the summer of 1924 with the Matteotti murder, as follows:[63]

It has been characteristic of the false position of the extreme left that its observations and its criticism have never been based on an examination, profound or superficial, of power relations and the general conditions of Italian society. Thus, it became very clear that the very method of the extreme left, which is claimed to be dialectical, is not the method of Marx's own materialistic dialectic, but the old method of conceptual dialectic of pre-marxist and even pre-hegelian philosophy.

Clearly, it is a matter of paraphrasing expressions recurring in Lenin's political writings. That they return with particular frequency precisely in relation to the question of the party is not only a consequence of political urgency, but also of the isolation of a line of analysis leading to the elaboration of the concept of the 'historical bloc': 'The complex, contradictory and discordant *ensemble* of the superstructures is the reflection of the *ensemble* of the social relations of production.' In the reciprocity between structure and superstructure, Gramsci says, lies 'the real dialectical process'.[64]

4 Introduction of the ethico-political element

In order to follow the concrete evolution of Gramsci's analysis in developing the notion of historical materialism as political science, it is necessary to pose a further question concerning the introduction of the ethico-political element. A brief note in the *Prison Notebooks* reads as follows:[65]

Elements of ethico-political history in the philosophy of praxis: the concept of hegemony, the re-evaluation of the philosophical front, the systematic study of the function of intellectuals in historical and governmental life, and the doctrine of the political party as the vanguard of every progressive historical movement.

On closer examination, the excerpt turns out to be a kind of conceptual summary of all of Gramsci's research. In fact, each of the individual stages articulating Gramsci's critical confrontation with the marxist tradition – from the recovery of the concept of the social relations of production as the axis of the doctrine, to the criticism of historical materialism as an interpretative canon, to the identification of the dialectic as the means for determining the unity of the social order – finds its arrival point and mode of expression in the introduction of the ethico-political element. All of Gramsci's research rotates around one question, best expressed in his own words: 'How does the historical movement arise on the structural basis?'[66]

Having abandoned the principle of linear causality, it is necessary to indicate how to overcome the dichotomy between structure and

superstructure, which has generated all sorts of economistic super-
stitions and led to the reabsorption of marxism within the framework of
traditional culture. The ethico-political dimension prevents historical
forces from turning into fantastic shadows of a 'hidden god'. They
become, instead, integral parts of a single social process. Thus, the
establishment of 'the "catharctic" moment', i.e. the identification of the
way in which the shift from economics to politics takes place, becomes
for Gramsci 'the starting point of all the philosophy of praxis',[67] and 'the
crux of all the questions that have arisen around the philosophy of
praxis'.[68] For this reason, the theory of hegemony is necessary to
preserve and fulfil the promises implicit in the marxist conception of
history. Likewise, the beginning of a concrete governmental experience
with the October Revolution has major theoretical significance:
'epistemological' relevance.

The theory of the intellectuals and of the political party are the
answers to the problem.[69]

> Every social group coming into existence on the original terrain of an
> essential function in the world of economic production, creates
> together with itself, organically, one or more strata of intellectuals
> which give it homogeneity and an awareness of its own function not
> only in the economic but also in the social and political fields.

The modern political party, the organisational form of a specific class in
late capitalism, performs a function without which social development is
no longer possible. Its function is similar to that which the state carries
out for the whole of civil society.

It is not the purpose of this essay to evaluate Gramsci's historical and
political analyses, but only to examine the theoretical framework which
sustained them. In order to do so, it is important to dwell for a moment
on Gramsci's interpretation of the *Preface* of 1859 which became pivotal
for all earlier expositions of historical materialism. Gramsci distinguishes
two parts within the *Preface*, attributing to each clearly distinct
functions in the theoretical construction of marxism. First, for Gramsci,
the claim that men become aware of structural contradictions at the level
of ideology entails no possibility of knowing the concrete forms of
development. It merely has philosophical meaning, at the level of the
theory of knowledge. Here Marx is understood as considering not only
the 'psychological and moral' meaning of ideologies as an aid in the
process of organising of the masses, but also a new way to pose the
problem of the 'objectivity' of knowledge.[70] Second, Gramsci takes it as a

fundamental theoretical claim necessary for a political and historical analysis that part in the *Preface* according to which social formations do not perish until they have fully developed all the productive forces that they can, and that mankind poses only problems for whose solutions the objective conditions already exist. Gramsci claims that:[71]

Only on this basis can all mechanicisms and every trace of the superstitiously 'miraculous' be eliminated, and it is on this basis that the problem of the formation of active political groups, and, in the last analysis, even the problem of the historical function of great personalities must be posed.

This means to break with the traditional interpretation based on a relation between the capitalist development of the productive forces and the working-class numerical, organisational and political growth. The Italian experience has shown that it is possible to have regressions, as well as 'withdrawals' from strategic positions already conquered (this is Lenin's teaching), thus necessitating a reconstruction of the movement. Gramsci does not underemphasise the objective role of the socio-economic sphere, but rejects the idea that it can explain the 'catharctic moment' as the process of the political organisation of the economic forces. Against Croce's theory of politics as passion, Gramsci argues that politics becomes permanent action and gives birth to permanent organisations precisely in so far as it identifies itself with economics.[72] The knowledge of this identify is a necessary starting point which by itself cannot explain the political outcome of on-going social antagonisms. In regard to the concept of necessity and regularity, Gramsci says.[73]

It is not a question of 'discovering' a metaphysical law of 'determinism', or even of establishing a 'general' law of causality. It is a question of bringing out how in historical evolution relatively permanent forces are constituted which operate with a certain regularity and automatism.

Thus, for Gramsci, the second part of the *Preface* of 1859 indicates that a given structure gives rise to a field of possibilities which relatively permanent and countervailing forces seek to utilise in opposite ways.

Thus, the Italian communal bourgeoisie did not succeed in going beyond the economic and corporative stage and in the epoch of developed capitalism, great mass movements can perish under the adversary's blows without the disappearance of the objective reasons for their existence. The very development of the working class into the dominant class which, through the management of the state, shows its ability to provide civil society with a totally different physiognomy, is not a spontaneous and automatic process. Only the introduction of the ethico-political element allows scientific knowledge to grasp the real nature of on-going social antagonisms.

Historical materialism can purify itself of economism only when it succeeds in providing a correct analysis of 'the forces active in the history of a particular period' and in determining 'the relation between them'.[74] There are three levels of analysis of power relations: 1 'a relation of social forces which is closely linked to the structure, objective, independent of human will'; 2 'the relation of political forces; in other words, an evaluation of the degree of homegeneity, self-awareness, and organisation attained by the various social classes'; and 3 the relation of military of 'politico-military' forces[75] – which becomes determining in the decisive moments of a crisis, when the fusion of economics and politics translates into actual force. So reformulated, the theory of historical materialism culminates in the theory of the political party as the historically determined form exemplifying a non-dichotomised relation between structure and superstructure.

The introduction of the ethico-political element grounds the criticism of the orthodox interpretation of historical materialism. From this, two important consequences follow for Gramsci's concept of political science. First, it is not a sociology in the positivist sense of twentieth-century Italian culture. (This, of course, does not affect Marx's 'fundamental innovation', the historicity of human nature.) Therefore, not only must the new marxist political science 'be seen as a developing organism' as far as 'both its concrete content and its logical formulation are concerned',[76] but all political forms cannot always be seen in terms of class conflict. Speaking about the possibility of writing a book 'that would constitute for marxism an ordered system as found in *The Prince* for contemporary politics', Gramsci says that 'the subject should be the political party, in its relations with the various classes and the state: not the party as a sociological category, but the party which wants to found the state'.[77] In other words, the party must be considered from the standpoint of its goal. Second, Gramsci's concept of political science is not a 'separate' zone of marxist theory. It can be derived only from a consideration of all of the doctrine's philosophical problems, by retracing all the main stages of Gramsci's philosophical reflection. That he devoted the best and most significant parts of his work to the elaboration of a marxist political science is a consequence of his notion of the historicity of marxism.

5 The historicity of marxism as a world view

When Gramsci in prison wrote that 'In the phase of struggle for hegemony it is the science of politics which is developed; in the state phase all the superstructures must be developed, if one is not to risk the dissolution of the state',[78] he was restating a vision of the development of marxism based on the functioning and growth of the working-class state. For Gramsci, the 'historicity' of marxism is strictly linked to the distinction between the period that precedes and the one that follows the taking of power and to the conviction that the experience of political direction entails the further elaboration of the doctrine's theoretical nucleus and not its modification (which would only serve to identify *historicity* with the *revision* of marxism).

Thus,[79]

only after the creation of the new state does the cultural problem impose itself in all its complexity and tends toward a coherent solution. In any case the attitude to be taken up before the formation of the new state can only be critical-polemical, never dogmatic; it must be a romantic attitude, but a romanticism which is consciously aspiring to its classical synthesis.

The contraposition of the critical and the dogmatic attitude is nourished by the same motives which led Gramsci to reject a systematic vision of marxism as a philosophy like all others that have emerged in the history of thought. The need not to lose the ground of criticism is Gramsci's expression of his awareness that the concept of the social relations of production poses an insuperable objective limit to marxism itself. The marxist philosopher, says Gramsci, also 'cannot escape from the present field of contradictions, he cannot affirm other than generically, a world without contradictions, without immediately creating a utopia'.[80] The elaboration of political science becomes crucial in Gramsci, given the impossibility of passing to a new phase until the existing social order has been effectively modified. What this means is that the scientific truths of marxism do not give rise to an ideology or to a general world-view, but to a new culture, to a new view of the world. Contrary to Plekhanov's and the Second International's perspective, this is not the product of marxist intellectuals, the movement's ideologues, or the upholders of orthodoxy, but an integral part of the development of social relations of production. The transformation of marxist science into culture, of marxist philosophy into a world-view, is a process accompanying the modification of on-going contradictions. In this historical perspective of the transition, the original theoretical claim whereby the concept of social relations of production allows marxism to choose a path different from the one followed by the whole history of philosophy translates into the project of 'a new culture in incubation which will develop with the development of social relations'.[81]

By concretely articulating the notion of the ethico-political, Gramsci is able to identify, not the content of this new culture, but features of the social and political process which will be its support and form of realisation. Elaborating this theory of the party, Gramsci postulates a historical development in which 'the formation of a "national-popular collective will" joins with an "intellectual and moral reform".' The birth, consolidation, and advancement of the political party up to when it takes power trigger modifications in the ideological and cultural, as well as economic and political character of the dominant 'historical bloc':[82]

> The modern prince, as it develops, revolutionizes the whole system
> of intellectual and moral relations in that his development means
> precisely that any given act is seen as useful or harmful, as virtuous or
> as wicked, only in so far as it has as its point of reference the modern
> prince himself, and helps to strengthen or to oppose him.

Only within the real historical life of the modern prince is the programme of 'economic reform' inextricably bound to 'intellectual reform'. What marxist criticism has singled out on the conceptual levels finds its historical existence with the development of an historical alternative. The individual philosopher's theoretical criticism as the expression of an absolute conception of doing philosophy, gives rise to the 'collective thinker'[83] through an examination of how existing social antagonisms find expression on the political level, Gramsci, consequently, deals with the development of marxism from a critical theory to a world-view in terms of the relation between intellectuals and the masses.

The entire discussion concerning philosophy and religion, its possible *rapprochement* with common sense, etc., is not meant to establish the theoretical status of marxist philosophy, but seeks to identify the whole trajectory of working-class experiences in developing from a subaltern to a ruling class. It is an important aspect of the theory of the party, which exemplifies, at the level of a moral reform, that role of reunifying the divisions on which bourgeois society is built. Here lies its revolutionary essence. This explains why 'the political development of the concept of hegemony represents a great philosophical advance as well as a politico-practical one.'[84]

To clarify how historical materialism, as an instrument of the working-class party, can trigger a reform which eventually comes to encompass the whole world-view of an age, Gramsci refers to 'the philosophical relevance' of Machiavelli's vindication of the autonomy of science and of political activity, and their implications for morality and religion. The transformation of Machiavelli's scientific discovery into machiavellianism indicates 'the gulf which exists between rulers and ruled', and that 'there exist two cultures – that of the rulers and that of the ruled'.[85] As the expression of a political party which is itself the expression of the fundamental social contradiction, marxist political science can begin to heal the break between the intellectuals and the 'simple' ones, in order to bring about 'an intellectual progress of the mass'.[86]

In this context, the relation between theory and practice, philosophy and religion, can be expressed in a new dialectic between intellectuals and the masses, reversing the existing trend. The definition of philosophy as a world-view comes to mean that[87]

> philosophical activity is not to be conceived solely as the 'individual' elaboration of systematically coherent concepts, but also and above all as a cultural battle to transform the 'popular mentality' and to diffuse the philosophical innovations which will demonstrate themselves to be 'historically true' to the extent that they become conretely – i.e. historically and socially – universal.

Universal thought can be reached only in a society which has overcome class divisions.

Thus, the historicity of marxism is inextricably connected with the problem of transition. It emphasises all the elements of the transformation of relations between state and civil society necessarily associated with the initial stage of the dictatorship of the proletariat. The identification of philosophy and history underlying all of Gramsci's marxism and in terms of which he reintroduces the concept of social relations of production indicates how to reach a superior cultural and social unity in terms of the ethico-political analysis.

6 Conclusion

With the notion of absolute historicism Gramsci pursues a kind of 'kantian' theoretical operation in order to re-examine the aims and limitations of philosophy and to stress the consequences of that recurring tendency to transcend these limitations even within marxist philosophy, whenever it loses sight of the concept of social relations of production. Thus, Gramsci sought to make marxism fully conscious of its own identity, to revive its revolutionary spirit, to eliminate the fifth columns nested within it, and to purify it of those old ways of thinking which it tended to reproduce.

The concept of revisionism in Gramsci undergoes an expansion which is related to his way of formulating the general theory of marxism. Far from referring to the interpretations of the doctrine's theoretical foundation *within* the labour movement, by revisionism Gramsci means every penetration of bourgeios ideology 'which sometimes creeps in the teachings of Engels and even of Marx, in the most dangerous way'.[88] Already in the Lyons theses we read:[89]

> After the victory of Marxism, the tendencies of a national character over which it had triumphed sought to manifest themselves in other ways, re-emerging within Marxism itself as forms of revisionism. ...
> The process of degeneration of the IInd International thus took the form of a struggle against Marxism which unfolded within Marxism itself.

In the prison writings we find the thesis that the revision of the doctrine can be understood only by analysing the relation between 'the philosophy of praxis and modern culture'. Since for Gramsci 'orthodoxy' means the 'self-sufficiency' of the philosophy of praxis, i.e. that it contains 'all the fundamental elements for building a total and integral world-view',[90] he leaves behind the concept of revisionism as it had been understood within the internal debates of German Social Democracy. The most dangerous revisionists are the orthodox marxists precisely because the theoretical essence of revisionism does not consist in distinguishing between what is dead and what is alive in Marx but, rather, in using his analytical framework according to criteria foreign to it.

To redefine the limits of philosophy means to outline the limits of the world and to furnish a more complete theoretical consciousness of its on-going contradictions. Not even marxism can go beyond the limitations of the mode of production. It would mean a falling back into utopianism (and every 'systematic' vision of marxism is utopian) but with this difference: while the old utopianism was the ideal expression of a new social class struggling against the existing order, the new utopianism threatens to reabsorb marxism into the old philosophy. The main concern of marxist philosophy will be to guard against the temptation to propose purely logical solutions to real contradictions. Its only task is to make them as clear as possible. It cannot add or take anything away. On the other hand, it is fatal to take that road which has already led the labour movement to become subaltern at the moment it claimed to offer alternative solutions. In 1929 Gramsci claimed that[91]

there is already a 'proletarian' intellectuality for the socialists, and it is constituted by the working *petit bourgeoisie*. A peculiar *civilisation* of the world of labour already exists and it is characterised by the ideology, feelings, aspirations and the amorphous dreams of the *travett*.

Thus, the criticism of individual philosophers is the same as that put forth against a new culture built by the intellectuals of the socialist movement. What allowed Gramsci to elaborate his position was the confrontation with German and Europèan Social Democracy's system-atisation of marxism and his clear perception of the dangers inherent in the construction of the first worker's state.

Here we find an extension of the concept of 'critique' in the subtitle of *Capital*: 'Classical economics has given rise to a "critique of political economy" but it does not seem to me that a new science or a new conception of the scientific problem has yet been possible.'[92] As 'critique' marxism can locate the historicity of the mode of production or, as Gramsci put it, of the 'determined market'. But it cannot give rise to a new science of economic facts which would require the existence of an ensemble of new facts. To consider marxism as a 'critique' with regard to every ideal cultural and political manifestation means, for Gramsci, to re-establish the limits of its intelligibility. It reiterates marxism's rupture with the existing cultural tradition and preserves it from the danger of being turned into a speculative doctrine by de-emphasising the givenness of the contradictions. According to Gramsci, the class adversary reasserts its domination and hegemony through individuating ever new levels in the 'unitary' recomposition of the social sphere, which will remain until they are theoretically and practically unmasked. This theoretical strategy corresponds fully with the political strategy.

Through uninterrupted critique it is necessary to progressively reduce the adversary's free space, and to make it possible to inflict the final blow. The primacy of political science as critique *par excellence* during a whole historical phase is not the result of underestimating theoretical marxism, but of the observation that the critique of the apologetic content, e.g. of the crocian interpretation of Italian history, cannot be considered definitive until one has reached a new level of the political organisation of the Southern peasants.

From a theoretical perspective, Gramsci's concept of 'critique' clearly differentiates between the marxist concept of science and positivist science. As theory, or science, marxism's 'only' is to indicate what is possible before and independently of all facts. The critique of political economy, by grasping the historicity of the mode of production, 'puts forward the "inheritor", the heir presumptive who must yet give manifest proof of his vitality'.[93] The task of science is to establish laws on the basis of already given facts. The task of marxist theory, as a theory of contradictions, is to establish only possibilities. Philosophy and critique made events transparent and provide a glimpse of the possibility, and only the possibility, of a new ensemble of facts. The realisation of this possibility falls completely outside of its field. In this sense, says Gramsci, one can predict only to the extent that one acts and, it could be added, one acts only to the extent that one modifies existing facts. Thus, to rediscover the limit of philosophy as the limits of the world means to rediscover the space that must be left to 'will' and 'praxis' as the realisation of the objective possibility to change not just individual facts, but the very limits of the world. The philosophy of praxis rediscovers the role of subjectivity since it has profoundly understood the distinction between what can be said and what can be shown. If what one cannot speak about should be left unsaid, the limit of what can be said can be practically altered by changing the world. Thus, the scientificity of marxism consists in locating as possible that whose existence the science of facts does not even suspect. But for this reason it refers immediately and to what is other than itself. Absolute historicism leads directly into political science, but the latter can rise only when the ground has been conceptually cleared up of every possible automatism or fatalism.

As already indicated, according to Gramsci, an understanding of the October Revolution requires the radical rejection of the whole interpretation of historical materialism provided by the Second International. As the previously mentioned Longobardi article argues[94]

If Marx writes that capitalist society, left to itself, would lead to an extreme centralisation of wealth, he never points out when such a process will be adequately advanced to make possible the expropriation of the monopolisers. And when he writes that the capitalist order will be destroyed only after having developed all the production forces which it is able to unleash, he leaves equally indeterminate the point in which this process can be considered concluded. The distinctive character of capital, notes Marx himself, is to develop indefinitely. The hour of death of capitalism, as that of the society which proceeded it, cannot be determined by an absolute accumulation of social wealth, but by the growing difficulty within which this process takes place, by the increasingly stronger reactions that it generates, and by the increased pressure of the proletariat. The truth is that the possibilities of success of a socialist revolution have no other measure but success itself.

European social democracy blames bolshevism for having carried out a socialist revolution in a country not yet ready for the transformation. Gramsci's answer does not stop with the documentation of the historical peculiarities of Russian society which have given rise to '1789 which is late and a vanguard revolution'. The problem is a theoretical one and has to do with the nature of Marx's 'prediction'. First of all, Gramsci rules out any catastrophic interpretation of the crisis, by ruling out a halt to the capitalist process of accumulation. Second, he denies that it is possible to talk about the crisis or the halting of the reproduction process of a capitalist society by restricting the analysis to the difficulties obtaining on the level of material production. Thus, on the basis of the *Preface* of 1859 it is possible to substitute for the concept of prediction that of the development of an objective possibility which, in order to be realised, must be expressed and articulated at the level of politics. No matter how deep, the contradictions of a society can never guarantee the passage to a new order unless they are organised. In this sense, the criterion that 'the possibilities of success of a socialist revolution have no other measure but success itself' is universal. This is not derived from the analysis of a given situation, but from a reinterpretation of the role of theory. To re-establish the nature and limits of theoretical 'prediction' means not only to rediscover the crucial role of the will (of being in history), but, at the level of analysis, to fill that vacuum left by an economistic interpretation of historical materialism.

Here is where the ethico-political comes in and, not accidentally, it has as its reference point that same *Preface* of 1859 which theoretically excludes the very possibility of formulating a fatalistic theory:[95]

society does not pose itself problems for whose solution the material preconditions do not already exist. This proposition immediately raises the problem of the formation of a collective will. In order to analyse critically what the proposition means, it is necessary to study precisely how permanent collective wills are formed, and how such wills set themselves concrete short-term and long-term ends – i.e. a line of collective action.

If, in Gramsci's interpretation, the first part of the *Preface* of 1859 emphasises the possibility of survival of a capitalist society, the second part points out the historically necessary, organic, and irreversible character of the birth and development of political and economic organisations of the working class. This entails the possibility of elaborating, not only the theory of the political party, but also the two major forms of revolutionary processes in capitalist society (the 'relationship of force' and that of 'passive revolution').

For Gramsci, the issue with regard to relations of force is clearly more complex than the respective strength of the armies in the field. It is rather a matter of grasping the complex way in which a class society is structured from the economic to the political sphere, and to represent its movement as a succession of the various outcomes of the confrontation between the struggling forces. In a passage where Gramsci tries to explain the methodology he used in the conflict between the Moderates and the Action Party, he writes:[96]

It seems obvious that the so-called subjective conditions can never be missing when the objective conditions exist, in as much as the distinction involved is simply one of a didactic character.
Consequently, it is on the size and concentration of subjective forces that discussion can bear, and hence on the dialectical relation between conflicting subjective forces.

With the re-elaboration of historical materialism in political science, Gramsci goes beyond what had divided 'revisionists' and 'orthodox marxists', precisely when he sought a different solution to the revisionists' objections. It has been pointed out that in his polemic against Croce's ethico-political, Gramsci always had Bernstein in mind.[97] Actually, the most significant and stimulating parts of his critical contribution consist in calling attention to the growing role of ideal forces and organised forces in the historical process: with the growth of all forms of regulations and guided intervention in civil society, the marxist prediction (identified with Kautsky's theory of the collapse) concerning the close relation between the development of productive forces and the advancing of the socialist revolution turns out to be inconsistent. The development of facts requires a theoretical revision. Contrary to Bernstein and Croce, who sought the definitive liquidation of marxism by elaborating the ethico-political, Gramsci's project is to accept the revisionists' objections by showing, through a radical rejection of the orthodox position, how they are totally compatible with the marxist theory of history.

But the importance of power relations in Gramsci's interpretation of historical materialism is better understood in connection with the concept of 'passive revolution'. For Gramsci, this concept refers to the character of the political struggle after a working-class withdrawal or a defeat and seeks to provide an adequate representation of the complex historical process resulting in the definitive supersession of an entire mode of production. Its polemical references are the theory of the crash and the jacobin tendency to compress the whole social significance of a revolutionary process into the violent break.

In this perspective, the course of the socialist revolution can no longer be understood by merely acknowledging the slow-down of the revolutionary process. It is necessary to bring about a change in the theoretical perspective which will allow an understanding of the contradictory manifestation of the on-going progressive tendency to replace a mode of production. Already in his political writing, Gramsci began to relate the epoch of the bourgeois revolution with that of the proletarian revolution:[98]

> As in the beginning of the nineteenth century when everyone's hopes were directed to the French Revolution, and in vain the reaction and the Holy Alliance raged against it, so today one looks to the Russian Revolution from Asia as well as from Europe.

In both instances there was an initial phase of war of movement: a jacobin experiment which succeeded in a given situation. Then it was followed by a much slower development, studded with 'restorations' which never amount to a return to pre-existing situations, but constitute different forms of the political management of an unchanged social content which, however, continues to spread and deepen. If advance into a territory that has not experienced jacobinism becomes increasingly more complex, the war of movement proves inadequate and must give way to a war of position. The French Revolution was not concluded in 1789, 1793, or even with the Napoleonic wars. It is equally true that the October Revolution did not end with either the assault on the Winter Palace or the civil war and war-communism, or with the introduction of the NEP:[99]

> Studies aimed at capturing the analogies between the period which followed the fall of Napoleon and that which followed the war of 1914–1918. The analogies are only seen from two viewpoints: territorial division, and the more conspicuous and superficial one of the attempt to give a stable legal organization to international relations (Holy Alliance and the League of Nations). However, it would seem that the most important characteristic to examine is the one which has been called that of 'passive revolution' – a problem whose existence is not manifest, since an external parallelism with the France of 1789–1815 is lacking. And yet, everybody recognises that the war of 1914–1918 represents an historical break, in the sense that a whole series of questions which piled up individually before 1914 have precisely formed a 'mound,' modifying the general structure of the previous process. ...

This historical example shows how the concept of passive revolution relates 'what is organic and what is conjunctural'. Passive revolution, based on the two methodological principles in the *Preface* of 1859, guarantees theoretical mastery over a multiform historical process which may confuse the distinction between what is organic and what is conjunctural. Losing sight of this distinction[100]

> leads to presenting causes as immediately operative which in fact only operate indirectly, or to asserting that the immediate causes are the only effective ones. In the first case, there is an excess of 'economism', or doctrinaire pedantry; in the second, an excess of 'ideologism'. In the first case, there is an overestimation of mechanical causes, in the second, an exaggeration of the voluntarist and individual element.

Thus, for Gramsci, the recognition of historical truth is impossible without an adequate theoretical instrument. For this reason, to define him as the theoretician of the revolution in the West appears reductive, in the light of the rediscovery of his political writings.

If, beginning in 1924, Gramsci's position is characterised by an emphasis on the specificity of the Western European situation with regard to czarist Russia, his contribution cannot be reduced to the recognition of this specificity. Furthermore, the more one investigates the unique character of the October Revolution, the more it becomes necessary to find at the theoretical level a unifying element between East and West in order to refute social democratic positions. It becomes necessary to show how this uniqueness does not invalidate the perspective with which the October Revolution exploded on the world scene.

The most favourable conditions for proletarian revolutions do not always necessarily exist in those countries where the development of capitalism and industrialism has reached the highest level. These conditions can obtain where the fabric of the capitalist system offers less resistance to an attack by the working class and its allies, because of structural weaknesses.[101] To theorise this possibility was not merely a matter of claiming the existence of conditions favourable to a revolutionary development *even* in countries which have not yet reached capitalist maturity, but also, and more importantly, to have completely changed the analytical tools. It meant primarily the abandonment of the traditional interpretation of historical materialism which had shown itself inadequate not only in the East, but also in the West: not only had it failed to understand the October Revolution, but it had also failed to develop a political strategy adequate for those capitalist countries where all the conditions seemed to be ripe. It was precisely in the West that it proved incapable of explaining that the development of the productive forces (which in capitalist societies can continue despite the onset of a crisis) not only constituted a further incentive to socialist revolution, but could also become a formidable obstacle to it. In the East as well as the West, marxism had to reject the interpretative scheme based on the relation of cause and effect between structure and superstructure. It had to reintroduce the concept of the social relations of production in political science, according to Gramsci's analysis of power relations. In fact, the multiplicity of historical situations was the major stimulus for rediscovering a unitary methodological analysis on the theoretical level. The question of the universality of leninism raises for Gramsci the problem of the relation between theory and history in terms of the political leadership.

The problem of the universality of leninism, i.e. 'whether a theoretical truth, whose discovery corresponded to a specific practice, can be generalised and considered as universal for a historical epoch', is dealt with in a note in the *Prison Notebooks* that discusses the Rome theses –

the bordigan document approved in 1922 by the Second Party Congress.[102] But rather than focusing on the allusive and loose language of the prison writings, it is better to examine here the text where Gramsci best expressed such a view during his years of political struggle. This is the extensive position presented by the Italian delegation at the Fifth Executive (and read by Scoccimarro) − which, through a polemic with Bordiga, defended leninism. The thesis set forth by Gramsci in prison is that the best proof of the 'concrete universality' of a theory lies in its incorporation into reality, 'and not simply in its logical and formal coherence'.[103] The position of the Italian delegation at the Fifth Executive pivots around the claim that 'actually, bolshevism has given us a tactical method of universal value'.[104] Bordiga's stand in relation to bolshevism 'showed a certain analogy with the view held in the past by Comrade Trotsky, when he contraposed to bolshevism his tactical method defined as "European Marxism" '.[105] Thus, the problem is still that of East−West relations and of the possible recomposition of each bloc's differences into a unitary methodological analysis, as in Lenin's conception of the dialectic. The political problem is to demonstrate how the tactical differences necessary for the variety of situations can remain compatible with principles. Bordiga's proposal, already contained in the Rome theses, was to establish irrevocable norms of behaviour. The danger of eclecticism arises − a danger which Bordiga had already identified at work in the political leadership of the Communist International. Bordiga's charge was refuted by reiterating Lenin's definition of eclecticism:[106]

> eclecticism consists in establishing tactics solely on the basis of a causal connection of two or more factors of the objective situation, rather than in examining such an objective situation on the basis of all its factors, in their totality, considering their unending development from all sides.

A correct tactical formulation is entrusted to an exhaustive knowledge of the historically concrete. This is how the marxist conception of theory is to be understood. In the contraposition of formal and dialectical logic there reappears the criticism of the role of the theory that does not seek to explain the world, but to superimpose itself on it. From a methodological viewpoint, the criticism of Bordiga is analogous to the critique of Bukharin's sociology and Plekhanov's conception of the dialectic. It is first a matter of re-establishing the boundaries of theoretical inquiry and historical analysis and, second, of establishing a possible connection:[107]

> Only the general lines guaranteeing faithfulness to principles and marking the boundaries within which party tactics must take place can be established *a priori*. It is not possible to go further than that, because the particularities of each moment of development cannot be known *a priori*.

Furthermore,[108]

> the tactical means the International is authorised to employ, find their limits only in the foundations of communist theory and programmes. Within these limits, it is inadmissible to predetermine tactical means. Their variety is determined by the given situations and by the experiences of the revolutionary struggle.

If the foundations of communist theory contain a criticism of the mode of production and determine the general features of its supersession, they cannot thereby describe the historical process through which such transcendence can occur. But politics is the way criticism takes on historical existence. To guarantee a method of political analysis means to discover the passage from theory to history. Dialectic as a method is the means through which marxism becomes the 'theory of history and politics'. As already stated in this 1925 text, 'Marxism is a method of historical analysis and political orientation.' But for this very reason, it is significant that 'Lenin refers to the past always with one purpose in mind – to learn from previous mistakes. And he resorts to fixed formulas only for one reason: to reiterate the value of the fundamental principles of communism.'[109] In short, only if one understands the fundamental distinction between the two terms can the dialectic be understood as the passage from theory to history. To say that leninism turns marxism into political theory does not exhaust Gramsci's judgment of its historical significance. It still overlooks the interpretation of the Marx–Lenin relationship. To examine Gramsci's analysis of this relation is to summarise his interpretation of marxism, and to understand this, one must re-examine the Comintern's elaboration of marxism–leninism during the bolshevisation of the communist parties.

By defining leninism as 'the marxism of the imperialist age', Lenin is presented both as Marx's true interpreter who avoided the 'falsifications' of the Second International and as someone who further developed marxism in the light of the problems of a new age. At any rate, the evaluation of Lenin's work takes place within the context of the history of marxism. For this reason, it can become the starting point for reconstituting an orthodoxy with retroactive implications. The theses approved at the Fifth Executive explicitly state that bolshevisation implies in every country the recovery of 'revolutionary traditions': 'To bolshevise the party means to make it, beginning with leninism, into the conscious continuation of all that which was really revolutionary and marxist in the First and Second Internationals'.[110] The names in the various countries associated with 'past generations of revolutionaries', whose heritage marxism–leninism must assume, turn out to be Guesde and Lafargue for France, Plekhanov for Russia, Liebknecht and Bebel for Germany. It can be inferred that the reason the 'first' Kautsky is not mentioned with a qualification similar to that used for Plekhanov – 'when he was still a marxist' – is that, being still alive, he still represented a strongly opposed political current. In a nutshell, the point is to restore that doctrinaire philosophical account which had characterised the Second International at its beginnings.

The theses on propaganda, approved at the Fifth World Congress in 1924, already spoke of 'a philosophical deviation of some of the intellectual centres of the parties of central Europe aiming at eliminating the materialist essence of dialectical materialism'.[111] In 1919 Lukács had rejected orthodoxy as the 'guardian of tradition',[112] and had argued that, for what concerns marxism, 'orthodoxy refers exclusively to *method*'.[113] In the attempt to resurrect a concept of orthodoxy meant to recover the tradition and philosophical materialism, the definition of leninism (aside from its role in the strategy of development of the soviet state and society) increasingly comes to coincide with a rehabilitation of the 'systematic' notion of marxism, which Gramsci saw as the main antagonist of 'absolute historicism'.

Gramsci's interpretation of leninism does not necessarily relate Lenin and the marxist *tradition*, but Lenin and Marx as such. His claim at the Lyon Congress that 'there is a fundamental analogy between the process of "Bolshevisation" being carried out today, and the activity of Karl Marx within the workers' movement',[114] advocates the recovery of the First International as the foundation of a comprehensive theoretical interpretation of marxism. The previously cited 1924 article already outlines a general interpretation. The theoretical authenticity of bolshevism is maintained on the basis of the October Revolution. Its faithfulness to Marx is not sought for in any formal continuity: in fact, there is no reference at all to matters of doctrine. In the second place, the continuity between Lenin and Marx is mediated by a critique of the marxism of the Second International which is not limited to its politics, but engulfs its theoretical foundations. What he sees as essential in Lenin's elaboration is to have restored to marxism its revolutionary theoretical nature and to have thereby rediscovered its philosophical nucleus.

In the 1924 text Lenin is seen as the 'great realiser' who has guided the Russian proletariat to victory: 'when major contemporary events will be a little more removed and visible under a proper perspective, leninism will be acknowledged as the practical realisation of marxism.' In the prison writings Gramsci discusses again 'Ilich's position', and states that 'the explanation is to be found in marxism itself as both science and action'.[115] In Gramsci's opinion, marxism–leninism finds a theoretical foundation in the doctrine's basic concepts independent of the historical events it designates. The relation between the two must be determined not on the basis of a tradition, but in terms of concepts proper to marxism.

After the October Revolution, marxism is no longer just a theory. The transition from science to action means the transition from theoretical possibility to historical effectiveness. Gramsci quickly adds that Marx's scientific contribution does not lie in any specific discovery which would include him in a gallery of great scientists, but in providing an account of mankind's development: no one before Marx 'has produced an original and integral conception of the world'.[116] No one else saw the possibility for a new phase of historical development as the necessary basis for a new way of thinking and the transcendence of all the antinomies plaguing human thought since its origins.

Lenin is the true heir to the *Theses on Feuerbach* because, by historically modifying social relations of production, he allowed marxism to leave the phase of critique and begin the positive creation of a new 'civilisation'. Gramsci cannot credit Marx with the creation of a new world-view, since he identifies this creation with the birth of new social relations of production. By abandoning capitalist relations of production it is possible to see the limit of the world which has also been the limit of philosophy. This is why 'to make a comparison between Marx and Ilich in order to create a hierarchy is stupid and useless. They express two phases: science and action, which are homogeneous and heterogeneous at the same time.'[117] Marx could claim that the solution of theoretical problems is 'by no means merely a problem of understanding, but a *real* problem of life, which *philosophy* could not solve precisely because it conceived this problem as *merely* a theoretical one'.[118] But he was unable to go further.

In Gramsci, the relation between Lenin and Marx is a result of his conception of marxism as absolute historicism. The same can be said of Engels' statement about the working class's inheritance of German classical philosophy. In the prison writings this question is dealt with once, where he argues that Marx's account of German classical philosophy cannot be considered definitive and must be re-elaborated in relation to the developments of bourgeois culture. This interpretation is already quite distant from the usual histories of marxism, according to which Engels' proposal is interpreted to mean that the labour movement's cultural tradition is inseparable from the highest theoretical achievements of the revolutionary bourgeoisie. Gramsci's marxism explicitly rejects any identification with traditions remote from political struggles and the working class's practical advances. This same notion is confirmed by the other more common statement, where marxism is seen as 'the theory of a class which seeks to become state'. With the introduction of modifications in social relations of production, marxism is no longer merely the theoretical critique of philosophical quandaries, but its 'real dialectic'. The proletariat becomes the heir to philosophy when, by creating a new kind of state, it proposes the first essential promise of a historical development leading to a new culture where philosophy will actually become a world-view and the individual philosopher's critique will be historically realised in a new relation between the intellectuals and the masses.

For Gramsci the strong presence of philosophical materialism in the Bolsheviks and in the leninist tradition is an embarrassment. Thus, it must be deprived of any theoretical import by giving it a purely historical meaning. In analysing the theoretical deformations marxism has undergone during its first stages as the 'conception of a subaltern social group', Gramsci writes that:

> In the history of culture, which is much broader than the history of philosophy, every time there has been a flowering of popular culture because a revolutionary phase was being passed through and because the metal of a new class was being forged from the ore of the people, there has been a flowering of 'materialism': concurrently, at the same time the traditional classes clung to philosophies of the spirit.

And he immediately adds: ' "Politically", the materialist conception is close to the people, to "common sense".'[119] The emphasis on philosophical materialism is to be seen as a tax paid by bolshevism for the backwardness of the environment in which it developed and functioned. Yet, it does not compromise its integrity: 'A man of politics writes about philosophy: it could be that his "true" philosophy should be looked for rather in his writings on politics.'[120]

There is consequently a contradiction between Lenin's political theory and his positions in philosophical battles. If, in Gramsci's opinion, there is continuity in Lenin's thought from beginning to end it is to be sought in the struggle against economism. The theory of hegemony, representing the only valid answer to the belated reassertion of the theory of permanent revolution, is only the final state of a theoretical battle originating in the theory of the party. The various 'counterrevolutionary' positions fought by Lenin are all summarised in economistic, syndicalist or reformist theories. The theory of spontaneity, which de-emphasises the role of the party and of theory since 'men act spontaneously, automatically, and only under the pressure of events', is but one of the consequences of that 'economistic theory' which, in its expressions as syndicalism and reformism, embraces the entire Second International. The general assumption is that economic struggles 'were able to lead automatically to the capitalist apocalypse from which the new society was to be born'.[121]

If what characterises Lenin's thought is the struggle against economism and the theory of the crash, then the problem arises of linking this with an appropriate philosophy. The rejection of economism by historical materialism cannot be considered definitive until it finds its philosophical extension. Gramsci seems to realise that through this contradiction internal to Lenin's thought, the latter's most important theoretical innovations could be reabsorbed by non-revolutionary perspectives. Many of the formulations of marxism-leninism after Lenin's death can be seen as prefiguring what was to become 'soviet marxism'. It is necessary to begin here to understand Gramsci's defence and explication of an interpretation of marxism-leninism strongly opposed by various sectors of the Communist International.

In response to Gramsci's thesis that 'leninism is a complete world-view, not exclusively confined to the process of proletarian revolution',[122] it is Bordiga in the Italian party who objects that the labour movement already has a complete world-view of its own in marxism, of which Lenin is not a revisionist – which would justify the expression 'leninism' – but a restorer. Bordiga's position followed from his affinity with the whole previous traditional interpretation of marxism. Even the major theoreticians of the German left who had violently broken with the marxism of the Second International were very cautious in accepting the new notion of marxism-lenism. Gramsci's acceptance of leninism as self-contained system of thought and his rejection of the marxism of the Second International stem from his belief that a 'return to Marx' is impossible outside of the development of the innovative elements brought about by the October Revolution. This is why in the 1925–6 writings bolshevisation is presented as a return to Marx, and the struggle for the diffusion of leninism is aimed against any form of revisionism.

When marxism-leninism reintroduced some aspects of the marxism of the Second International and leninism tended to become the connecting point for a 'revolutionary tradition' uncritically including undigested fragments from the past, Gramsci brought in Labriola against Plekhanov. His 'formulation of the philosophical problem' became the startingpoint for developing that world-view entrusted with preserving the original features of political leninism. Labriola was present in Gramsci's early works, but his interpretation of historical materialism appeared already obsolete.[123] When he reappeared in 1925 as a rediscovery it was the Labriola of *Socialism and Philosophy* and not the Labriola of the *Essay on the Materialist Conception of History*. What was emphasised were not the anti-determinist interpretations of historical materialism, but Labriola's approach to the philosophy of marxism. If, in his early writings, Gramsci tried to bring in Labriola in his anti-positivist polemics, he now saw his full meaning within the theoretical experience of the Second International. It is significant that Labriola's name appears in the report to the Central Committee which officially opened the campaign for bolshevisation in the Italian party after the conclusion of the Fifth Executive.[124] In the postscript to a note to Togliatti sent along in October 1926 with his written report of the debates in the Russian party, Gramsci wrote: 'I am waiting for the corrected and collated text of Antonio Labriola's letters, with Rjazanov's preface. It is needed for the first issue of *L'Ordine Nuovo*. The utmost speed is necessary.'[125] The decision to publish the letters to Engels, which were to appear in the *Stato Operaio* immediately after his arrest, was connected with a theoretical and political struggle.

In the prison writings Gramsci did not completely develop this new world-view. He merely drafted a project whose realisation was entrusted to the theoretical developments of working-class political hegemony in a specific territory. At this point we can ask once again whether it is possible to speak of a general theory of marxism in Gramsci. The answer is no, if leninism is seen by Gramsci as the launching pad for a new chapter of marxism. Lenin outlines a positive tendency for all of marxist theory and not just parts of it. In Gramsci's opinion, however, the realisation of this tendency implies a 'new synthesis', at the level of cultural and political development of marxism.

As the theoretician of the concept of hegemony, Lenin has necessitated a 're-evaluation of the philosophical front'. He has not, however, explicitly provided the weapons necessary for such a re-evaluation, which can emerge only from a critical reconsideration of the relations between marxism, the labour movement and modern culture. In Gramsci's *What Is To Be Done?* the party is the bearer of a revolutionary theory to the extent that marxism is critically related to all the existing forms of consciousness, from the masses' common sense to the best representatives of European culture. When Gramsci unequivocally stated that in the previous history of the movement marxism had been defeated, that it had failed to fulfil its task 'to supersede the highest cultural manifestation of the age, classical German philosophy, and to create a group of intellectuals specific to the new social group whose conception of the world it was',[126] he was not only critical of the Second International, but also historically and theoretically removed from Lenin's thought.

The Russian working class has succeeded in becoming the heir to classical German philosophy by creating its own state, but in order to break other links in the chain it is essential that marxism rediscovers its own identity.[127]

> To maintain that the philosophy of praxis is not a completely
> autonomous and independent structure of thought in antagonism to
> all traditional philosophies and religions, means in reality that *one has
> not severed one's links with the old world, if indeed one has not
> actually capitulated.*

The 'Kantian' operation Gramsci pursues, continually testing his concept of absolute historicism, is the indispensable premise for recreating that new synthesis between materialism and idealism that had been lost in Marx's interpretations. Yet, it does not amount to a new synthesis. Nor did Gramsci ever pretend that it did. Having completed the critique of the individual philosopher in the various forms in which it has continued to be reproduced both inside and outside marxism, only the movement as a whole will be able to carry out this new synthesis.[128]

The task which at the beginning of the movement was performed by single intellectuals (like Marx and Engels) and by workers with scientific capability (like the German worker Dietzgen) is today carried out by the communist parties and the International as a whole.

This new development of marxism carried out by the collective intellectual has, so far, not taken place. Gramsci's project remains a project. The working class's practical advances have been accomplished, as Togliatti would stress, 'in action'. They have not brought forth notable studies or developments in political science. The same could be said of the other gramscian project of the development of marxism as an integral world-view for the construction of a different society. The fact remains that no intellectual has emerged to master it and make it work. Certainly, it has been possible to turn Gramsci's marxism into a 'fragmentary marxism'. His interpretation of historical materialism as a science of history and politics has provided useful indications for a historiography which, however, has remained underdeveloped. In its first phase absolute historicism turned into a vaguely defined historicist tradition which was already the cultural formation of traditional intellectuals. When the studies on marxist theory were resumed, absolute historicism aroused unjustified diffidence based on the belief that Gramsci's work denied the role of theory. They were somewhat justifiable, perhaps, when they realised that, with Gramsci, even within the labour movement there was no creative role for the individual philosopher as such, and absolute historicism and the science of history and politics required a different mode of theoretical production.

To claim that Gramsci's work amounts to a general theory means to reject the 'fragmentary Gramsci' but to simultaneously assert that the gramscian interpretation of marxism develops through a systematic confrontation with all of the doctrine's crucial points and that individual answers are in a relation of reciprocal implications. It is an 'organic and indivisible system' from which its individual constitutive elements cannot be separated. The aim is to filter marxism through a sieve to purify it of the encrustations built upon it during a whole phase of its history, to provide it with a renewed awareness of its identity, and to establish the possibilities for its further development.

So far the movement has not been adequate to the task: Gramsci's theoretical project has itself become a victim of the passive revolution. But the passive revolution is still in progress. Maybe it will be necessary to rely on its developments for an answer to that question which still keeps Gramsci's work suspended and fluctuating between two opposed poles: whether it contains a hearty utopia, full of useful cultural notations, or whether, instead, it is an attempt to determine the active theoretical and political behaviour of the working class in the declining phase of the mode of production when the danger grows that what is dead may devour what is alive. In the last analysis, this divergence has a practical content. Speaking of the concept of passive revolution, Gramsci once maintained that it 'presupposes, indeed postulates as necessary, a vigorous antithesis which can present intransigently all its possibilities for development'.[129] But with these words he was summing up the meaning of all his theoretical research.

Notes

This chapter was originally published in *Annali del Instituto Feltrinelli*, Milan, 1973. English translation by William Boelhower, Maria Antonietta Sergi and Franca Bernabei first published in *Telos*, no. 36, 1978.

1 Palmiro Togliatti, 'Il Leninismo nel Peniero e nell'Azione di Gramsci', *Antonio Gramsci*, Rome, 1958, p. 35.
2 Antonio Gramsci, *Selections from the Prison Notebooks*, ed. and trans. Q. Hoare and G. Nowell Smith, London, Lawrence & Wishart, 1971, p. 386.
3 Giorgio Plekhanov, *Le Question Fondamentali del Marxismo*, Milan, 1947, pp. 23 ff. English translation, *Fundamental Problems of Marxism*, trans. J. Katzer, London, Lawrence & Wishart, 1969.
4 'Leninismo', *l'Unita*, 10 September 1925.
5 Gramsci, op. cit, pp. 455–6.
6 Ibid., p. 464.
7 Ibid., p. 463.
8 Ibid., p. 390.
9 Antonio Labriola, *Socialism and Philosophy*, trans. Ernest Untermann, Chicago, 1907, p. 62.
10 Ibid., pp. 77–8.
11 Recently, Sereni has pointed out some decisive textual similarities between some passages of Labriola's exposition of historical materialism and the young Lenin's discussion of the concept of social-economic formation. Cf. Emilio Sereni, 'Da Marx a Lenin: la Categoria di "Formazione Economico-Sociale" ', in *Lenin Teórico e Dirigente Revoluzionario, Quaderni di Critica Marxista*, 4, pp. 50–7.
12 Labriola, *Socialism and Philosophy*, pp. 42–3.
13 Frederick Engels, 'Ludwig Feuerbach and the End of Classical German Philosophy', in K. Marx and F. Engels, *Selected Works*, vol. 2, Moscow, 1962, p. 365.

14 Gramsci, op. cit., p. 355.
15 Ibid., p. 405.
16 Ibid., pp. 355–6.
17 Gramsci, 'Della Sospensione di un Congresso di Filosofi', *l'Unita*, 1 April 1926.
18 Cf. Loyd D. Easton and Kurt H. Guddat, *Writings of the Young Marx on Philosophy and Society*, Garden City, N.Y., 1967, p. 53.
19 Gramsci, *Il materialismo storico e la filosofia di Benedetto Croce*, Turin, 1948, p. 217. (This part has not been included in the English translation of the *Prison Notebooks*.)
20 Gramsci, 'Produzione e Politica', *L'Ordine Nuovo*, 24–31, January 1920.
21 Franco De Felice, *Serrati, Bordiga, Gramsci*, Bari, De Donato, 1971, p. 303.
22 Gramsci, *Il Materialismo Storico*, p. 233.
23 Ibid., p. 191.
24 Gramsci, *Prison Notebooks*, p. 399.
25 Gramsci, *Socialismo e Fascismo*, Turin, 1966, p. 13.
26 Gramsci, *La Costruzione del Partito Comunista 1923–1926*, Turin, 1971, p. 272.
27 E. C. Longobardi, 'Marxismo, Labourismo e Bolscevismo', *L'Ordine Nuovo*, third series, 15 November, 1924.
28 Gramsci, 'The Russian Utopia', in Pedro Cavalcanti and Paul Piccone, eds, *History, Philosophy and Culture in the Young Gramsci*, St Louis, Telos Press, 1975, p. 149.
29 Ibid., p. 39.
30 Gramsci, *Letters from Prison*, selected and trans. Lynne Lawner, New York, 1973, p. 235.
31 Gramsci, *La costruzione*, p. 432.
32 Gramsci, *Il Materialismo Storico*, p. 191.
33 Gramsci, *La costruzione*, pp. 336–7.
34 Ibid., p. 308.
35 Ibid., p. 309.
36 Gramsci, *Passato e Presente*, Turin, 1954, pp. 183–4.
37 'Fünfter Kongress der kommunistischen Internationale', in *Protokoll*, Hamburg, 1924, p. 513, *The Communist International, 1923–28: Documents*, ed. J. Degras, Oxford University Press, 1960, pp. 160–1.
38 Nikolai Bukharin, *Theorie des historischen Materialismus*, Hamburg, 1922, p. 8.
39 The text of this 'translation' can be found in the archives of the Italian Communist Party.
40 Gramsci, *Prison Notebooks*, p. 436.
41 Ibid., p. 427.
42 Ibid., p. 437.
43 Togliatti, 'Lezione di Marxismo', *Rinascità*, vol. 2, no. 3, March, 1945.
44 Gramsci, *Prison Notebooks*, p. 456.
45 Ibid., p. 435.
46 Karl Marx, *The Poverty of Philosophy*, Moscow, Progress Publishers, 1973, pp. 102, 109, sixth and seventh observations.

47 Gramsci, *Prison Notebooks*, p. 431.
48 V. I. Lenin, 'On the Question of Dialectics', in his *Collected Works*, Moscow, 1961, vol. 38, pp. 335–63.
49 Lenin, 'Once Again on the Trade Unions', in *Collected Works*, vol. 32, Moscow, 1965, pp. 93–4.
50 Lenin, 'Il Materialismo Militante', *L'Ordine Nuovo*, third series, 15 March 1924, cf. ibid., vol. 33, pp. 227–36.
51 Ibid., vol. 21, p. 236.
52 Ibid., vol. 22, p. 316.
53 Cf. 'Annotazioni di Lenin al Libro di Bucharin sull'Economia del Periodo di Transizione', in *Critica Marxista*, vol. 5 no. 4–5 (1967), p. 308.
54 Lenin, 'Philosophical Notebooks', in his *Collected Works*, vol. 38, p. 159.
55 Ibid., p. 230.
56 Ibid., p. 196.
57 Ibid., p. 182.
58 Gramsci, *Letters from Prison*, p. 240. Translation modified.
59. Mario Garuglieri, 'Ricordo di Gramsci', in *Società*, 7–8, July–December, 1946, p. 697.
60 Gramsci, *Prison Notebooks*, p. 428.
61 Togliatti, *Opere*, ed. Ernesto Ragionieri, vol. I, 1917–26, Rome, 1967, p. 652.
62 Ibid., vol. 2, 1926–9, Rome, 1972, p. 21.
63 Gramsci, *La costruzione*, p. 102.
64 Gramsci, *Prison Notebooks*, p. 366.
65 Gramsci, *Il Materialismo Storico*, p. 203.
66 Gramsci, *Prison Notebooks*, p. 431.
67 Ibid., p. 367.
68 Ibid., p. 432.
69 Ibid., p. 5.
70 Ibid., p. 371.
71 Ibid., p. 432.
72 Ibid., pp. 139–40.
73 Ibid., p. 412.
74 Ibid., p. 177.
75 Ibid., pp. 180–3.
76 Ibid., pp. 133–4.
77 Gramsci, 'Marx e Machiavelli', a previously unpublished passage of the *Prison Notebooks*, ed. Valentino Gerratana, *Rinascità*, 14 April 1967.
78 Gramsci, *Prison Notebooks*, p. 404.
79 Ibid., p. 398.
80 Ibid., p. 405.
81 Ibid., p. 398.
82 Ibid., p. 133.
83 Ibid., p. 341.
84 Ibid., p. 333.
85 Ibid., p. 134.
86 Ibid., p. 333.

87 Ibid., p. 348.
88 Gramsci, *La costruzione*, p. 476.
89 Ibid., p. 489. English translation in *Selections from Political Writings 1921–26*, ed. and trans. Q. Hoare, London, Lawrence & Wishart, 1978, pp. 340–1.
90 Gramsci, *Il Materialismo Storico*, p. 157.
91 *Socialismo e Fascismo*, pp. 137–8.
92 Gramsci, *Prison Notebooks*, p. 411.
93 Ibid.
94 Longobardi, 'Marxismo, Labourismo e Bolscevismo'.
95 Gramsci, *Prison Notebooks*, p. 194.
96 Ibid., p. 113.
97 Nicola Badaloni, 'Gramsci et le problème de la Révolution', translated in this volume, pp. 80–109.
98 Gramsci, *La costruzione*, p. 323.
99 Gramsci, *Prison Notebooks*, p. 106.
100 Ibid., p. 178.
101 Gramsci, *La costruzione*, p. 492.
102 Gramsci, *Prison Notebooks*, p. 201.
103 Ibid.
104 *Protokoll der erweiterten Exekutive der Kommunistischen Internationale*, (Moscow, 21 March – 6 April 1925), Hamburg, 1925, p. 291.
105 Ibid.
106 Ibid., p. 103.
107 Ibid., p. 102.
108 Ibid., p. 103.
109 Ibid., p. 104.
110 *Erweiterte Exekutive*, March/April 1925, *Thesen und Resolutionen*, Hamburg, p. 18.
111 This is from the translation in *L'Ordine Nuovo*, 3rd series, 1 November 1924.
112 Georg Lukács, *History and Class Consciousness*, trans. R. Livingstone, London, 1971, p. 24.
113 Ibid., p. 1.
114 Gramsci, *La costruzione*, p. 482, *Political Writings*, p. 313.
115 Gramsci, *Prison Notebooks*, p. 381.
116 Ibid., p. 382.
117 Ibid.
118 Karl Marx, *The Economic and Philosophic Manuscripts of 1844*, ed. Dirk J. Struik, New York, 1971, pp. 141–2.
119 Gramsci, *Prison Notebooks*, p. 396.
120 Ibid., p. 403.
121 Cf. 'Leninismo', *l'Unità*, op. cit.
122 Amadeo Bordiga, 'Il Pericolo Opportunista dell'Internazionale', *l'Unità*, 30 September 1924.
123 Leonardo Paggi, *Gramsci e il Moderno Principe*, Rome, Riuniti, 1970, pp. 18–23.
124 Gramsci, *La costruzione*, p. 54, *Political Writings*, p. 288.

125 Ibid., p. 125, *Political Writings*, p. 426.
126 Gramsci, *Prison Notebooks*, p. 393.
127 Ibid., p. 462. Paggi's italics.
128 Gramsci, *La costruzione*, p. 251.
129 Gramsci, *Prison Notebooks*, p. 114.

5 Hegemony and ideology in Gramsci

Chantal Mouffe

The theory of ideology was for a long time one of the most neglected areas of the marxist analysis of society. Yet this is a key area involving some extremely important issues which are not only theoretical but also political. It is vital, therefore, to attempt to understand the nature of those obstacles which have hindered the formulation of a theory which offers an adequate explanation of the significance and role of ideology, since it is no exaggeration to say that these have constituted the main impediment to the development of marxism, both as a theory and as a political movement.

At first sight the answer seems fairly simple. The various obstacles all seem in effect to proceed from the unique phenomenon which a vast body of contemporary literature has termed *economism*. However, the apparent obvious simplicity of the term hides a whole series of problems which begin to emerge as soon as one attempts a rigorous definition of its specificity and extent. Although it is clear that all forms of economism imply a misrecognition of the distinct autonomy of politics and ideology, this generic definition is inadequate, as it gives rise to two possible spheres of ambiguity. The first stems from the fact that the notion of the economic is indeed ambiguous and far from being clear itself (it is not clear for example, what is the relative importance attributed to the forces of production and the relations of production in this area). The second is the result of the vagueness and imprecision characterising the mechanism of the subordination of politics and ideology to economics, since this is always defined resorting to purely allusive metaphors, ('subordination', 'reduction', 'reflexion'). In this way one is left with the possibility of the existence of complex forms of economism which are not easy to detect since they do not appear as such at first sight.

168

1 Economism and ideology

It is here that we can locate the reason for the complexity of the problem of economism in relation to the theory of ideology, since the former occurs in numerous forms some of which have only rarely been identified. The economistic problematic of ideology has two intimately linked but quite distinct facets. The first one consists in seeing a causal link between the structure and the superstructure and in viewing the latter purely as a mechanical reflection of the economic base. This leads to a vision of ideological superstructures as epiphenomena which play no part in the historical process. The second facet is not concerned with the role of the superstructures but with their actual nature, and here they are conceived as being determined by the position of the subjects in the relations of production. This second aspect is not identifiable with the first since here it is in fact possible to attribute 'differential time sequences' and even a certain efficacy to the ideological superstructures.

It is important to understand the various forms in which these two aspects have been combined in the marxist tradition. They can in fact be divided into three main phases: the first, which is the one in which the two aspects have combined, constitutes the pure and classic form of economism; in the second there is a move away from the classic view as the two aspects begin to be dissociated; finally, in the third phase there is a break with the two aspects of economism, and the theoretical bases for a rethinking of historical materialism in a radically anti-economistic perspective are established.

There are various reasons why the distinction of these three moments is necessary for an accurate understanding of economism. First of all, although it is generally agreed that the Second and Third Internationals were economistic, the particular forms of economism involved have not been adequately specified, with the result that reductionism and epiphenomenonism have tended to be identified with each other, or at least to be seen in a relation of mutual implication. As regards the 'superstructural' marxist interpretations (Lukàcs, Korsch, etc.), it is important to see that they only partially break with economism because although they reject the epiphenomenalist concept of ideology, class reductionism is none the less still present. Finally, it must be realised that the third moment is only just beginning and that the superseding of both aspects of economism is a theoretical task which for the most part still remains to be carried out.

Antonio Gramsci must surely be the first to have undertaken a complete and radical critique of economism, and it is here that his main contribution to the marxist theory of ideology lies. It is the object of this article, therefore, to analyse Gramsci's contribution within this perspective. First, however, it is important to recognise the particular difficulties that such a reading would involve. Some of these are inherent in any attempt at what is called a 'symptomatic reading', while others stem from the particular nature of Gramsci's writings and their fragmentary character. The main pitfall to be avoided at all costs, is an instrumental reading of Gramsci, one which takes advantage of the unsystematic nature of his work to extrapolate passages in an arbitrary fashion in order to back up a thesis bearing little relation to his thought. If symptomatic readings involve *practising a problematic* it is vital to make the latter explicit in order to avoid transferring to the text in question the contradictions of the conceptual system upon which the analysis is based. In addition one should not lose sight of the fact that the problematic underlying the analysis of the text is *external* to it, and that the unity of the text is often established along quite separate lines from the problematic itself. To avoid any ambiguity I shall start by defining the fundamental principles of the anti-reductionist problematic which is the basis of this reading of Gramsci. It should then be possible to judge whether the hypothesis with which I intend to proceed, which consists in attributing to Gramsci the merit of having laid the foundations of such a conception, can be accepted or not.

Principles of a non-reductionist conception of ideology

The non-reductionist conception of ideology which constitutes the theoretical foundation of this symptomatic reading of Gramsci is based on the following principles:

1   The notion of the concrete as overdetermination of contradictions. Faced with a hegelian-type conception which reduces each conjuncture to a process of the auto-development of a single contradiction, which as a result reduces the present to an *abstract* and *necessary* moment of a linear and predetermined development, I accept Althusser's conception which establishes the primacy of the notion of conjuncture in the analysis of the concrete, and considers every conjuncture as an overdetermination of contradictions each one of which can be thought *abstractly* in conceptual independence from the others. This constitutes the basis of a non-reductionist conception of the political and the

ideological given the fact that reductionism stems precisely from marxism's adoption of a hegelian historicist model. This leads to a consideration of all contradictions as moments in the development of a single contradiction – the class contradiction – which as a consequence leads one to attribute a class character to all political and ideological elements. The central problem of contemporary marxism lies in the elaboration of a non-reductionist theory of ideology and of politics which will account for the determination in the last instance by the economic.

2 How is this need for a conception which is both marxist and non-reductionist expressed in the concrete case of the theory of ideology? Following Althusser on this point, I understand by ideology a practice producing subjects.[1] The subject is not the originating source of consciousness, the expression of the irruption of a subjective principle into objective historical processes, but the *product* of a specific practice operating through the mechanism of interpellation. If, according to Althusser's conception, social agents are not the constitutive principle of their acts, but supports of the structures, their subjective principles of identity constitute an additional structural element resulting from specific historical practices. In this case how are the principles of overdetermination and of the determination in the last instance by the economic combined? Let us first take overdetermination.

The social agent possesses several principles of ideological determination, not just one: he is hailed (interpellated) as the member of either sex, of a family, of a social class, of a nation, of a race or as an aesthetic onlooker etc., and he lives these different subjectivities in which he is constituted in a relation of mutual implication. The problem consists in determining the *objective* relation between these subjective principles or ideological elements. In a reductionist perspective each of these has a necessary class-belonging. But if, on the contrary, we accept the principle of overdetermination, we must conclude that there can exist no necessary relation between them, and that it is consequently impossible to attribute a necessary class-belonging to them. However, it is here that the second principle – the determination in the last instance by the economic – intervenes. To stress determination in the last instance by the economic is equivalent to saying determination in the last instance by the social classes inasmuch as we define classes as constituting antagonistic poles in the dominant relations of production. This brings us, therefore, to the following assertion: if the ideological elements referred to do not *express* social classes, but if nevertheless classes do in the last instance, determine ideology, then we must thereby conclude that this determination can only be the result of the establishing of an articulating principle of these ideological elements, one which must result in actually *conferring upon them* a class character. This point, however, leaves a whole series of questions unresolved, and it is in this area that the elaboration of the anti-reductionist conception of ideology still remains to be done. In effect the assertion that the class character of an ideology is conferred upon it by its own articulating principle suggests the area in which the solution is to be found, but this in itself does not provide the theoretical answer to the problem.

The two points above have dealt with the theoretical bases of a non-reductionist conception of ideology, and the ground still to be covered in order to achieve a rigorous formulation of this conception has been indicated. The central concern of this article is to determine the ways in which these problems were recognised as such by Gramsci and to see what kind of solutions he proposed. I will attempt to show how the gramscian conception of *hegemony* involved, *in the practical state*, the operation of an anti-reductionist problematic of ideology. I shall go even further and maintain that it is this whole anti-reductionist conception of ideology which is the actual condition of *intelligibility* of Gramsci's conception of hegemony, and that the difficulties encountered in the interpretation of this conception stem from the fact that this anti-reductionist problematic has not so far been stressed.

Before going on to analyse Gramsci's conception it will first be necessary to take a detour via the Second International. In effect, economism did not present itself to Gramsci as an abstract or academic problem since it was on the contrary deeply embedded in the political practice of the Second International and was the root cause of the massive defeats suffered by the German and Italian working-class movements in the decade following the First World War. It is within this context that Gramsci's thought gains its significance and is to be understood.

The Second International and economism

The Second International's theory of the collapse of capitalism was based on an interpretation of Marx's thought whereby the proletarian revolution was the necessary and inevitable consequence of the development of the economic contradictions of the capitalist mode of production. Ideology did not have any autonomy since the development of socialist consciousness was the corollary of the numerical growth of the proletariat as a class, and of the exacerbation of economic contradictions. On the other hand, socialist consciousness was identified with the consciousness of the social agents, and the latters' principle of identity was to be found in the class to which they belonged. The two forms of economism were therefore combined: that is to say the epiphenomenonist conception of the role of ideology and the reductionist conception of its nature. This type of interpretation of marxism had its epistemological foundations in a positivist conception of science which viewed historical materialism in terms of a model of scientificity then prevalent in the physical sciences.[2] This gave rise to the assumption that the validity of Marx's theory depended on the empirical proof of the three laws considered to constitute the basis of his analysis of the capitalist mode of production: increasing concentration, overproduction, and proletarianisation. The conviction that these laws would be enacted and that they would automatically bring about the proletarian revolution led the defenders of the catastrophe theory to assert the inevitable nature of socialism. As Kautsky wrote in his commentary on the Erfurt programme:[3]

> We believe that the collapse of the existing society is inevitable because we know that economic development naturally and necessarily produces contradictions which oblige the exploited to combat private property. We know that it increases the numbers and strength of the exploiters whose interests lie in the maintenance of the existing order, and that it finally brings about unbearable contradictions for the mass of the population which is left only with the choice between brutalisation and inertia or the overturning of the existing system of ownership.

The Second International was strongly reductionist from an ideological point of view, and since it considered that all ideological elements had a necessary class-belonging it concluded from this that all elements belonging to the discourse of the bourgeoisie had to be decisively rejected by the working class whose aim had to be to cultivate pure proletarian values and to guard against all external contamination. This is how democracy came to be considered the typical ideological expression of the bougeoisie

In order to understand how such an interpretation of marxism was able to come into being it is important to recapture the historical climate of those years. On the one hand there was a strong bourgeoisie which had succeeded in extending its hold over the whole of society and in articulating the democratic demands to its class discourse. On the other hand there was the working class organised into powerful unions and mass parties, which made it possible to achieve success in its struggle for economic demands. This situation caused a twofold tension in socialist thought between (a) the need to establish a radical break between socialist ideology and bourgeois ideology, which was the only way to ensure the independence of the socialist movement at a time when the bourgeoisie still excercised a considerable power of attraction, and (b the need to establish a point of contact between the revolutionary objectives of the workers' movement and its growing success in the field of reforms within the capitalist system. Kautsky's economism constituted a full reply to these two needs. Since the bourgeoisie had succeeded in assimulating popular and democratic ideology to its discourse kautskyism concluded that democracy was necessarily a bourgeois ideology. Democracy therefore ceased to be seen, as in the young Marx, as the terrain of a permanent revolution begun by the bourgeoisie but concluded by the proletariat, and became instead a class ideology. The class criterion began to become the fundamental criterion at all levels and this is how one of the fundamental characteristics of economism originated, that is to say, class reductionism. On the other hand, if the working class was to take no part in the direction of other social forces and was to limit itself to the defence of its own interests, then revolution could not be the result of the conscious intervention of the working class presenting itself as a political alternative for all the exploited, but had instead to represent the unfolding of the possibilities inherent in the economic contradictions. From this ensues the theory of the collapse of capitalism. However, since this collapse was seen as merely the result of the play of economic forces, the latter were considered to contain all the elements necessary to explain the historical process. As a consequence, political and ideological factors simply became epiphenomena, which constitute the second characteristic of Kautsky's economism.

This mechanistic conception was to undergo a crisis on several points at the beginning of the twentieth century. But the development of the critique of kautskyan dogmatism had its own particular characteristics: in its most diverse and even antagonistic forms, the critique indicated the contradictions and inconsistencies of kautskyism without, however, abandoning its presuppositions. What is more, these critiques constituted both a negation of kautskyism as a system and a development of the various potentialities present in its ideological presuppositions. This tendency is particularly clear in the case of Bernstein and in the debate on revisionism. As a result of the non-realisation of predictions based on the theory of the collapse of capitalism and also of certain glaring contradictions in the theory of the spontaneous determination of the socialist consciousness of the working class – as in the case of the British working class – Bernstein was driven to reject marxism which he declared incapable of understanding real historical developments. Bernstein was to replace the marxist vision of scientific socialism with a view of socialism as an 'ethical ideal', as a type of society towards which humanity should voluntarily orientate itself by virtue of moral principles.

Bernstein had understood that in view of the new conditions in which capitalism was developing, the theory of catastrophe could no longer be upheld and that in advanced capitalist countries the superstructures played an increasingly important part. This is why, unlike Kautsky, he saw the importance of the working-class struggle being extended to the political and ideological fields. It was, therefore, this recognition of the need to pose the problem of ideology in a radically different way which led Bernstein to challenge the economistic version of marxism. However, since he identified Marx's doctrine with the theory of catastrophe, his critique of economism led him to reject marxism outright. In effect he considered that the attribution of an active role to ideologies had necessarily to contradict the marxist theory of history. Thus Bernstein's break with marxism is to be located within the theoretical domain constituted by the ideological presuppositions of the Second International which were never seriously challenged. If on the one hand he identified marxism and the theory of catastrophe, on the other he identified democracy and bourgeois parliamentarianism. This is why it is impossible to use Bernstein's revisionism as a basis for a theory of the autonomy of the political and the ideological as *specific objective levels*. For him objectivity meant determination, and the only form of determination with which he was acquainted was mechanical economic determinism. As a result, although he did intuit the fact that class reductionism and economic determinism had prevented marxism from understanding the specific problems of the age of monopoly capital, the only alternative intellectual expression open to him lay in the opposite. extreme, in a flight from objectivity, an irruption of subjectivity – the ethical ideal – into history. This gave rise to his recourse to kantian ethics. From Sorel to Croce, all the tendencies which at the beginning of the century attempted to oppose the dominant positivist trend, did so in the name of voluntarism, of subjectivism or even of irrationalism. There was no other solution in an intellectual world where mechanical determination and objectivity had become synonymous.

Leninism and its consequences

If reductionism and epiphenomenalism had ended up by being inextricably linked in the thought of the Second International, then the historic experience of the Russian Revolution was to lay the basis for the breaking up of this unity. On the one hand the revolution had triumphed in the European countries where it was least expected – in complete contradiction with the theory that revolution was the result of the mechanical unfolding of economic forces. It was obvious that this revolution had resulted from political intervention in a conjuncture which traditional Marxism had considered could never bring about a socialist outcome. As a result, this discredited the type of political reasoning which linked all historical changes to the relation between the forces of production and the relations of production, and it also called into question epiphenomenist presuppositions. On the other hand, Lenin's analysis of combined development, and the transformation of democratic slogans into socialist ones during the Russian Revolution, brought new prestige to the analyses made by the young Marx on the subject of the dialectic between democracy and classes, and it established a link between the Russian Revolution and the cycle of permanent revolutions which had been interrupted by the failure of the 1848 revolutions. In this way the reductionist presupposition was also seriously called into question.

Nevertheless, Lenin's analyses on this subject are on the one hand extremely succinct and on the other fairly ambiguous, since in various ways they did remain prisoner to the old problematic. In fact, it was Lenin's *political practice* rather than his actual thought which really proved to be a transforming force which shattered the narrow economistic confines of Western marxist thought at the beginning of the century.

There were three possible attitudes which could further develop the new point of departure represented by leninism. One of these was to see revolution as the result of the irruption of consciousness and will into history in opposition to fatalism and the determinism of economic forces. This represented the continuation of the voluntarist subjectivism of the pre-war period. The young Gramsci saw the Bolshevik triumph as the revolution against 'Capital'; Sorel saw it as the triumph of 'the method of liberating violence' and of the will. In the confusion of the post-war world in which an infinite variety of anti *status quo* ideologies flourished and proliferated, bolshevism had become for numerous sections of society the symbol of a revolutionary *élan* which spurned all restrictions and objective conditions.

Another possible attitude consisted in trying to make the primacy of consciousness and the autonomy of the political moment compatible with an objective class logic. This was possible as long as one defined classes by their position in the process of production while at the same time making class consciousness the highest moment in their process of self-development. It is this sort of conception which defines the parameters of Lukàcs' project in his *History and Class Consciousness* and this is why he only half succeeded in superseding economism. In effect although by his insistence on the decisive function of class consciousness he was anti-economist because of the *efficacity* which he attributed to ideology, he was incapable of overcoming reductionism in his conception of the *nature* of ideology. For him ideology was identified with class consciousness, and he therefore defined it as the 'imputed consciousness' of a social class which is determined by the place which it occupies in the relations of production. This means that Lukàcs broke with the Second International's epiphenomenalism but not with class reductionism. He used the heritage of leninism in a one-sided fashion and only continued one of the two potential lines of development which this had opened up.

The third attitude was that of trying to extract all the theoretical consequences from Lenin's political practice, and this led to a complete and radical questioning of all aspects of the economistic problematic. Unfortunately, the extremely active period of theoretical elaboration of the 1920s was followed by the sterile silence of the stalinist era which effectively blocked the development of marxism for several decades. And yet, at that time there was one solitary effort made in this third direction. During his long years of captivity, in his reflections on the causes for the defeat of the working-class movement and the victory of fascism, alone in the isolation of his cell, Antonio Gramsci arrived at the source of all the errors: the lack of understanding of the nature and role of politics and ideology. In his *Prison Notebooks* this was to lead him to rethink all the problems central to marxism in a radically anti-economistic perspective, and hence to develop all the potentialities present in leninism.

2 Gramsci and hegemony

Having now sketched in broad outline the marxist problematic which provided the background against which Gramsci's thought developed, we must now return to the central problem of this article, that is, Gramsci's contribution to the marxist theory of ideology. Let us first restate our main argument: this consists in showing that a radically anti-economistic problematic of ideology is operating *in the practical state* in Gramsci's conception of *hegemony* and that it constitutes its actual condition of *intelligibility*. I shall therefore begin by analysing the texts where Gramsci presents the concept of hegemony, in order to define its meaning and to study its evolution. I shall then discuss the implications which it has for the marxist theory of ideology.

The concept of hegemony first appeared in Gramsci's work in 1926 in *Notes on the Southern Question*. It was introduced in the following way:[4]

> The Turin communists posed concretely the question of the
> 'hegemony of the proletariat': i.e. of the social basis of the proletarian
> dictatorship and the workers' State. The proletariat can become the
> leading (*dirigente*) and the dominant class to the extent that it succeeds
> in creating a system of alliances which allows it to mobilise the
> majority of the working population against capitalism and the
> bourgeois State. In Italy, in the real class relations which exist there,
> this means to the extent that it succeeds in gaining the consent of the
> broad peasant masses.

This work marked a step forward in Gramsci's thought. Naturally he had understood the importance of an alliance with the peasantry before 1926, since already in 1919, in an article entitled 'Workers and Peasants', he had insisted on the role which the peasants had to play in the proletarian revolution. It was in his *Notes on the Southern Question*, however, that he was to put the question of this alliance in terms of hegemony for the first time and to stress the political, moral and intellectual conditions which were necessary to bring this about. Hence he insisted, for example, on the fact that the working class had to free itself entirely of corporatism in order to be capable of winning over the Southern intellectuals to its cause, since it was through them that it would be able to influence the mass of the peasantry. The existence of an intellectual and moral dimension in the question of hegemony was already something typical of Gramsci and was later to take on its own importance. However, we are still at the stage of the leninist conception of hegemony seen as the leadership of the proletariat over the peasantry, that is to say that it was political leadership which constituted the essential element of this conception in view of the fact that hegemony was thought of in terms of a *class alliance*. It is only later in the *Prison Notebooks* that hegemony in its typically gramscian sense is to be found, and here it becomes the indissoluble union of political leadership and intellectual and moral leadership, which clearly goes beyond the idea of a simple class alliance.

The problematic of hegemony is to be found right from the first of the *Prison Notebooks*, but with an important innovation: Gramsci no longer applies it only to the *strategy* of the proletariat, but uses it to think of the practices of the ruling classes in general:[5]

> The following historical and political criterion is the one on which research must be based: a class is dominant in two ways, that is to say it is dominant and ruling. It rules the allied classes and dominates the opposing classes.

There is no doubt that in mentioning the direction of the allied classes Gramsci is referring here to hegemony, and there are innumerable statements to this effect throughout the *Prison Notebooks*. For example, a few pages further on in the same *Notebook* 1, in his examination of the role of the Jacobins in the French Revolution, he declares:[6]

> not only did they organise a bourgeois government, i.e., make the bourgeoisie the dominant class – they did more. They created the bourgeois State, made the bourgeoisie into the leading, hegemonic class of the nation, in other words gave the new State a permanent basis and created the compact modern French nation.

He indicates that it was by forcing the bourgeoisie to overcome its corporatist nature that the Jacobins managed to make it a hegemonic class. They in fact forced it to widen its class interests and to discover those interests which it had in common with the popular sectors, and it was on this basis that they were able to put themselves in command and to lead those sectors into the struggle. Here, therefore, we find once more the opposition between corporatist and hegemonic classes encountered in *Notes on the Southern Question*, but this time it is applied to the bourgeoisie. Gramsci had in fact begun to understand that the bourgeoisie had also needed to ensure itself popular support and that the political struggle was far more complex than had ever been thought by reductionist tendencies, since it did not consist in a simple confrontation between antagonistic classes but always involved complex relations of forces.

Gramsci analyses the relations of forces in all societies and studies the transition from a corporate to a hegemonic stage in a fundamental passage in *Notebook* 4.[7] He begins by distinguishing three principal levels at which the relations of forces exist:

1   the relation of social forces linked to the structure and dependent on the degree of development of the material forces of production;
2   the relation of political forces, that is to say the degree of consciousness and organisation within the different social groups;
3   the relation of military forces which is always, according to Gramsci, the decisive moment.

In his analysis of the different moments of political consciousness he distinguished three more degrees:

a   the *primitive economic* moment in which the consciousness of a group's own professional interests are expressed but not as yet their interests as a social class;
b   the *political economic* moment which is the one in which the consciousness of class interests is expressed, but only at an economic level;
c   the third moment is that of *hegemony*, 'in which one becomes aware that one's own corporate interests, in their present and future development, transcend the corporate limits of the purely economic class, and can and must become the interests of other subordinate groups too.'[8] For Gramsci this is where the specifically political moment is situated, and it is characterised by ideological struggle which attempts to forge unity between economic, political and intellectual objectives, 'placing all the questions around which the struggle rages on a "universal", not a corporate level, thereby creating the hegemony of a fundamental social group over a series of subordinate ones.'[9]

This text (which was to be reworked by Gramsci into its definitive form two years later in *Notebook* 13) is, I believe, one of the key texts for an understanding of the gramscian conception of hegemony and it is surprising that until now little importance has been attached to it.[10] It is here in fact that Gramsci sets out a very different conception of hegemony from the one found in *Notes on the Southern Question*, since here it is no longer a question of a simple political alliance but of a complete fusion of economic, political, intellectual and moral objectives which will be brought about by one fundamental group and groups allied to it *through the intermediary of ideology* when an ideology manages to 'spread throughout the whole of society determining not only united economic and political objectives but also intellectual and moral unity.'[11] From *Notebook* 4 the leninist conception of hegemony is doubly enriched: firstly its extension to the bourgeoisie and then the addition of a new and fundamental dimension (since it is through this that unity at the political level will be realised), that of intellectual and moral direction. It was only later that Gramsci was to develop all the implications of this enrichment, but from *Notebook* 4 onwards hegemony does assume its specifically gramscian dimension. It is therefore already possible on the basis of what has so far been discussed, to advance a tentative initial definition of a *hegemonic class*: it is a class which has been able to articulate the interests of other social groups to its own by means of ideological struggle. This, according to Gramsci, is only possible if this class renounces a strictly corporatist conception, since in order to exercise leadership it must genuinely concern itself with the interests of those social groups over which it wishes to exercise hegemony – 'obviously the fact of hegemony presupposes that one takes into account the interests and the tendencies of the groups over which hegemony will be exercised, and it also presupposes a certain equilibrium, that is to say that the hegemonic groups will make some sacrifices of a corporate nature.'[12] This conception of hegemony has certain very important consequences in relation to the way in which Gramsci envisaged the nature and the role of the state.[13]

> It is true that the State is seen as the organ of one particular group, destined to create favourable conditions for the latter's maximum expansion. But the development and expansion of the particular group are conceived of, and presented, as being the motor force of a universal expansion, of a development of all the 'national' energies. In other words the dominant group is coordinated concretely with the general interests of the subordinate groups, and the life of the State is conceived of as a continuous process of formation and superseding of unstable equilibria (on the juridical plane) between the

interests of the fundamental group and those of the subordinate groups – equilibria in which the interests of the dominant group prevail, but only up to a certain point, i.e. stopping short of narrowly corporate economic interest.

It is, therefore, the problematic of hegemony which is at the root of this 'enlarging of the state' whose importance has quite rightly been stressed by Christine Buci-Glucksmann.[14] This was to permit Gramsci to break with the economistic conception of the state, only envisaged as a coercive bureaucratic apparatus in the hands of the dominant class, and to formulate the notion of the *integral state* which consisted of 'dictatorship + hegemony'. This is not the place to analyse Gramsci's contribution to the marxist theory of the state (which is also of the utmost importance), so I shall limit myself to pointing out that this enlargement of the state works on two levels: first, it involves the enlarging of the social base of the state and the complex relations established between the state, the hegemonic class and its mass base; second, it also involves the enlarging of the state's functions, since the notion of the integral state implies the incorporation of the apparatuses of hegemony, of civil society, to the state.

Concerning the methods by which a class can become hegemonic, Gramsci distinguishes two principal routes: the first is that of transformism and the second is that of expansive hegemony. Let us first take *transformism*. This is the method by which the Moderate Party during the Risorgimento managed to secure its hegemony over the forces fighting for unification. Here what was involved was 'the gradual but continuous absorption, achieved by methods which varied in their effectiveness, of the active elements produced by allied groups – and even those which came from the antagonistic groups ...'[15]. This naturally was only a bastard form of hegemony and the consensus obtained with these methods was merely a 'passive consensus'. In fact the process whereby power was taken was termed a 'passive revolution' by Gramsci, since the masses were integrated through a system of absorption and neutralisation of their interests in such a way as to prevent them from opposing those of the hegemonic class. Gramsci contrasted this type of hegemony through absorption by what he called successful hegemony, that is to say, *expansive hegemony*. This had to consist in the creation of an active, direct consensus resulting from the genuine adoption of the interests of the popular classes by the hegemonic class, which would give rise to the creation of a genuine 'national-popular will'. Unlike the passive revolution, in fact, where vast sectors of the popular classes are excluded from the hegemonic system, in an expansive hegemony the whole society must advance. This distinction of two methods of hegemony makes it possible to specify further the tentative definition of hegemony already put forward. In fact, if hegemony is defined as the ability of one class to articulate the interest of other social groups to its own, it is now possible to see that this can be done in two very different ways: the interests of these groups can either be articulated so as to neutralise them and hence to prevent the development of their own specific demands, or else they can be articulated in such a way as to promote their full development leading to the final resolution of the contradictions which they express.

These texts prompt a series of further observations. First, only a fundamental class (that is to say one which occupies one of the two poles in the relations of production of a determinate mode of production) can become hegemonic, as Gramsci unequivocally states: 'though hegemony is ethico-political, it must also be economic, must necessarily be based on the decisive function exercised by the leading group in the decisive nucleus of economic activity.'[16] This condition not only restricts the possible number of hegemonic classes, it also indicates the possible limitations of any forms of hegemony. If in fact the exercise of hegemony involves economic and corporate sacrifices on the part of the aspiring leading class, the latter cannot, however, go so far as to jeopardise its basic interests. Sooner or later, therefore, the bourgeoisie comes up against the limitations of its hegemony, as it is an exploiting class, since its class interests must, at a certain level, necessarily clash with those of the popular classes. This, says Gramsci, is a sign that it has exhausted its function and that from then on 'the ideological bloc tends to crumble away; then "spontaneity" may be replaced by "constraint" in ever less disguised and indirect forms, culminating in outright police measures and *coups d'etat*.'[17] Thus only the working class, whose interests coincide with the limitation of all exploitation, can be capable of successfully bringing about an expansive hegemony.

The most important aspect of Gramsci's hegemony still remains to be studied. This is the aspect of *intellectual and moral leadership* and the way in which this is achieved. In fact, all the points which have been raised could be entirely compatible with a conception of hegemony seen as alliance of classes. However, if Gramsci's hegemony were limited to political leadership it would only differ from Lenin's concept in that Gramsci does not restrict its use to the strategy of the proletariat, but also applies it to the bourgeoisie. Now it has been pointed out that the conception of hegemony is doubly enriched with respect to Lenin, as it also involves the addition of a new dimension which is inextricably linked to political direction, and that is intellectual and moral leadership. As a result, the establishing of hegemony became a phenomenon which went far beyond a simple class alliance. In fact, for Gramsci — and it is this which constitutes his originality — hegemony is not to be found in a purely instrumental alliance between classes through which the *class demands* of the allied classes are articulated to those of the fundamental class, with each group maintaining its own individuality within the alliance as well as its own ideology. According to him hegemony involves the creation of a *higher synthesis*, so that all its elements fuse in a 'collective will' which becomes the new protagonist of political action which will function as the protagonist of political action during that hegemony's entire duration. It is through ideology that this collective will is formed since its very existence depends on the creation of ideological unity which will serve as 'cement'.[18] This is the key to the indissoluble unity of the two aspects of gramscian hegemony, since the formation of the collective will and the exercise of political leadership depends on the very existence of intellectual and moral leadership. To account for these two aspects and the way in which they are articulated undoubtedly constitutes the major difficulty to be faced in any study of the conception of hegemony in Gramsci's thought. It is this, moreover, which explains why a comprehensive definition of hegemony has not been established so far despite the abundant literature existing on this subject. In fact, most interpretations unilaterally stress one or the other aspect which gives rise to widely differing and often opposing interpretations according to whether political direction or moral and intellectual direction is stressed.[19] The few interpretations which do try to account for both aspects at once, do so on the basis of an erroneous conception of one or the other of the two, or else of the link between them.[20]

If, therefore, we wish finally to manage to establish a comprehensive definition of Gramsci's conception of hegemony which accounts for its specificity and does not ignore any of its potentialities, it is important to be able to think theoretically the kind of relation established between its two components, that is, the secret of their unity, and to see what are the main characteristics resulting from this. To do this the following question needs to be answered: how can one forgo genuine ideological unity between different social groups in such a way as to make them unite into a single political subject? To answer this problem it is of course necessary to discuss the conception of ideology which is present – both explicitly and implicitly – in Gramsci's work. It will then be shown how it is impossible to give a coherent account of the specificity of Gramsci's conception from the perspective of an economistic problematic of ideology.

3 Hegemony and ideology

The best point of departure for an analysis of the conception of ideology operating in the gramscian problematic of hegemony is to study the way in which he envisaged the process of the formation of a new hegemony. The notes referring to how a new collective will must be formed through moral and intellectual reform which will be the work of the 'Modern Prince' are, therefore, the most revealing on this subject.[21] But first the few texts in which Gramsci explicitly sets out his conception of ideology must be discussed.

The problematic of ideology

Gramsci immediately places himself on entirely different ground from those viewing ideology as false consciousness or as a system of ideas, and he rebels against all epiphenomenalist conceptions which reduce it to mere appearances with no efficacy:[22]

> The claim, presented as an essential postulate of historical materialism, that every fluctuation of politics and ideology can be presented and expounded as an immediate expression of the structure, must be contested in theory as primitive infantilism, and combated in practice with the authentic testimony of Marx, the author of concrete political and historical works.

According to Gramsci, the starting point of all research on ideology must be Marx's assertion that 'men gain consciousness of their tasks on the ideological terrain of the superstructures'.[23] So that the latter, he declares, must be considered 'operating realities which possess efficacy'[24], and if Marx sometimes terms them illusions it is only in a polemical sense in order to clearly specify their historical and transitory nature. Gramsci was to formulate his own definition of ideology as the terrain 'on which men move, acquire consciousness of their position, struggle'.[25] Ideology, he declares, must be seen as a battle field, as a continuous struggle, since men's acquisition of consciousness through ideology will not come individually but always through the intermediary of the ideological terrain where two 'hegemonic principles' confront each other.[26] The self's acquisition of consciousness is in effect only possible through an ideological formation constituted not only of discursive elements, but also of non-discursive elements which Gramsci designates by the rather vague term 'conformism'. His intention becomes clear, however, when he indicates that the acquisition of this necessary consciousness through conformism results in the fact 'that one is always mass-man or collective man'.[27] One finds here, in fact, the idea that the subjects are not originally given but are always produced by ideology through a socially determined ideological field, so that subjectivity is always the product of social practice. This implies that ideology has a material existence and that far from consisting in an ensemble of spiritual realities, it is always materialised in practices. The nature of ideology as practice is further reinforced by the identification Gramsci establishes between ideology and religion (in the crocean sense of a word-view with its corresponding norms of action), as it serves to stress that ideology organises action. In effect Gramsci considers that a world-view is manifest in all action and that this expresses itself in a very elaborate form and at a high level of abstraction − as is the case with philosophy − or else it is expressed in much simpler forms as the expression of 'common sense' which presents itself as the spontaneous philosophy of the man in the street, but which is the popular expression of 'higher' philosophies.[28] These world-views are never individual facts but the expression of the 'communal life of a social bloc', which is why Gramsci calls them 'organic ideologies'.[29] It is these which 'organise the human masses' and which serve as the informative principle of all individual and collective activities, since it is through these that men acquire all their forms of consciousness.[30] But if it is through organic ideologies that men acquire all their forms of consciousness, and if these organic ideologies are world-views of determinate social blocs, this means that all forms of consciousness are necessarily political. This enables Gramsci to make the following equation: philosophy = ideology = politics. This identification has generally been misunderstood and it is this which underlies all the misinterpretations of Gramsci's historicism which present it as a hegelian reading of marxism.[31] In fact what Gramsci was trying to do was to think the role of subjectivity, but so as not to present it as the irruption of the individual consciousness into history. To achieve this he posits consciousness not as originally given but as the effect of the system of ideological relations into which the individual is inserted. Thus it is ideology which creates subjects and makes them act.

Ideology as a practice producing subjects is what appears to be the real idea implicit in Gramsci's thoughts on the operative and active nature of ideology and its identification with politics. However, he did not have the necessary theoretical tools at his disposal to express this intuition adequately, and he had to content himself with making allusions to it using very ambiguous formulas strongly influenced by crocean historicism. Let us take, for example, the definition of ideology as 'a conception of the world implicitly manifest in art, in law, in economic activity, in all individual and collective manifestations of life'.[32] If this definition is examined in the light of the one in which ideology is seen as a world-view with its corresponding norms of action and Gramsci's repeated insistence on the fact that ideology is the terrain on which men acquire all their forms of consciousness, then it becomes plain that this definition (far from having to be interpreted as showing that Gramsci is dealing with a hegelian problematic of expressive totality in which ideology plays the central role), must be understood as an allusion to the fact that it is through ideology that all possible types of 'subjects' are created.

Another very new aspect of the gramscian problematic of ideology is the importance which he attributes to the *material and institutional nature of ideological practice*. In effect Gramsci insists on the fact that this practice possesses its own agents, that is to say, the *intellectuals*. They are the ones in charge of elaborating and spreading organic ideologies,[33] and they are the ones who will have to realise moral and intellectual reform.[34] Gramsci classes the intellectuals into two main categories depending on whether they are linked to one of the two fundamental classes (organic intellectuals), or to classes expressing previous modes of production (traditional intellectuals). Apart from stressing the role of the intellectuals, Gramsci insists on the importance of the material and institutional structure for the elaboration and spreading of ideology. This is made up of different *hegemonic apparatuses*: schools, churches, the entire media and even architecture and the name of the streets.[35] This ensemble of apparatuses is termed the *ideological structure* of a dominant class by Gramsci, and the level of the superstructure where ideology is produced and diffused is called *civil society*. This constitutes the ensemble of 'private' bodies through which the political and social hegemony of a social group is exercised.[36]

It is now obvious that we are far from the economistic problematic of ideology and that Gramsci is clearly situated on a different terrain. What is quite new in him is the awareness of the material nature of ideology and of the fact that it constitutes a practice inscribed in apparatuses which plays an indispensable practical-social role in all societies. He intuited the fact that this practice consists in the production of subjects, but he did not quite manage to formulate this theoretically. Besides, one should never forget that all these new ideas are expressed by Gramsci in an ambiguous form which is now outdated. Since, as has already been indicated, the only intellectual tradition available to assist in the elaboration of an anti-economistic problematic was Croce's historicism. In any case, Gramsci never set out to elaborate a theory of ideology and his thought is not presented in a systematic way. Having said all this, however, it does nevertheless seem possible to assert that Gramsci's problematic anticipated Althusser in several respects: the material nature of ideology, its existence as the necessary level of all social formations and its function as the producer of subjects are all implicit in Gramsci, although it was Althusser who was to be the first to formulate this conception in a rigorous fashion.

A non-reductionist conception

Gramsci's contribution to the marxist theory of ideologies, however, is not limited to his having shown that they were objective and operative realities, as real as the economy itself, and that they played a crucial role in all social formations. Such a conception, however, only definitively supersedes the first facet of economism and still leaves room for the possible existence of complicated forms of reductionism. Now Gramsci was not simply content to criticise the epiphenomenal conception as he went much further and queried the reductionist conception which made ideology a function of the class position of the subjects. There can be no doubt that it is here that the most important and original aspect of his contribution is to be found. Unfortunately, it is also the least understood aspect, and this explains why all the potentialities which this opened out to marxist analysis have virtually remained undeveloped.

It must be admitted here that this is a much more difficult area, since Gramsci never presented the anti-reductionist problematic in an explicit fashion, although it does exist *in the practical state* in the way in which he conceived hegemony. This problematic must, therefore, be clearly brought out, and it must be shown that it provides the *actual condition of intelligibility* of Gramsci's hegemony. However, before embarking on a study of texts which will serve as points of reference, it is worth briefly recapitulating the three principles underlying the reductionist problematic of ideology, since this will make it easier to bring out the difference between Gramsci's conception and this one. The three principles are as follows:

1 all subjects are class subjects;
2 social classes have their own paradigmatic ideologies;
3 all ideological elements have a necessary class belonging.

Gramsci's opposition to the first principle emerges clearly at once. According to him the subjects of political action cannot be identified with social classes. As has already been seen, they are 'collective wills' which obey specifically formed laws in view of the fact that they constitute the political expression of hegemonic systems created through ideology. Therefore, the subjects (the social classes) which exist at the economic level, are not duplicated at the political level; instead, different 'inter class' subjects are created. This constitutes Gramsci's break with the first principle of reductionism and provides him with the necessary theoretical basis to enable him to think hegemony beyond a simple class alliance as the creation of a superior unity where there will be a fusion of the participant elements of the hegemonic bloc. We know that this fusion will be realised through ideology, but the question remains, how and on what basis? We have now, in effect, reached the point of having to answer our previously formulated question: how can genuine ideological unity between different social groups be created?

There are two possible solutions to the problem. The first is the only one which can be formulated within a reductionist problematic of ideology (as exemplified by principles 2 and 3). It consists in viewing this ideological unity as the imposition of the class ideology of the main group upon the allied groups. This leads one to define a hegemonic class as one which has been capable of creating ideological consensus with other groups on the basis of the role played by its own ideology as the dominant one, and to reduce the problematic of ideology to a mere phenomenon of ideological inculcation. This, for example, is the kind of solution underlying Nicos Poulantzas's interpretation of Gramsci's conception of hegemony.[37] According to him, in so far as hegemony in Gramsci refers to a situation in which class domination involves a function of direction by means of which active consent of the dominated class is created, then this is similar to Lukàcs' nation of class-consciousness–world-view, and hence to the hegelian problematic of the subject. He declares that if this kind of problematic is transposed to marxism, then it leads to the conception that class is the subject of history, the genetic totalising principle of the instances of a social formation. In this context it is the ideology consciousness world-view of the class viewed as the subject of history, that is of the hegemonic class, which founds the unity of a formation, in so far as it determines the adhesion of the dominated classes within a determinate system of domination.[38]

Such an interpretation of Gramsci's thought is only possible if one identifies hegemony with the imposition of the dominant ideology (understood here in the lukàcsian form of the dominant class's world-view–class consciousness). I think that what has so far been demonstrated is already sufficient to show that this is a completely incorrect interpretation of Gramsci's thought. This does, in fact, prevent Poulantzas from grasping the full extent of Gramsci's conception of hegemony and it leads him to find some incoherent elements in it especially as regards the extension of this conception to the strategy of the proletariat. Poulantzas declares this extension unacceptable since it implies 'that a class imposes its own world-view on a formation and therefore actually conquers the place of the dominant ideology before the conquest of political power'.[39] Now, not only does Gramsci indicate the possibility of a class becoming hegemonic before the seizure of power, but he insists on the *necessity* of its doing so. Can one really talk of incoherence on his part? If so, then it must seriously affect the whole of his work in view of the importance which this conception plays in his thought. On the other hand, could this not rather indicate a way of understanding hegemony which differs from the one which Poulantzas attributes to him, that is to say a conception which assumes that the problem of the creation of an ideological unity is tackled on the basis of a non-reductionist conception of ideology? In fact, this is the case, and it is this which explains why this fundamental aspect of Gramsci's thought remained for a long time completely unnoticed, since it was absolutely *unthinkable* within the reductionist problematic dominating marxist thought.[40]

So we must now present the second solution – the one to be found in Gramsci – to the problem of the possibility of forming ideological unity between different social groups. It is a solution which, of course, does not consist in the imposition of the class ideology of one of the groups over the others. An analysis of the way in which Gramsci visualises the process leading to the constitution of a new hegemony through *intellectual and moral reform* will throw light on the subject.

As already previously mentioned, the importance of intellectual and moral reform lies in the fact that the hegemony of a fundamental class consists in the creation of a 'collective will' (on the basis of a common world-view which will serve as a unifying principle) in which this class and its allies will fuse to form a 'collective man':[41]

> From this one can deduce the importance of the 'cultural aspect', even in practical (collective) activity. An historical act can only be performed by 'collective man', and this presupposes the attainment of a 'cultural-social' unity through which a multiplicity of dispersed wills, with heterogeneous aims, are welded together with a single aim, on the basis of an equal and common conception of the world.

The creation of a new hegemony, therefore, implies the transformation of the previous ideological terrain and the creation of a new world-view which will serve as a unifying principle for a new collective will. This is the process of ideological transformation which Gramsci designates with the term 'intellectual and moral reform'. What is important now is to see how this process is envisaged by Gramsci. The two following passages are extremely significant in this context:

> What matters is the criticism to which such an ideological complex is subjected by the first representatives of the new historical phase. This criticism makes possible a process of differentiation and change in the relative weight that the elements of the old ideologies used to possess. What was previously secondary and subordinate, or even incidental, is now taken to be primary – becomes the nucleus of a new ideological and theoretical complex. The old collective will dissolves into its contradictory elements since the subordinate ones develop socially ....[42]

> How, on the other hand should this historical consciousness, proposed as autonomous consciousness, be formed? How should everyone choose and combine the elements for the constitution of such an autonomous consciousness? Will each element imposed have to be repudiated *a priori*? It will have to be repudiated inasmuch as it is imposed, but not in itself, that is to say that it will be necessary to give it a new form which is specific to the given group.[43]

Here Gramsci indicates extremely clearly that intellectual and moral reform does not consist in making a clean sweep of the existing world-view and in replacing it with a completely new and already formulated one. Rather, it consists in a process of transformation (aimed at producing a new form) and of rearticulation of existing ideological elements. According to him, an ideological system consists in a particular type of articulation of ideological elements to which a certain 'relative weight' is attributed. The objective of ideological struggle is not to reject the system and all its elements but to rearticulate it, to break it down to its basic elements and then to sift through past conceptions to see which ones, with some changes of content, can serve to express the new situation.[44] Once this is done the chosen elements are finally rearticulated into another system.

It is obvious that viewed in this way moral and intellectual reform is incomprehensible within a reductionist problematic which postulates the existence of paradigmatic ideologies for each social class, and the necessary class-belonging of all ideological elements. If, in effect, one does accept the reductionist hypothesis, moral and intellectual reform can only amount to replacing one class ideology by another. In the case of the hegemony of the working class, therefore, the latter would have to extricate the social groups which it required as allies from the influence of bourgeois ideology and impose its own ideology upon them. In order to do this it would have to combat bourgeois ideology by totally rejecting all its elements since these would be intrinsically and irremediably bourgeois, and since the presence of one of these elements within social-ist discourse would prove that working class ideology had been contaminated by bourgeois ideology; in this event ideological struggle would always be reduced to the confrontation of two closed and previously determined systems. This, of course, is not Gramsci's conception, and the information so far available already makes it possible to assert that his conception of ideology *cannot be reductionist* since in that case the way in which he visualises moral and intellectual reform would be totally incomprehensible.

What, then, is the conception of ideology developed in Gramsci's theory of hegemony? In order to clarify this it is first necessary to determine what kind of answers Gramsci gives to the following questions:

1   What constitutes the unifying principle of an ideological system?
2   How can one determine the class character of an ideology or of an ideological element?

This brings us to one of the least developed aspects of Gramsci's thought and we will have to be content with a few rather imprecise indications which will need to undergo the test of a symptomatic reading. To begin with, let us recall the elements of the problem which have already been analysed. We know that according to Gramsci hegemony (which is only possible for a fundamental class) consists in the latter exercising a political, intellectual and moral role of leadership within a hegemonic system which is cemented by a common world-view (organic ideology). We also know that intellectual and moral leadership exercised by the hegemonic class does not consist in the imposition of the class ideology upon the allied groups. Time and time again Gramsci stresses the fact that every single hegemonic relation is necessarily 'pedagogic and occurs amongst the different forces of which it is composed'.[45] He also insists that in a hegemonic system there must exist democracy between the ruling group and the ruled groups.[46] This is also valid at the ideological level, of course, and it implies that this common world-view unifying the hegemonic bloc is really the organic expression of the whole bloc (and here we have the explanation of the chief meaning of the term 'organic ideology'). This world-view will therefore include ideological elements from varying sources, but its unity will stem from its articulating principle which will always be provided by the hegemonic class. Gramsci calls this articulating principle a *hegemonic principle*. He never defines this term very precisely, but it seems that it involves a system of values the realisation of which depends on the central role played by the fundamental class at the level of the relations of production. Thus the intellectual and moral direction exercised by a fundamental class in a hegemonic system consists in providing the articulating principle of the common world-view, the value system to which the ideological elements coming from the other groups will be articulated in order to form a unified ideological system, that is to say an organic ideology. This will always be a complex ensemble whose contents can never be determined in advance since it depends on a whole series of historical and national factors and also on the relations of forces existing at a particular moment in the struggle for hegemony. It is, therefore, by their articulation to a hegemonic principle that the ideological elements acquire their class character which is not intrinsic to them. This explains the fact that they can be 'transformed' by their articulation to another hegemonic principle. Ideological struggle in fact consists of a process of *disarticulation–rearticulation* of given ideological elements in a struggle between two hegemonic principles to appropriate these elements; it does not consist of the confrontation of two already elaborated, closed world-views. Ideological ensembles existing at a given moment are, therefore, the result of the relations of forces between the rival hegemonic principles and they undergo a perpetual process of transformation.[47]

It is now possible to answer our two questions:

1   The unifying principle of an ideological system is constituted by the hegemonic principle which serves to articulate all the other ideological elements. It is always the expression of a fundamental class.

2   The class character of an ideology or of an ideological element stems from the hegemonic principle which serves as its articulating centre.

However, we are still a long way from having solved all the problems. There remains for example the problem of the nature of those ideological elements which do not have a necessary class character. It is not clear what they express, and Gramsci does not give us an answer. But, in spite of this, it is possible to find a few very significant definite pointers to a solution. In a passage where he reflects on what will determine the victory of one hegemonic principle over another, Gramsci declares that a hegemonic principle does not prevail by virtue of its intrinsic logical character but rather when it manages to become a 'popular religion'.[48] What are we supposed to understand by this? Elsewhere Gramsci insists that a class wishing to become hegemonic has to 'nationalise itself',[49] and further on he declares:[50]

the particular form in which the hegemonic ethico-political element presents itself in the life of the state and the country is 'patriotism' and 'nationalism', which is 'popular religion', that is to say it is the link by means of which the unity of leaders and led is effected.

In order to understand what Gramsci means it is necessary to relate all these statements to his conception of the 'national-popular'. Although this conception is not fully formulated, it plays an important role in his thought. For Gramsci everything which is the expression of the 'people-nation' is 'national-popular'.[51] A successful hegemony is one which manages to create a 'collective national-popular will', and for this to happen the dominant class must have been capable of articulating to its hegemonic principle all the national-popular ideological elements, since it is only if this happens that it (the class) appears as the representative of the general interest. This is why the ideological elements expressing the 'national-popular' are often at stake in the fierce struggle between classes fighting for hegemony. As regards all this Gramsci points out some changes of meaning undergone by terms like 'nationalism' and 'patriotism' as they are appropriated by different fundamental classes and articulated to different hegemonic principles.[52] He also stresses the role which those terms play as a link leading to the creation of the union between leaders and led and in providing a base for a popular religion.

It is now possible to understand Gramsci's statement in which he declares that a hegemonic principle asserts itself when it manages to become a popular religion. What he means is that what has to be chiefly at stake in a class's struggle for hegemony is the attempt to articulate to its discourse all national-popular ideological elements. This is how it can 'nationalise itself'.[53]

The conception of ideology found in the practical state in Gramsci's problematic of hegemony consists therefore of a practice which transforms the class character of ideological elements by the latter's articulation to a hegemonic principle differing from the one to which they are at present articulated. This assumes that these elements do not in themselves express class interests, but that their class character is conferred upon them by the discourse to which they are articulated and by the type of subject thus created.

Hegemony and war of position

It is only now that the anti-reductionist problematic of ideology implied by Gramsci's hegemony has been made explicit that it is possible to really grasp the meaning and *full extent* of his concept of hegemony: a class is hegemonic when it has managed to articulate to its discourse the overwhelming majority of ideological elements characteristic of a given social formation, in particular the national-popular elements which allow it to become the class expressing the national interest. A class's hegemony is, therefore, a more complex phenomenon than simple political leadership: the latter in effect is the consequence of another aspect which is itself of prime importance. This is the creation of a unified coherent ideological discourse which will be the product of the articulation to its value system of the ideological elements existing within a determinate historical conjuncture of the society in question. These elements which have no necessary class-belonging rightly constitute for this reason the terrain of ideological struggle between the two classes confronting each other for hegemony. Therefore if a class becomes hegemonic it is not, as some interpretations of Gramsci would have it, because it has succeeded in imposing its class ideology upon society or in establishing mechanisms legitimising its class power. This kind of interpretation completely alters the nature of Gramsci's thought because it reduces his conception of ideology to the traditional marxist conception of false consciousness which necessarily leads to presenting hegemony as a phenomenon of ideological inculcation. Now, it is precisely against this type of reductionism that Gramsci is rebelling when he proclaims that 'politics is not a *"marché de dupes"'*.[54] For him, ideology is not the mystified-mystifying justification of an already constituted class power, it is the 'terrain on which men acquire consciousness of themselves', and hegemony cannot be reduced to a process of ideological domination.

Once the real meaning of Gramsci's hegemony has been understood, all the pseudo-incoherences disappear from his thought. For example, the problem of knowing why Gramsci can use this conception both to designate the practices of the bourgeoisie and those of the working class becomes clear as does the reason for his envisaging the possibility of a class becoming hegemonic before the seizure of power. It is, in fact, the link which had been established between hegemony and ideological domination which made it impossible to grasp the internal coherence of Gramsci's thought and which made it appear full of discrepancies. Once, however, the problematic of ideology which is operating in the practical state in Gramsci's conception of hegemony, has been established, all the other conceptions fall quite naturally into place in a perfectly structured ensemble and the underlying meaning of his thought is revealed in all its coherence. I shall only take one example, but it is a crucially important one since it is the conception upon which Gramsci bases his entire strategy of transition to socialism in the West: I am referring to the *war of position*.

Gramsci's thought on the strategy of the working class in its struggle for socialism is organised around the conception of hegemony. This thought has its starting point in the enlarging of the phenomenon of hegemony which Gramsci began to consider applicable to the bourgeoisie as well, since he understood that state power was not limited to the power of a single class and that the bourgeoisie had managed to ensure itself a 'historical base', a group of allies led by it through its hegemonic apparatuses. In this way it had created a 'collective man' which functioned as an autonomous political subject. From here Gramsci reaches the conclusion that political struggle does not only take place between the two fundamental antagonistic classes, since the 'political subjects' are not social classes but 'collective wills' which are comprised of an ensemble of social groups fused around a fundamental class. If, therefore, the struggle between the antagonistic classes constitutes, in the final instance, the determining level of all political struggle, the struggle of all the other groups within a social formation must nevertheless be articulated to it. These other groups will provide the 'historical base' of a dominant class and it is on this terrain that the struggle for hegemony – by means of which a fundamental class tries to win over the other social groups – takes place. The revolutionary process can, therefore, not be restricted to a movement organised on strict class lines which would tend to develop a pure proletarian consciousness detached from the rest of society. The road to hegemony in fact makes it imperative to take into account a double process: the self awareness of oneself as an autonomous group, and the creation of a basis of consensus:[55]

> A study of how these innovatory forces developed, from subaltern groups to hegemonic and dominant groups, must therefore seek out and identify the phases through which they acquired: i. autonomy *vis-à-vis* the enemies they had to defeat, and ii. support from the groups which actively or passively assisted them; for this entire process was historically necessary before they could unite in the form of the State. It is precisely by these two yardsticks that the level of historical and political consciousness which the innovatory forces progressively attained in the various phases can be measured – and not simply by the yardstick of their separation from the formerly dominant forces.

It is, therefore, vital for the working class not to isolate itself within a ghetto of proletarian purism. On the contrary, it must try to become a 'national class', representing the interests of the increasingly numerous social groups. In order to do this it must cause the disintegration of the historical bases of the bourgeoisie's hegemony by disarticulating the ideological bloc by means of which the bourgeoisie's intellectual direction is expressed. It is in fact only on this condition that the working class will be able to rearticulate a new ideological system which will serve as a cement for the hegemonic bloc within which it will play the role of a leading force. This process of disarticulation–rearticulation constitutes in fact the famous 'war of position' which Gramsci conceives as the revolutionary strategy best adapted to countries where the bourgeoisie has managed to firmly establish its hegemony due to the development of civil society. Unless one has grasped the real meaning of

Gramsci's concept of hegemony – which consists in the capacity of a fundamental class to articulate to its discourse the ideological elements characteristic of a given social formation – then it is impossible to understand the nature of the war of position. In effect the war of position is the process of ideological struggle by means of which the two fundamental classes try to appropriate the non-class ideological elements in order to integrate them within the ideological system which articulates itself around their respective hegemonic principles. This is, therefore, only a stage in the struggle, the one in which the new hegemonic bloc cements itself, but it is a decisive moment since Gramsci states, 'in politics, once the war of position has been won, it has been won definitively.'[56] It will in fact only be a question of time before the military relations of forces begin to lean towards the bloc of socialist forces as soon as all the popular forces rally to socialism and the bourgeoisie finds itself isolated. As a result, far from designating a reformist strategy as certain interpretations of Gramsci maintain,[57] the war of position represents the translation into political strategy of a non-reductionist conception of ideology and politics. This stresses the fundamental role of ideological struggle and the form of popular war which the struggle for socialism must assume: 'in politics the war of position is the conception of hegemony.'[58] This statement of Gramsci's can only be understood in the light of the anti-reductionist problematic of ideology which has been presented as the very condition of intelligibility of his conception of hegemony. Only when this has been grasped can one glimpse all the political consequences involved. These are crystallised into a conception of socialist revolution seen not as a strictly proletarian one but as a complex process of political and ideological transformations in which the working class plays the leading role. The war of position understood as the struggle for hegemony within all the anti-capitalist sectors also explains Gramsci's insistence on the 'national' character of the struggle.[59]

the international situation should be considered in its national aspect. In reality, the internal relations of any nation are the result of a combination which is 'original' and (in a certain sense) unique; these relations must be understood and conceived in their originality and uniqueness if one wishes to dominate them and direct them. To be sure, the line of development is towards internationalism, but the point of departure is 'national' – and it is from this point of departure that one must begin.

Conclusion

In this article I have argued that in Gramsci's conception of hegemony one finds in the practical state a radically *anti-economistic* problematic of ideology and that it constitutes the condition of intelligibility of the specificity of his conception of hegemony. However, I am not claiming that all the problems of the marxist theory of ideology are solved by Gramsci — even in the practical state. In any case the conceptual tools which he had to use have been completely superseded, and nowadays we are equipped to deal with the problem of ideology in a far more rigorous fashion thanks to the development of disciplines such as linguistics and pyscho-analysis. Nevertheless, Gramsci's contribution to the marxist theory of ideology must be considered of crucial importance for several reasons:

1   Gramsci was the first to stress the material nature of ideology, its existence as a necessary level of all social formations, its inscription in practices and its materialisation into apparatuses.

2   He broke away radically from the conception of ideology as false consciousness, i.e. a distorted representation of reality because it is determined by the place occupied by the subject in the relations of production, and he anticipated the conception of ideology as a practice producing subjects.

3   Finally, he also queried the general principle of reductionism which attributes a necessary class-belonging to all ideological elements.

As regards the first two points, Gramsci's thought has been taken up and thoroughly developed by Louis Althusser — although the latter reached the same point of view in quite a different way — and so his ideas have spread through the althusserian school. As regards his criticism of reductionism, however, it is unfortunate that his contribution has not been fully recognised as it is in this area that the theoretical potentialities of his thought urgently need developing. This is particularly so since the marxist theory of ideology has not yet managed to free itself entirely of the reductionist problematic and hence remains trapped by insidious forms of economism.

The topicality and importance which Gramsci's work has for marxist researchers working in the field of ideology lies in the fact that Gramsci's conception points the way to a possible solution to the most serious problem of marxist theory of ideology. The problem consists in superseding economism while at the same time adhering to the problematic of historical materialism. In fact once the elementary phase of ideology seen as an epiphenomenon has been superseded, marxist theory still has to face the following difficulty: how to show to what extent ideological practice actually has real autonomy and efficacity while still upholding the principle of the determination in the last instance by the economic. This is a problem which Althusser himself has not yet been capable of solving satisfactorily, and it is why he has recently been accused of economism.[60] However, if his critics propose a solution which effectively resolves the problem of economism, this is done at the expense of abandoning historical materialism. In effect, by identifying economism with the thesis of the determination in the last instance by the economy, and by proposing the total autonomy of ideological practices as a solution, they call into question the basic tenets of historical materialism.

In Gramsci's work the outline of another kind of solution to the problem can be found and it is worth analysing it before deciding whether the solution to the problem of economism is really impossible within the theoretical framework of marxism. As presented here the problematic of hegemony contains in the practical state the broad outlines of a possible articulation between the relative autonomy of ideology and the determination in the last instance by the economy. In fact the conception of ideology brought out by Gramsci's conception of hegemony attributes real autonomy to it, since the ideological elements which ideological practice aims at transforming do not possess a necessary class-belonging and hence do not constitute the ideological representation of interests existing at the economic level. On the other hand, however, this autonomy is not incompatible with the determination in the last instance by economy, since the hegemonic principles serving to articulate these elements are always provided by the fundamental classes. Here, of course, I am only designating the area where a solution might be found, and if work is to be done in this direction there are a large number of problems still to be solved before it will be possible to formulate a theoretical solution. It does nevertheless seem to be an area which ought to prove fruitful.

Finally, I wish to indicate another area in which Gramsci's conception of hegemony opens out extremely fruitful perspectives. This is to be found in his *conception of politics*. Gramsci was extremely aware of this since after all he declared that economism had to be combated 'not only in the theory of historiography but also – and more especially – in political practice and theory', and that 'in this area the struggle can and must be conducted by developing the concept of hegemony.'[61] The ways in which economism manifests itself in the field of politics are extremely varied and range from the 'wait-and-see' attitude of the Second International to the 'purism' of the extreme left. These are two apparently opposing forms and yet they do both express the same lack of understanding of the true nature of politics and its role in a social formation. The fundamental error of the economistic conception – its epiphenomenalist and reductionist conception of the superstructures – manifests itself in this domain by an *instrumental* conception of the state and of politics. In identifying the state with the repressive apparatus it reduces the field of politics, since its vital relation with the ideological struggle is severed. Gramsci's 'enlarged' notion of the state which is correlative to the role attributed to hegemony, recuperates this forgotten dimension of politics, and ideological struggle becomes a fundamental aspect of political struggle. Politics thereby ceases to be conceived as a separate specialist activity and becomes a dimension which is present in all fields of human activity. In effect, if no individual can become a subject except through his participation in a 'mass-man', there is not one aspect of human experience which escapes politics and this extends as far as 'common sense'.

This conception of politics should make it possible to devise a completely new approach to the problem of *power* which has generally not been satisfactorily treated by marxists. Actually, once the hegemonic dimension of politics which expresses itself in Gramsci's notion of the 'integral state' has been re-established, and once it has been accepted that the supremacy of a class is not solely exercised by means of its domination over adversaries, but also by means of its role of leadership over allied groups, then one can begin to understand that far from being localised in the repressive state apparatuses, power is exercised at all levels of society and that it is a 'strategy' – as Michael Foucault puts it. So this is yet another field of research opened up by Gramsci's non-reductionist conception of hegemony, and it is an extremely topical one.

It is in fact quite remarkable to see the extraordinary way in which some contemporary research – such as that of Foucault or Derrida which brings out a completely new conception of politics[62] – converges with Gramsci's thought, and having recognised the anti-reductionist character of his thought I do not think it too hazardous to predict that the topicality of Gramsci's work and his influence will go on increasing in the future.

Notes

This chapter was was translated into English by Denise Derôme.

1 Louis Althusser, *Lenin and Philosophy and Other Essays*, London, New Left Books, 1971, pp. 160–5.

2 For a thorough analysis of the epistemological foundations of the marxism of the Second International as well as of Bernstein's revisionism, see Leonardo Paggi's excellent introduction to Max Adler's book, *Il socialismo e gli intellettuali*, Bari, De Donato, 1974.

3 Karl Kautsky, *Das Erfurter Programm*, Stuttgart, Verlag von J. H. W. Diek, 1892, p. 106. This is cited by Lucio Colletti in his introduction to Bernstein's book, *I presupposti del socialismo e i compiti della socialdemocrazia*, Bari, Laterza, 1974, p. xix.

4 Antonio Gramsci, 'Quelques Thèmes sur la Question Meridionale'. This is published in the appendix of Marie-Antonietta Macciochi, *Pour Gramsci*, Paris, Seuil, 1874, p. 316. English translation in *Selections from Political Writings 1921-26*, ed. and trans. Q. Hoare, London, Lawrence & Wishart, 1978, p. 443.

5 Antonio Gramsci, *Quaderni dal Carcere*, vol. 1, ed. V. Gerratana, Turin, Einaudi, 1975 (all the references to the *Prison Notebooks* are to this edition). English translation in *Selections from the Prison Notebooks*, ed. and trans. Q. Hoare and G. Nowell Smith, London, Lawrence & Wishart, 1971, p. 57.

6 *Quaderni*, vol. 1, p. 51, *Prison Notebooks*, p. 79. It is important to stress the fact that for Gramsci hegemony only refers to the moment of leadership and does not include the moment of domination, since several interpretations which declare that domination is part of hegemony reach conclusions which completely alter the character of Gramsci's thought. See for example, Luciano Gruppi, *Il concetto di egemonia in Gramsci*, Rome, Editori Riuniti, 1972, and Massimo Salvadori, 'Gramsci e il PCI: due concezioni dell 'egemonia', *Mondo Operaio*, vol. 2, November 1976, in this volume, pp. 237–58.

7 *Quaderni*, vol. 1, pp. 457–9, *Prison Notebooks*, pp. 180–3. This text was reworked by Gramsci two years later and is to be found in its definitive form in *Notebook* 13. See *Quaderni*, vol. 3, pp. 1583–6.

8 Ibid.

9 Ibid.

10 These texts have not passed totally unnoticed. Several works on Gramsci (for example Leonardo Paggi's article 'Gramsci's General Theory of Marxism' in this volume pp. 113–67) do attribute some importance to them, but not as regards the conception of hegemony.

11 *Quaderni*, vol. 3, p. 1584, *Prison Notebooks*, pp. 180–5.

12 Ibid., vol. 1, p. 461.

13 Ibid., vol. 3, p. 1584, *Prison Notebooks*, p. 182.

14 For an analysis of Gramsci's contribution to the marxist theory of the state, see Christine Buci-Glucksmann, *Gramsci et l'État*, Paris, Fayard, 1975.

15 *Quaderni*, vol. 3, p. 2011, *Prison Notebooks*, p. 59.

16 Ibid., vol. 1, p. 461, *Prison Notebooks*, p. 161.

17 Ibid., vol. 3, p. 2012, *Prison Notebooks*, pp. 60–1.
18 Ibid., vol. 2, p. 1380.
19 If political leadership is exclusively stressed this leads to the reduction of Gramsci's hegemony to the leninist conception of hegemony as an alliance of classes. In his intervention at the Cagliari Congress in 1968 ('Gramsci e la concezione della società civile', translated in this volume as 'Gramsci and the Conception of Civil Society', pp. 21–47), Norberto Bobbio was the first to insist on the specificity of Gramsci's conception and on the importance which the latter attributed to moral and intellectual direction. However, the interpretation which Bobbio gave of this does not succeed in making clear its articulation to the economy and leads to an excessively 'superstructural' interpretation of Gramsci's thought.
20 A typical example of this kind of interpretation consists in presenting hegemony as an alliance of classes in which one of the two imposes its class ideology on the other. This problem will be dealt with again in the third part.
21 These are mainly to be found in *Notebook* 13, 'Noterelle sulla politica del Machiavelli', *Quaderni*, vol. 3, pp. 1555–652, *Prison Notebooks*, pp. 123–202.
22 *Quaderni*, vol. 2, p. 871, *Prison Notebooks*, p. 407.
23 Ibid., vol. 1, p. 437, *Prison Notebooks*, p. 365.
24 Ibid., vol. 2, p. 869, *Prison Notebooks*, p. 377.
25 Ibid., vol. 1, p. 337, *Prison Notebooks*, p. 377.
26 Ibid., vol. 2, p. 1236.
27 Ibid., p. 1376, *Prison Notebooks*, p. 324.
28 Ibid., p. 1063, *Prison Notebooks*, pp. 323–6.
29 Ibid., p. 868, *Prison Notebooks*, p. 376.
30 Ibid., p. 1492.
31 Most authors who criticise Gramsci for this reason base themselves on the critique of historicism developed by Louis Althusser in *Lire le Capital*, where, wrongly in my view, he assimilates Gramsci's problematic to that of Lukàcs, cf. Louis Althusser, *Reading Capital*, London, New Left Books, 1970, especially the chapter 'Marxism is not a Historicism'.
32 *Quaderni*, vol. 2, p. 1380, *Prison Notebooks*, p. 328.
33 Ibid., vol. 3, p. 1518, *Prison Notebooks*, p. 12.
34 Ibid., vol. 2, p. 1407, *Prison Notebooks*, pp. 60–1.
35 Ibid., vol. 1, p. 332.
36 Ibid., p. 476, *Prison Notebooks*, p. 12.
37 Nicos Poulantzas, *Political Power and Social Classes*, London, New Left Books, 1973.
38 Ibid., p. 138.
39 Ibid., p. 204.
40 This is why even those writers who *intuited* the radical newness of Gramsci's conception of hegemony did not manage to think it. In my view this is the case of C. Buci-Glucksmann, op. cit. As regards work on Gramsci in English, the dominating tendency has been to identify hegemony with ideological domination. For exceptions to this see S. Hall, B. Lumley and G. McLennan, 'Politics and Ideology: Gramsci', *Cultural Studies*, 10, 1977;

Raymond Williams, *Marxism and Literature*, Oxford University Press,
1977. The way in which these authors pose the problem of hegemony bears
similarities in several respects to the way in which it is seen in this article.

41 *Quaderni*, vol. 2, p. 1330, *Prison Notebooks*, p. 349.
42 Ibid., p. 1058 (author's italics), *Prison Notebooks*, p. 195.
43 Ibid., vol. 3, p. 1875 (author's italics).
44 Ibid., vol. 2, p. 1322.
45 Ibid., p. 1331, *Prison Notebooks*, p. 350.
46 Ibid., p. 1056, *Prison Notebooks*, p. 56 n.
47 Ibid., vol. 3, p. 1863.
48 Ibid., vol. 2, p. 1084.
49 Ibid., vol. 3, p. 1729, *Prison Notebooks*, p. 241.
50 Ibid., vol. 2, p. 1084.
51 This is a conception which Gramsci develops above all as regards its
   application to literature (*Quaderni*, vol. 3, pp. 2113–20, *Prison Notebooks*,
   pp. 421 ff.), but he does indicate that all ideological or political
   manifestations can have a 'national-popular' character when there exists an
   organic link between the intellectuals and the people.
52 *Quaderni*, vol. 2, p. 1237.
53 Gramsci's indications naturally do not provide a solution to the problem of
   the nature of the non-class ideological elements. They simply suggest the
   type of response which Gramsci could have had in mind. This problem
   does, however, require a rigorous theoretical solution. One possible line of
   research seems to have been developed by Ernesto Laclau in his book
   Politics and Ideology in Marxist Theory, London, New Left Books, 1977,
   where he deals with the specificity of the popular-democratic contradiction.
54 *Quaderni*, vol. 3, p. 1595, *Prison Notebooks*, p. 164.
55 Ibid., p. 2289, *Prison Notebooks*, p. 53.
56 Ibid., vol. 2, p. 802, *Prison Notebooks*, p. 239.
57 Parry Anderson supports this view in his article, 'The Antinomies of
   Antonio Gramsci', *New Left Review*, no. 100, 1977. His interpretation of
   Gramsci exemplifies the fact that the lack of understanding of the nature of
   Gramsci's hegemony and the anti-reductionist problematic of ideology
   which it implies makes it impossible to grasp either the specificity of
   Gramsci's thought or its coherence.
58 *Quaderni*, vol. 2, p. 973, *Prison Notebooks*, p. 239.
59 Ibid., vol. 3, p. 1729.
60 On this subject see, Paul Hirst, 'Althusser and the Theory of Ideology',
   Economy and Society, vol. 5, no. 4, 1976.
61 *Quaderni*, vol. 3, p. 1596, *Prison Notebooks*, p. 165.
62 Foucault's recent work since *L'Ordre du Discours* has led him to stress
   increasingly the political function of intellectuals, and Derrida's work at
   GREPH (Groupe pour la recherche de l'enseignement de la philosophie et
   de l'histoire) has led him to uncover the political dimension of philosophical
   practice. Their research converges towards a new conception of politics and
   power which is anticipated on several points by Gramsci's thought.

Part three

State, politics and revolutionary strategy

6 State, transition and passive revolution

Christine Buci-Glucksmann

1 By way of a starting-point: passive revolution and the marxian problematic of transition

It is not until 1933, in a somewhat enigmatic passage, that Gramsci links the concept of passive revolution, of 'revolution without revolution' – already to be found in his first notebook, where he analyses the Risorgimento – to the global problematic of transition outlined in Marx's *Preface* to the *Critique of Political Economy*:[1] 'It would seem that the theory of the passive revolution is a necessary critical corollary to the Introduction to the *Critique of Political Economy*.' Insofar as it is a corollary it must be related to the theoretico-political principles that pertain to every transitional phase:[2]

> The concept of 'passive revolution' must be rigorously derived from the two fundamental principles of political science:
> 1 that no social formation disappears as long as the productive forces which have developed within it still find room for further forward movement;
> 2 that a society does not set itself tasks for whose solution the necessary conditions have not already been incubated etc.

Yet as a *critical* corollary it seems to concern an issue that is strangely absent from Marx's *Preface* · the role and nature of the transitional state, the always 'radical' or 'passive' revolutionary character of the transition, in short, its historical specificity. This addition is, therefore, far from neutral in character, and Gramsci stresses that the principles themselves of the transition 'must first be developed *critically* in all their implications, and purged of every residue of mechanism and fatalism'.[3] In other words, in reinstating the political form and dimension of the

207

transition, Gramsci – like Lenin before him – puts an end to mechanistic-economistic interpretations of Marx's *Preface*, the outcome of which is always the same: a general, utopian theory of transition and the hypostasis of a model valid for every transition. But that is not all. A critical and dialectical approach to the transition of 'passive revolution' must take into account certain elements of a *political theory of transition*, which studies the process as a specific product of a given, historical relation and 'equilibrium of forces'. But why 'passive revolution', why 'revolution-restoration', and not the strategic model of the October Revolution, with its direct revolutionary attack on the state, and its 'frontal' seizure of power? In what does this *critical* function of passive revolution consist, both theoretically and politically?

It would be easy to restrict the scope of the concept of passive revolution in such a way that it covered only a detailed examination of the historical forms of bourgeois revolution. Gramsci does indeed exemplify it by reference to the passive revolution of the Risorgimento, whose structural and political properties he contrasts with the form of a 'war of manoeuvre' and 'popular revolution' through 'explosion' which characterise the French Revolution. All the same, in contrast to any positivist-historicist attempt to confine its application to the historical moment in which it takes effect and in which it is developed, Gramsci considerably enlarges the concept of passive revolution, endowing it with a general methodological and theoretical import.

The passive revolution becomes a potential tendency intrinsic to every transitional process: 'the thesis of the "passive revolution" as an interpretation of the Risorgimento period, *and of every epoch characterised by complex historical upheavals*'.[4] Certainly, revolution-restoration, in the sense in which Italian liberals made use of it during the Risorgimento, could not provide a programme of political intervention for the working class. For to a certain extent every passive revolution develops a 'conservatism or moderate reformism' which breaks up the free political dialectic of class contradiction and neutralises and channels popular initiative in its, extremely partial, attempt to satisfy some of the latter's demand 'by small doses, legally, in a reformist manner';[5] so equally there is the extent to which the passive revolution tends to resolve the problems of transformation and *leadership* (hegemony) in favour of the state (domination), its administrative and police apparatuses.[6] As soon as the state becomes the means of social reproduction in all its aspects 'political leadership becomes merely an aspect of the function of domination'[7] and the masses are ultimately treated as 'mass of manoeuvre'. It is obvious that Gramsci is perfectly aware of the political costs and of the 'danger of political defeatism' that *stem from* an 'anti-democratic operation of this kind'. Yet despite the fact that it does not constitute a strategy for the working class it remains none the less – on condition that the struggle is waged against every form of historical fatalism – a dialectical conception and a criterion of interpretation 'in the absence of other active elements to a dominant extent'.[8] Furthermore, as it functions as an interpretation and critical corollary of the marxian problematic of transition, its conceptual scope extends beyond the historical processes of the Risorgimento or of the political economy of fascism, in such a way as to expose the morphology of advanced capitalism, and to reveal the politico-economic obstacles that are put in the way of any frontal attack on the state, any more or less jacobinist strategy of 'permanent revolution'. It is as if the relations of capitalist production were possessed of a certain capacity for internal adaption to the developments of the forces of production, a certain plasticity, which allows them to 'restructure' in periods of crisis. That this *is indeed the case*, and that Gramsci became increasingly conscious of the fact during his work in prison (let us say in 1933–4) is revealed in the single draft of a text of 1934 on *Americanism and Fordism*. Here, for the first and last time, we have a quite explicit attempt by Gramsci to discover in americanism a specific model of development of capitalism, which has passed from the crisis of 1929 into passive revolution: 'The question of whether americanism can constitute ... a gradual evolution of the same type as the "passive revolution" examined elsewhere'.[9]

It therefore appears that Gramsci's theoretico-political interest in the dialectic of transition-passive revolution, and the new approach to the forms and difficulties of the revolutionary process to which it leads him, cannot possibly be separated from the morphological transformations of capitalism and of socialism during the 1930s – from the failure of the proletarian revolution in the West, and emergence of the Fascist State, the revolution of capitalism from above following the crisis of 1929 (the 'New Deal'), and the aggravation of contradictions in the construction of socialism. This kind of alteration in the strategic terrain modifies, both historically and practically, the context of the transition, creating new relations between economics and politics (state capitalism), between hegemonic 'apparatuses' and the state, between institutional forms and the masses. And all of this finds its explanation because Gramsci reappropriates the leninist concept of hegemony, and endows it – right from the time of his first *Notebook* – with *new functions* and a *much wider scope.* In contrast, then, to the manner in which the subject is still treated in *Questione meridionale*, the concern is now no longer simply with 'the social base of the proletarian dictatorship and of the workers' state', with the way in which 'the proletariat can become the leading (*dirigente*) and the dominant class to the extent that it succeeds in creating a system of class alliances';[10] or rather, one might say instead that an *a priori* condition of such a conception is an analysis of the political forms in which the bourgeoisie constitutes its own power bloc: an interrogation of the divergent forms of hegemony in their relations with the state and with civil society. This explains why it is that, so far from being marginal, the concept of passive revolution as a critical corollary of the marxian problematic of transition possibly allows for a new, global interpretation of the forms of involvement of politics in the overthrow of a mode of production. If we take the study of *a politics of transition* to consist in a critical analysis of the dialectic between historical bloc and institutional forms, then passive revolution emerges as 'a general principle of political art and science'.[11]

In the most general sense, we can say that in contrast to every catastrophist or economistic conception of the crisis as a revolutionisation of the masses (the conception of the Third International during the 1930s), and in opposition to every reduction of the revolutionary process to a frontal encounter, to a violent and jacobin social collapse, Gramsci endows the processes of passive revolution, whose tendency is always to 'reduce the dialectic to an evolutionary process of reform', with an almost 'epochal' significance. Is it perhaps necessary to regard it first and foremost as a principle of historical periodisation, a new tendency of advanced capitalism? Or should we go further than that, as Leonardo Paggi, somewhat peremptorily suggests: if it is seen to apply to the *East as much as to the West, the concept of passive* revolution constitutes 'an adequate representation of the complex historical process resulting in the definite supersession of an entire mode of production'.[12]

On that view, one can proceed from an initial hypothesis which modifies the interpretation of the strategical difference between 'war of manoeuvre' (characteristic of the East, the frontal attack of 1917) and the 'war of position' (the stragegy of hegemony, characteristic of the West). In fact, it is not just two strategies that Gramsci opposes to each other, but rather *two wars of position*: the war of the dominant class in its various forms of passive revolution is opposed to the *asymmetrical* war of the subaltern classes in their struggle for hegemony and a political leadership over society. What I mean by this is that despite a sameness in form, hegemony differs in content. When the reference is to the forms of passive revolution of the dominant classes in the economic and political context its role is not identifiable with that which it plays in determining a 'socialisation of politics' that can activate a mass cultural revolution (leading to changed institutions, styles of life, behaviour, consumption) and can transform class relations and the equilibrium of power within society and the state. It should be understood that it is by virtue of these new relations between the problematic of transition and passive revolution that Gramsci is able to explore in detail a new strategy for the working class in the West (the famous war of position) differing in kind from the strategy of frontal attack of the war of movement of 1917.

Besides, this opposition between East and West – from the point of view of the superstructures and their effects in a revolutionary process – is already to be found in Lenin, not to mention Trotsky's speech to the Fourth Congress of the International. Gramsci himself refers explicitly to the strategy of the single front, to Lenin's position in 1921–2, as the point from which all his thoughts on the war of position develop.[13]

If this distinction in terms of strategy does indeed allow for a renewed and more profound approach to questions about the state and about the relations between *political forms* and economic and social factors, is it not rather because Gramsci provides certain elements whereby the *political morphology* of the processes of transition themselves can be characterised? And he does so because he makes the relations in the transition period of parties-state-alliances his point of departure. Given this, it means that if we are to use Gramsci as a yardstick, whether theoretically or politically, then we must do more than repeat him; it means rather that we must use this complex dialectic of the political forms of transition which he studies, in its negative as much as in its positive aspects, as our genuine yardstick. If it is true that the transition to socialism associated with Eurocommunism is based on democratic strategies necessarily consisting in *mass democratic revolutions* that forge new links between representative democracy and democracy of the base, between hegemony and pluralism, must they not primarily be *anti-passive revolutions*?

2 On the theory of passive revolution

1 On the dysymmetry of class struggles and their difficulties

From *Ordine Nuovo* to the *Notebooks*, Gramsci's political thought,

though progressively enriched in the process of his development of a
new strategy of Western revolution, remains singularly constant in its
insistence that 'the transformation of the working class into a hegemonic
class, becoming State', depends entirely upon its capacity to develop a
new political practice that is not symmetrical with that of the dominant
classes. The reason for this is simple, and not essentially ideological; it
lies in the respective positions of the classes in their relations to the state
and to the historical processes of transition. The bourgeoisie, by contrast,
is constituted and reconstituted within and through the state: 'The
historical unity of the ruling classes is realised in the State, and their
history is essentially the history of States and of groups of States'.[14]
Certainly this is potentially so in the case of the working class also, for
the subaltern classes 'are not unified and cannot unite until they are able
to become a "State"'.[15] But this process in which they become
autonomous is never completed but is always an *on-going constitution*, a
permanent process of political 'recomposition' of alliances, that is based
on the construction of a new relation between production and politics.
For if it is the state that provides the standpoint of the dominant classes,
it is primarily economic and civil society that does so in the case of the
working class. Even in this respect, the history of the subaltern classes is
asymmetrical, 'their history, therefore, is intertwined with that of civil
society, it is a "disjointed" and *discontinuous* function of the history of
civil society, and *thereby* of the history of states and groups of states'.[16] A
discontinuous history, a history of a *mediated* relation to the state – in
short, a history of an asymmetrical autonomisation which aims to
construct new political forms (councils, unions and parties).

This was true in the case of the dual strategy of the Factory Councils
of 1919–20, which sought simultaneously to construct from the factory
upwards forms of worker-democracy conducive to the *reunification* of
the entire working class and to the establishment of its autonomy, and to
use these new democratic forms as a means to resolve the crisis of
society and the parliamentary state, and to replace the latter by a
worker's and peasant's state.

In 1926, when he once more reverts to the experience of *Ordine
Nuovo*, Gramsci exposes both its limits and its irreversibly positive
character: 'The self-government of the working class', its democratic
inventiveness, its initiative.[17] Nor was he later to change his mind on that
particular point. In fact in 1934 we find him writing in the *Notebooks*
that 'it is precisely the workers who are the bearers of the new and more
contemporary demands of industy'.[18]

This is to be understood in a *political* sense: in contrast to the bourgeois-technicist conception, Gramsci's understanding of production is always political. In actual fact: 'The political constitution of the state has a good deal more importance for production than does the alteration of a technology or labour process'.[19]

It is in these relations between production and the state, between economics and politics, that the core of the problem lies. From that point of view Gramsci is to draw *new* conclusions about the failure of the Italian working class in face of fascism. The hegemonic practice of the working class places it in a much more conflict-ridden and difficult position than one might possibly think because of the complexity of the political mediations, their powers of resistance in a period of crisis, and the effects of a state which is identifiable neither simply with the government nor simply with a repressive apparatus. It cannot, therefore, develop its hegemonic strategy of expansionary movement from the *bottom upwards* without resistance to the effects of the state and its political mechanisms on its own practice.

This is equally true in the case of the 'modern prince', the revolutionary party, which has to reveal its unity in its *political* relationship with the masses rather than allow it to become a mere technical instrument or bureaucratic device; in short, a mere fact of organisation which conceals the 'active social bloc of which the party is the guide'.[20]

The autonomy which arises within the factory is therefore constantly menaced by *factional corporatism*, continually 'broken by the initiative of the dominant groups', forever in the grip of a certain socio-political instability of the bourgeoisie and of its dominant groups, which are even able to generate new parties 'intended to conserve the assent of the subaltern groups and to maintain control over them'.[21]

The allusion here is clear: the formation of new bourgeois parties (cf. the fascist party) corresponds to a *situation of hegemonic crisis* in which the entire state is involved; to a crisis of relations between rulers and ruled which strikes at the historical basis of the state and the whole complex of its hegemonic apparatuses.

This conception of crisis, which is that of the *Prison Notebooks*, in fact reveals a different structure from that of the model analysed by Lenin and revised by Gramsci in 1919–20, which regards the crisis in terms of a collapse of the state effected within that same state as a result of global *revolutionary crisis*. One reason for this is that the resolution of the hegemonic crisis can take the form of a *reduplication of bourgeois power* (and not of the power of the proletariat). This is something that Gramsci had already diagnosed in 1921 in his exposure of the *twofold nature assumed by the state apparatus* in time of crisis, which has the form of a violent and complicit co-existence of two repressive and punitive apparatuses: fascism and the bourgeois state.[22] But above all, it is because the crisis occurs within an unstable equilibrium of forces that demands that greater attention be paid to two connected and complementary phenomena. On the one hand, there are the effects of the form of the state and of its crisis upon the great mass of the people, and on the historical basis of the state; they occur simultaneously with the emergence of a disparity between civil society and political society. On the other hand, there are the attempts that are made during the crisis to restructure capital and the political forms of its existence (state, party, mass movement).

In this sense, the hegemonic crisis is not a revolutionary type of crisis that goes wrong. It is not only at the political level that it imposes new problems, but also at the level of historical materialism. And in this respect again, the experience of the Factory Councils well exemplifies Gramsci's conclusions. Contrary to what one might, somewhat naively, suppose the relationship between the forces at play in the 'catastrophic equilibrium' type of crisis is not such as to create division in the forces that are opposed externally to the working class; instead it is the particular strengths and weaknesses of the working class itself that are involved:[23]

> In Italy there existed an unstable equilibrium between the social forces engaged in struggle. The proletariat was *too strong* in 1919–20 for it any longer passively to submit to capitalist oppression. But its organising forces were uncertain, hesitant, internally *weak*, because the socialist Party was merely the amalgamation of at least three parties; in 1919–20 Italy lacked a well organised revolutionary party that was fully committed to the struggle.

We cannot, therefore, approach questions about the autonomisation of the working class and of its forms of organisation (party, unions, democracy of the base) independently of questions about the relations of forces of the classes themselves and their effects *internally* within the state. So it is no surprise that Gramsci relates the two principles proclaimed by Marx in the Preface to the *Critique of Political Economy* to the analysis of the relations of force in their three constitutive phases of the economic, the political and the politico-military. But we would be much mistaken at this point to interpret these three phases in terms of a linear, evolutionary model, as an untroubled progression. In fact, these three moments define a *new object of analysis*, already outlined by Marx in his historico-political writings (from the *Eighteenth Brumaire* to the *Civil War in France*), namely, *a theory of the structure of the conjuncture*, which opens the way to an understanding of the conditions and processes of transition.

To locate the problematic of transition purely at the level of the objective contradictions in the mode of production is to fail to recognise the role in transition of the relations: classes/state/parties/historical bloc, and thereby to neglect the critical corollary of the marxian problematic that is contained in the dialectic of hegemony and domination. Inversely, the *addition* of an analysis of the political form of transition – in the transition itself – means, as Gramsci himself indicates, that we are guaranteed of a development of the leninist concept of hegemony; but at the same time it also quite certainly means that we must go beyond certain of its premises, that we must retranslate it. Is it not precisely by contrasting hegemony with passive revolution that we today appreciate the full meaning and import of this reinterpretation?

If one charts the development in the prison writings of the theory of passive revolution through its various elaborations and qualifications, one is bound to be struck by its lack of homogeneity, by the relatively gradual emergence of the problematic of transition-passive revolution as a whole. It is a development that is best described as transforming a *historical concept into a general theoretical concept* in a way that sheds a fairly immediate light upon Gramsci's marxism, upon the relations of production between theory and history, and upon his conception of the intellectuals and of culture in the 'war of position of the dominant classes'.

Let us first discuss the historical concept. The notion of passive revolution is concerned with two major historical processes each one corresponding to a stage in the development of the capitalist mode of production. On the one hand, there is the Risorgimento, where it is the element of passive revolution in the superstructure that is accentuated; on the other hand, there is fascism-americanism, where the stress is laid on passive revolution in the organisation of work and of the productive forces as a result of new relations between politics and economics (state capitalism). It is not so much my intention in any re-examination of these two models to question their historical validity, which has been the subject of numerous researches and debates, so much as to understand in what way the theory of the passive revolution alters the gramscian problematic of the state and of the revolutionary processes that are found present.(in the West) prior to the seizure of power, but also (in the East) subsequent upon that seizure of power. My point is that the accompaniment of the theory is a *critical* re-evaluation of the role of the political element in the transition, of its effects upon civil society and of the political 'management' of the transition. Once the state is no longer seen as *external* to the process of transition (as a mere *instrument* – a view that characterises the unilateral conception of the state criticised by Gramsci), but is regarded as an integral component of transition, the real dialectic between *domination* (coercion; force) and *hegemony* (in which consent is organised) cannot fail to 'correct' i.e. to fulfil, in an anti-economistic sense, the two major principles proclaimed by Marx. It is for this reason that the theory of passive revolution and its critique leads to a new vision of the relations of the state in transition. Or rather, it leads to a rejection of any 'statism' of and in the transition, to a reformulation of socialism in terms of a transitional society, a historical bloc.

2 Of passive transitions or 'dictatorship without hegemony'

Gramsci does not fail to stress on various occasions that the Risorgimento as a model of the formation of a unitary national state is a passive transition, which simultaneously and in highly contradictory fashion, embraces both (bourgeois) 'revolutionary' elements and elements of 'restoration' (compromises with the former dominant strata, absence of a mass popular revolution). The contradiction in the formula *revolution-restoration* (a formula borrowed from Quinet) is a reflection of the role itself of the masses in the transition, of their relations with the existing forms of power – of the form and of the *contents* of politics. To the extent that revolutionary innovation and progress take place 'in the absence of popular initiative' or active hegemonic intervention on the part of the masses as a whole, and even in opposition to certain forms of sporadic revolt, the historical process is *passive* and conservative in character. Nevertheless, it remains a case of *revolution* (however diluted) and as such it therefore occurs in response to 'certain popular demands', including, as Gramsci makes clear in the second draft of the same note, the 'demands at the base'.[24] It remains to be explained why the dialectic of old and new, of innovation and conservation, continues to go along with a 'moderate reformist conservatism' which is later to find its intellectual interpretation in crocean historicism. Why are the historical antagonisms subsumed in conservatism?

Gramsci's reply is particularly illuminating: the revolution is passive when the state is replaced by a ruling class, when the aspect of *domination* (coercion) predominates over that of *leadership* (hegemony as organised consent).

This occurs during the Risorgimento: 'The Piedmontese State becomes the *real motor* of unity after 1848'.[25] From then onwards, in contrast to the French jacobins, the Italian liberals 'conceive unity as the extension of the Piedmontese State and of dynastic patrimony, not as a *national movement of the base* but as a conquest of rulership'.[26] This is expressed even more explicitly in a piece (of which there is only a single draft) written after 1933: 'The function of the Piedmont in the Italian Risorgimento is that of a "ruling class".'[27]

In any consideration of these formulations it must be stressed that the proportions in which the element of state domination and that of hegemonic consent are respectively combined depends on the relations between the ruling class and the state in transition, and therefore on the mass (or non-mass) character of the process. In revolutionary movement 'from above' it is domination that is given a certain priority, while the existence of a national movement 'of the base' gives more weight to hegemony. But there is more to it than this: Gramsci explicitly refers to the role of the 'enlargement of the state' in a historical period of transition. Let us note that he is by no means simply dealing with a specific case of transition (as it happens, that of the development of capitalism in Italy) but with what in fact is a historical tendency of the bourgeoisie. In effective contrast to other classes in earlier modes of production, and also in contrast to the way in which the working class becomes autonomous, the bourgeoisie maintains a specific relationship with the state. This is a relationship of hegemonic expansion within the union of society and the self-constitution of class:[28]

> The revolution of the bourgeois class in its conception of right and thus in the function it assigns to the state has its especial character in its desire for conformism (hence the ethical character of right and State). Previous dominant classes were essentially conservative in the sense that they did not tend to elaborate an organic passage from other classes to their own, to enlarge, that is, their sphere of class 'technically' and ideologically; the conception was that of a closed caste.

This kind of *enlargement* of the state in transition presupposes a certain historical capacity to absorb and assimilate all the levels of society, creating a global and universal formation. The state does not exist without consent, without organised hegemonic apparatuses, without concern for the specific relations between economic society, civil society and political society. In contrast to every narrow conception of the state,[29]

it should be remarked that the general notion of the state includes elements which need to be referred back to the notion of civil society (in the sense that one might say that State = political society + civil society, in other words, hegemony is protected by the armour of coercion).

Hence the reason why Gramsci abandons every instrumentalist conception of the state which would regard it either solely as government (in conformity with the liberal social-democratic tradition) or else simply as a monolithic repressive apparatus devoid of all socio-political contradiction (the view that informs the entire economistic-maximalist tradition and is found moreover in stalinism). In this sense – and I have elsewhere developed the point in detail[30] – Gramsci breaks with the whole instrumentalist approach that characterises the Second International and certain currents of the Third, in favour of a new vision of the state which is more than a mere 'complement' to the marxist-leninist theory of the dictatorship of the proletariat. This is because the problematic of the enlarged state allows for *a critical reformulation of the problematic of transition.* By that I mean that the concept of the enlarged state, of the 'integral state' remains empty unless one distinguishes between two radically opposed types of state enlargement and transition – as Gramsci himself suggests in his treatment of the Risorgimento.

1   The enlargement of the state may have its roots in the *base* in the form of a democracy of the base, and be founded upon the democratic creativity of the masses and the extension of their hegemony. Where this is the case, the hegemonic aspect tends to prevail over that of state domination (though the latter as such is never absent). Has such an enlargement of the state anything in common with the stalinist theory and practice of state reinforcement through the reabsorption of civil society, the reduction-suppression of its contradictions, and the reproduction of the distinction between rulers and ruled that is a feature of every state? On the contrary, this enlargement of the state is the grounds for a 'socialisation' of politics, and for a re-evaluation of the role played by social factors and hegemonic struggle during the transition,

that conforms with the ultimate aim of the withering away of the state.

2   The 'passive revolution', by contrast, issues in a kind of 'statisisation' of the transition which destroys the impact of every popular initiative at the base and of every alteration of the relations rulers–ruled within the superstructures and their institutions. When domination prevails over leadership, when the ruling class loses its own expansionary basis in the masses, when the state replaces class as the motor of socio-economic development, the inevitable result is what Gramsci calls a *dictatorship without hegemony*. Thereupon, the hegemonic apparatuses, including party and union, become 'ideological state apparatuses' as is the case with stalinist or neo-Stalinist 'transmission belts'.

The real meaning of the Risorgimento is therefore to be discovered at a level beyond that of concrete analysis: it lies in the fact that its study, in the light that it sheds upon the causes and effects of passive revolution and in its production of certain definite instruments for a political theory of the transition, allows us to distinguish between two types of transition. It might be objected at this point that I am reading too much into the words of Gramsci's text. That is not so because Gramsci himself endows his pronouncements with a general application precisely in the kind of *problems* that he detects in them.

Problem 1 : Is it not the case perhaps that the role of the state in the Risorgimento is equivalent to that of a party? 'Thus Piedmont had a function which can, from certain aspects, be compared to that of a party i.e. of the leading personnel of a social group (and in fact people always spoke of the "Piedmont party").'[31]

Problem 2 : Is it not possible that the Piedmont case offers us a more general methodological and theoretical lesson regarding the 'canons' of historical interpretation set out by Marx in the Preface to the *Critique*?[32]

The important thing is *to analyse more profoundly the significance of a 'Piedmont' type of function in passive revolution* – i.e. the fact that a State replaces the local social groups in leading a struggle of renewal. It is one of those cases in which these groups have the function of 'domination' without that of 'leadership': dictatorship without hegemony.

This much is clear: the 'Piedmont' is only a particular instance of passive revolutions (note the plural), and it behoves us to analyse it as such in depth because of the understanding it allows us not only of other historical processes but also, in the long run – as we shall come to discover – of other passive revolutions. So in what respects exactly does it provide an example? What are its causes, its effects, its conclusions?

If the Italian bourgeoisie as a class has been incapable of leading a radical bourgeois democratic process and of unifying the people, it is above all because of a certain inversion of the relations between economy and politics in the transition. The specific efficacy of superstructures depends in large measure on the strength of earlier socio-economic development: now, in Italy, 'there did not exist a strong and diffused class of the economic bourgeoisie'.[33] For this reason, in contrast to the principles set out by Marx in the Preface: 'the problem was not so much to liberate the economic forces that had already developed ... as to create the general conditions that would allow these forces to arise.'[34] The case presents an odd inversion of the marxian principles of transition: the state, so far from resting upon a developed economic and civil society, had to create the conditions of its development beginning with its own apparatus. Such a situation – which is precisely that which occurs in the USSR after the civil war – cannot but be prejudicial to the autonomy of a class, its *hegemony*, relative to the state. In the event that the state becomes a partisan-state (or even a party-state), hegemony is restricted not only in its mass basis, but also within the class itself: 'the hegemony will be exercised by *a part* of the social group over the entire group, and not by the latter over other forces in order to give power to the movement'.[35] This loss of hegemony, which is typical of passive and statist transitions, inevitably leads to the introduction of bureaucratic-elitist mechanisms of social reproduction, to forms of 'bureaucratic centralism':[36]

> the prevalence of bureaucratic centralism in the State indicates that the leading group is saturated, that it is turning into a narrow clique which tends to perpetuate its selfish privileges by controlling or even by *stifling* the birth of oppositional forces.

From these reflections upon the passive transition of the State, Gramsci draws two conclusions:

1   If the class is to avoid being replaced by the state it must gain hegemony (ideological, cultural, political) both *before* and *after* the seizure of power; this implies the existence of non-state institutional forms which encourage a dynamic development of the base and generate mechanisms for the 'socialisation of politics'.

2   This new interpretation of transitional processes in terms of the dialectic of hegemony and domination goes to confirm the specificity of the transition typical of the West. The opposition between the respective strategies of the war of manoeuvre and the war of position, between East and West, refers to a kind of *proportionality* that exists between the different aspects of the social complex. In contrast to the situation in the East, where the state was everything and civil society was but primordial and gelatinous, we have the situation of the most advanced states, where civil society has become 'a very complex structure and one which is resistant to the catastrophic "incursions" of the immediate economic element (crisis, depressions etc.)'.[37]

If what is indicated by these and yet other, equally well-known remarks is that the strategy of revolution in the West acquires a specific nature, it is none the less necessary to make that nature precise. It is not so much, as some would hold, that gramscian thought about the state privileges the hegemonic-war of position aspect over the aspect of war of movement-domination to such an extent that it ceases to allow for any coercive element of domination (which is in fact false). Nor is it even that the primacy accorded the war of position eliminates any aspect of rupture or movement. For Gramsci is careful to make it clear that the *strategic* primacy of the war of position implies, in so far as its tactics are concerned, recourse to elements of the war of movement, of rupture with the dominant socio-political equilibrium. In this sense, the 'war of position' is never pure. Nor was it so in the case of the Risorgimento, for the war of manoeuvre, and the aspect of popular initiative had their representative in Mazzini. But it was the element represented by Cavour and by the Piedmontese State, the war of position, that was dominant. In other words, the nature and outcome of the transitional process and the form assumed by the state involved in it are entirely dependent upon who it is in any given historical situation who takes initiative *for* the transition and *during* it, and who is therefore in a position to assess its long-term political and historical consequences. Here again, in the asymmetry of forces that existed at the objective and subjective levels the Risorgimento offers us an example. For while 'Cavour was aware of his role (at least up to a certain point) inasmuch as he understood the role of Mazzini, the latter does not seem to have been aware either of his own or of Cavour's'.[38]

This disparity in knowledge of historical roles (and therefore of their respective strategies), this measure of disproportion between the war of movement and the war of position, that is an ever present feature of transition, becomes incorporated into a general 'principle of political science'. Thus, when the relationship between civil society and political society is 'well-adjusted', as it is in the West, we must expect to find that its forms of political life are complex, and that the political sphere has been re-defined for *all* classes in society. By this I mean that the dominant classes are in a position to combat even a 'war of position'. In this sense, the theory of passive revolution as a critical supplement to the marxian problematic of transition is not limited to 'passive transitions': it has to do also with the modes of *passive restructuring* of capitalism itself.

3   On the passive revolutions of dominant classes: the war of position

If it is the structural character of 'passive transitions' to bring into prominence the specific weight of the processes whereby hegemony is replaced by a statist and bureaucratic domination, that is no reason for us to conclude that the theory of passive revolution is strictly superstructural, that it begets a kind of dualist reformism between base and state, production and politics. It is not in fact like that; indeed, the very reformulation of the transition to socialism in terms of historical bloc tends in a quite opposite direction. For not only does Gramsci define the formation of the historical bloc in terms of the actual unity of infrastructure and superstructure, of objective and subjective conditions; he also formulates the *conditions* of this unity, and thereby endorses the principles of transition pronounced by Marx.

The first condition is well-known. In contrast to a simple alliance of classes and social forces, the formation of a historical bloc implies a transformation of respective social roles within the alliance and an alteration of the forms of political power. It implies, that is, transformations of the dialectical and organic relations between intellectuals and people, leaders and led, rulers and ruled, all of which are implicated in the cultural revolution that is a necessary condition of a new state practice, a new type of state.[39] But the *expansive* unity of the 'historical bloc' also differs from every bureaucratic organisation of a simple 'power bloc', which favours domination and leads to a passive relationship (at its best, it is administrative-repressive, at its worst ...) between the masses and social institutions. The historical bloc is the antithesis of passive revolution and imposes a second condition, that which Gramsci calls 'homogeneity' between infrastructure and superstructure. It therefore overcomes the strictly 'economic-corporate' stage in which the state is merely an economic agent. The reformulation of transition contained in the strategy of the historical bloc is therefore the positive circumscription of that which the passive revolution negatively delimits; it is as if the binomial of historical bloc – passive revolution – defines the two limits, the two critical corollaries of the 'canons' of transition proclaimed by Marx once the economistic-mechanistic conception of the transition has been jettisoned. If this is true, it is immediately apparent that the critique of economism has nothing to do with a voluntaristic dismissal of the economy, nor with a neo-crocean absorption of history into its ethico-political totalisation. Instead, the critique defines the terms of a non-economistic conception of the economy itself, in the light of which the processes of passive revolution are reinterpreted as a counter-attack of capital. Its point of departure is the capitalist organisation of work and the new relations between the economic and the political, the masses and the state, that come into being in the post-1930s era. And it is precisely that which is its concern.

The idea that fascism is the twentieth-century's historical equivalent of nineteenth-century liberalism, that it is a *new form* of passive revolution, 'a "war of position" in the economic field',[40] is not discounted. It seems clear in fact that Gramsci himself had for a long time preferred to think in terms of the relations between caesarism and fascism in order to provide a better definition of the crisis of fascisisation (of hegemony) – whose accompaniment is an equilibrium of forces of a catastrophic kind – and of its consequence: the totalitarian state. And it is certain that from the time of *Notebook* 8 (1931–2) the two fundamental concepts of passive revolution and war of position are always involved in the analysis of fascism.[41] The concept itself of passive revolution comes to be modified and eventually designates an immanent tendency of capitalist development of the American type.

If the war of position is really a new offensive strategy of the working class in the West, which is capable (by virtue of the fact that it takes the conquest of civil society to be a presupposition of the overthrow of the state), of dealing with the 'hegemonic apparatuses' and the complex of processes involved in state penetration of the economy, all its consequences must be examined from the standpoint of the strategy of the dominant classes. It is *from* and *within* the economy, *from* and *within* the hegemonic apparatuses, that the countertendencies of capitalism, its 'passive revolutions' begin and develop. In contrast to all approaches to fascism that concentrate upon its political character, upon its totalitarianism and upon its mechanisms of ideological or state repression, Gramsci – although he by no means excludes that approach – develops what is none the less a different analysis; this analysis was already central to the strategy of the Factory Councils in 1919–20, and is based on the relations between the reorganisation of the productive forces and the forms of political existence. Does not fascism as a form of state totalitarianism in fact conceal a new form of reformism linked to state capitalism?

The war of position in the field of the economy begins with the capitalist reorganisation of the productive forces and is based on the contradictory introduction of a half-measure of economic planning:[42]

> Is not fascism precisely the form of 'passive revolution' belonging to the twentieth century? ... One could conceive it as follows: the passive revolution comes about through a 'reformist' transformation of the economic structure which replaces its individualistic character by a planned economy (a regulated economy).

The emergence in this fashion of a 'mixed' form of economy that is *passive in character* (which Gramsci relates to corporatism) in fact implies a new role for the state in the economy. The second draft of this same note is much more explicit on the point:[43]

> there is a passive revolution involved in the fact that, through *legislative intervention by the State* and by means of the corporative organisation, relatively far-reaching modifications are being introduced into the country's economic structure in order to accentuate the 'plan of production' element.

Of course, this involves no alteration in the profit and control of the transitional dominant and ruling classes since the 'revolution' remains passive and the productive forces are developed under their direction. But it can happen that certain forms of alliance are undermined since the passive revolution creates a period of expectation and hope, especially in certain social groups such as 'the great mass of urban and rural petit-bourgeois'.[44] This is why this 'species of reformism' is not simply the effect of a certain politics, but is rather – as both americanism and fordism demonstrate – the outcome of an 'immanent necessity to organise the economy in a systematic fashion'. Or better still, it expresses this 'new mechanism of accumulation and distribution of finance capital based directly on industrial production'.[45]

In contrast to the 'catastrophist' view of capitalism elaborated in the analysis of the Third International in its 'shift' of 1929–30, Gramsci admits the possibility of a capitalistic development of the productive forces in *determinate sectors*, on condition that this is based on the state both economically, ideologically and morally (increase in the moral coercion exercised by the state apparatus). In this sense, the state itself becomes the 'biggest plutocratic organism, a holding company for the great mass of savings of the small capitalists'.[46] From then on, the equilibrium of consent and coercion typical of classical parliamentary political hegemony can no longer rely on the cohesion of its institutional structures or of its mass basis. Certainly Gramsci has not yet penetrated beyond the horizon of the leninist critique of 'bourgeois' parliamentarism (it will need the harsh lesson of anti-fascism and of stalinism before the relations between representative democracy and socialism come to present themselves in radically new terms and democracy is seen as the strategic axis of transition). Nevertheless he does insist upon the specificity and diversity of the forms of state and hegemony, and it is the dialectic of state-civil society as determinant upon these forms and upon the problematic of the 'withering away' of the state, to which he refers.

The gradual displacement of civil society by the 'total' (totalitarian) state, takes place via state penetration into the economy and mass institutions. In contrast to this process of consolidation of the state, the withering away of the state (that characterises communism) presupposes the self-regulation and expansion of civil society to the detriment of political society. This means that the dialectic of state-civil society, far from being a neo-crocean-hegelian regression in comparison to the marxist analysis of the mode of production, as Althusser has thought, is really the opposite. This is because, in the first place, this dialectic underpins Marx's political thought, his critique of the superstitious view of the state as something separate and centralised, engulfing all social forces in a monstrous bureaucratic and parasitical mechanism; but above all it is because this dialectic permits an anti-economistic approach to the economy itself, a re-evaluation of the role of the social in its relations with the political and an analysis of political forms from which to conduct a 'left' critique of stalinism in terms of 'passive revolution'. In contrast to the 'classic' parliamentary state which remains relatively autonomous of civil society (in equilibrium with it) the changes undergone by the state in the post-1930s period introduce a new relationship between the economy and politics which is *non-*

instrumental. The social division of labour, the relations of production, no longer merely constitute the support for a state that is produced externally, but are rather the 'casemates' or 'organisational reserves' of a state organised production, which cannot leave the masses out of its sphere of operation. Between the form of the state and the laws of capital accumulation, the relations become more functional, less mediate. In short, the passive revolution arises, as does hegemony, in the factory itself. It is here that the originality of Gramsci's analysis of taylorism and fordism lies: he discovers the countertendencies of capitalism in the forms themselves of the organisation of labour; he re-explores the political dimension that is a central feature of the Factory Council strategy in the light of new developments in capitalism; in short, he studies the relations between productive forces and political forms.

In fact, the vehicles of the American type of 'passive revolution' are the reorganisation of the wage-earner (the politics of high wages), the development of differential practices within the working class, and the creation of a new, fragmented proletariat, which is parcellised and interchangeable. The development of the productive forces, their 'rationalisation', takes place under the direction of the dominant classes and they exercise a monopoly over initiative and over the working class to the extent that the latter lacks any autonomous and conscious leadership. As Badaloni has correctly observed: 'The passive revolution corresponds to a situation in which the unifying element of politics in its link with the new productive forces has failed to appear'.[47] It is not simply by chance, therefore, that when confronted by this absence of political socialisation, Gramsci recalls, even in the *Notebooks*, the experience of *Ordine Nuovo* 'which upheld its own type of "americanism" in a form acceptable to the workers'.[48] Hegemony arises in the ownership and control over the labour-process; it depends upon the presence of political forms at the base (such as the councils) which are capable of realising the *unity* of the class as a class of 'producers'.

All the same, in face of the new forms of mass control at the level of the factory which are developed by americanism and experimented with by fascism (the state union, corporatism), Gramsci refers to the experience of *Ordine Nuovo* more as a form of anti-passive revolution than as a basis for a state of councils of the pyramidal and centralised type that came into being in 1919–20. For a state of that kind, which is based on a two-fold system of power, is precisely the outcome of a war of movement, of a frontal attack, and it is highly improbable, if not impossible, that that could ever occur in the West.

Though a strange theoretical involution, it is at this point that the binomial: passive revolution/anti-passive-revolution, taylorism/fordism-councils, brings us back *directly* to Marx (even if Lenin's remarks on the constitution of the working-class state always remain an inevitable mediation). The reference to Marx lies in the fact that the passive revolution is in reality that *critical corollary* which allows us to forge a new link between the critique of political economy and the theory of the revolution via the idea of a kind of expansivity of politics into the base.[49] In effect, the development of taylorism/fordism, and more generally of americanism, represents the capitalist response to the law of the falling rate of profit discovered by Marx. Or better, perhaps, this law 'must be studied on the basis of taylorism and fordism'.[50] In contrast to all economistic interpretations of this law, which privilege the development-reorganisation of the *material* forces of production, Gramsci stresses, in addition to this, the decisive role that is played by the 'selection of a new type of worker' which 'makes it possible, by means of tayloristic rationalisation of operations, to achieve a much greater relative and absolute productivity'.[51] It is the form of the working class, its internal modifications, that determines the nature of the law both morphologically and politically, that gives to it its *tendential* character – since there can be no tendential law which does not have its counter-tendency i.e. that is without its political variant, that does not give rise to relations of force in the economy – or, in Gramsci's words, 'Since the law is the contradictory aspect of another law, that of relative surplus-value which determines the molecular expansion of the factory system.'[52] The passive revolution as a process of capitalist rationalisation of work, therefore, remains contradictory in the long run because it generates its antithesis: the molecular expansion of the factory system. But in terms of political strategy, what is further needed is a war of position that resists and hampers the effects of this rationalisation; the massification-division that it produces must be opposed by a reunification at the base along the lines of Marx's 'collective labourer'. When he explicitly links the council movement with Marx's theoretical category of the 'collective labourer', Gramsci aims to define a new relationship between economy and hegenomy – to make the concept of hegemony a critical principle that stands opposed to any economistic interpretation of *Capital*. If it is true that the passive revolution tends to harmonise technological needs with the interests of the dominant classes, hegemony and its political forms at the base of society allow for the possibility of discord between them in that they create the conditions for a new historical synthesis in which technical exigencies are united with the interests of a still subaltern class. The anti-passive revolution takes place through the emergence of a new consciousness on the part of the producers;[53] via a 'socialisation of the political'.

Let us attempt a provisional conclusion on this issue: if there can be a *political form* which allows for the reunification of a parcellised, 'rationalised' working class that is permanently subjected to the effects of capital's passive revolution, then it means that hegemony is founded in the economy: 'though hegemony is ethical-political, it must also be economic'.[54] But there is no reason to think that this applies only to capitalism; it equally allows us to come to terms with the contradictions and 'deviations' of socialism. Commenting on Trotsky's americanism in 1921, on his desire to 'give supremacy in national life to industry and industrial methods, to accelerate, by means of external coercion, the growth of discipline and order in production' (all of which occurs under Stalin), Gramsci notes that there is a real risk that this kind of americanistic-military mode of development ends up in a new form of bonapartism;[55] in other words, in a form of caesarism in which the passive revolution at the superstructural level (the substitution of state for class) is united with americanism in the division of labour; a strange combination in which the working class loses twice over its *expansive* hegemony. The result is an absence of any real and authentic socialist historical bloc. We can easily invert this idea, in which case the question becomes: in what sense does the historical bloc, insofar as it represents a reformulation of the problematic of transition, constitute an anti-passive revolution?

3   By way of conclusion: transition conceived as anti-passive revolution

The foregoing analyses of passive revolution, and the problems which they generate, allow us at this point to formulate a certain number of hypotheses and conclusions which can serve as a basis for further discussion. The complexity of the revolutionary strategy appropriate to the West is revealed to be even more 'complex' than one might initially have thought. The first conclusion about strategy that Gramsci draws from the failure of the proletarian revolution in the West is that it is necessary to conduct a protracted 'war of position' in order to undermine the ensemble of organisational reserves developed by the bourgeoisie, by its state and by its hegemonic apparatuses. But this strategy is in permanent conflict with another war of position that is contained in the various forms of capital's passive revolution and the new types of reformism these create. This is why, even if the reinstation and development of the leninist concept of hegemony allows for the analysis of a *new object*, namely the complex of power structures found in the West (structures by and large absent in Russia, and which are obstacles to any form of frontal attack, to any repetition of the October 'model'), there is no need to leap to the conclusion that this object has a strictly superstructural character. For there are two conclusions concerning the dialectical relations between the economico-social and the political that can be drawn from the passive revolution, and which serve as critical corollaries to the principles stated by Marx in the *Preface* to the *Critique of Political Economy*:

1   A process of transition from one mode of production to another remains passive and confined to the level of the state when it is based on an absence of hegemony at the economic level; this is a typical inversion of Marx's principle since the state serves as the *instrument* for the development of the productive forces. We know the price of this type of passive revolution: 'forced' accumulation based principally on the peasants (see Gramsci's notes on the absence of agrarian reform in the Risorgimento and in a more general sense on the place of the *Questione meridionale* in passive revolutions[56]), substitution of a bureaucratised party-state for class, loss of hegemony. ... In short, the absence of any socialist historical bloc.

2   Conversely, the realisation of the hegemony of the ruling classes within an 'economistic' restructuring of the productive forces paralyses the process of working-class autonomisation, strikes at its alliances and alters the relations between the economic and the political level; the state itself becomes 'an instrument of "rationalisation", of acceleration and of taylorism. It operates according to a plan'.[57] In such conditions, the factory itself becomes the centre of reunification of the social and the political. Every strategy of the 'war of position' is founded upon 'the whole organisational and industrial system'.[58]

These two critical corollaries therefore modify the topology of the classic schema of infrastructure-superstructure and thus the locus of politics as a determinant element in the overthrow of the mode of production. As soon as the state penetrates the economy and hegemonic apparatuses of civil society, it exists simultaneously both *within* and *outside* the economic base it is a political force both *within* the socio-economic realm and *outside* civil society. When Gramsci takes up certain points made by Lenin in his later years on the displacement of the position of politics in a transitional process, he *discovers a certain historicity* in the relation between the form of politics and the form of theory:[59]

> To the economic-corporate phase, to the phase of struggle for hegemony in civil society and to the phase of State power there correspond specific intellectual activities which cannot be arbitrarily improvised or anticipated. In the phase of struggle for hegemony it is the science of politics which is developed; in the State phase all the superstructures must be developed, if one is not to risk the dissolution of the State.

Such a passage acquires its full significance in regard to his own work in prison; Gramsci was able neither to 'improvise' nor to 'anticipate' arbitrarily the historico-theoretical phase whose prospectus he offers as a kind of critical and utopian vista: the development of all the superstructures, of a homogeneous and expansionary historical bloc whose end result is the withering away of the state. Gramsci located himself quite precisely in a phase of struggle for hegemony in the face of the processes of passive revolution whether in the West or in the East. The extension of Marx's celebrated text on the correspondence between the forces and relations of production so as to include all the relations between base and superstructure functions as a kind of *critical norm* which allows him to understand the whole pathological history of the processes of passive revolution: the history of Italy and of Europe, the authoritarian and bureaucratic deformations of the transition from one mode of production to another. From this non-linear history, which appeals to a 'pessimism of the intelligence' the better to develop an 'optimism of the will', Gramsci is to draw a single conclusion: it is necessary to *break* with every economistic conception of social reality. The rupture precisely concerns the conception of the state and its power; it consists in the passage from an instrumental and 'restricted' conception of the state (which sees it merely as government or as coercive apparatus) to a wider conception (domination plus hegemony). Yet such a break still bears the marks of a contradictory tension in the double role that it assumes is played by the concept of hegemony.

In effect, as recent debates have shown, hegemony serves both as a concept in the theorisation of the state and as a concept in its critique. In the one case, it functions as a corrective to any reductive analysis of the state in terms of political society and allows the concept of the state to include the totality of superstructures in their relations with the mass basis (hegemonic apparatuses). In the other case, it permits a critique of a political pathology (dictatorship without hegemony) and invites us to consider in what ways the domain of the state can and should be limited in a situation of class leadership and *real historical* bloc.

In contrast to all interpretations which attempt to resolve this antinomy by privileging one or another of its terms – in the one case, hegemony is regarded as a straightforward expansion of dictatorship,[60] in the other as a strategy leading to the removal of every coercive aspect of state action – Gramsci appears to incorporate both aspects of the contradiction when he offers a reinterpretation of the problematic of transition in terms of passive revolution. If, as certain passages suggest, one can interpret the morphology of transition as a politics in which *two kinds of wars of position* (not just one) are counterposed, and if these two wars remain profoundly asymmetrical in form, we cannot expect to draw any straightforward conclusion. The concept of hegemony is itself redoubled in an asymmetric fashion depending on whether it refers to the strategy of the dominant classes or to that of the subaltern classes in their struggle to replace the leadership of society.

For the dominant classes the extension of the state is always biased towards its 'reinforcement', with the proviso that this reinforcement relies upon mechanisms brought into operation through passive revolution, and takes place by means of new forms of *mass* (of the masses) integration within the state and hegemonic institutions. The presence of the masses in these institutions, the fact that the state becomes an ever more condensed embodiment, a materialisation (in its apparatuses) of the totality of social relations of force, brings about a radical alteration in the relations between war of position and war of manoeuvre:[61]

> The massive structures of the modern democracies, both as State organisations, and as complexes of associations in civil society, constitute for the art of politics as it were the 'trenches' and permanent fortifications of the front in the war of position: they render merely 'partial' the element of movement which before used to be 'the whole' of the war, etc.

The possibility of conducting a war of position in such conditions (the moment of rupture always remains, but it is 'partial') is linked to the capacity of the working class and its allies to invest these positions, to develop *a strategy of anti-passive revolution*. Gramsci outlines a certain number of institutional points of contact for this strategy. While it is useless to search for any kind of political pluralism at the level of the state in the gramscian analysis, what we do find instead is an *institutional pluralism* that matches the treatment he accords the state in the problematic of transition. Over and above the forms of democracy of the base, Gramsci stresses the decisive role of the party as the 'modern prince', that is to say, as a *mass* party. The insistence upon its mass character, the critique of any form of bureaucratic centralism and the argument in favour of a democratic centralism that can unite the political leadership to the movement at the base, are certainly not new. They are to be found, for example, in the polemical correspondence between Gramsci and Togliatti on the matter of opposition in the USSR in 1926. Gramsci does not hide his disapproval of the effects produced by the centralist-authoritarian methods of the Communist Party of the Soviet Union (CPSU), when he notes that such methods cannot fail to crystallise 'both left and right wing deviations', to impair the 'function of leadership that the Communist Party of the USSR had achieved under Lenin's impulse'[62] and, furthermore, to undermine the very capacity for 'revolutionisation' of the masses in the West.

All the same, even if the idea is not that original, it acquires a new theoretical dimension from the moment in which Gramsci connects the problem of bureaucratic centralism with the passive revolution itself and with its effects. As witness to this, there is a decisive passage in which Gramsci, commenting on the critical character of the theory of passive revolution in relation to the two principles proclaimed by Marx in the *Preface*, adds: 'revision of certain sectarian ideas on the theory of the party, theories which precisely represent a form of fatalism of a "divine right" type; development of the concepts of mass party and small élite party, and *mediation between the two*'.[63]

The full import of such a *mediation*, which modifies the classic form of the party such as Lenin envisaged it, and postulates a new dialectic of the economico-social and the political which alters the very frontiers of politics, extending them to the diverse positions occupied by hegemony (hegemonic apparatuses, the intellectuals), is discoverable in the strategic effects of passive revolution. For the working class, the extension of the state constitutes a strategy of transition. Hence we find again the two forms of its enlargement which were mentioned before; but they co-exist in an unresolved historical and political antinomy. If Gramsci explores the conditions of an anti-passive revolution, he none the less does not provide any *resolution of it in terms of the state*, for the reason that there is no theory of the state in transition which is adequate to such a historical process. It does not exist, and in a certain sense, for historical and theoretical reasons, it could not exist. In that it reflects for the first time upon the relations between theory of passive revolution and theory of transition, is not Gramsci's marxism as a *marxism of transition* also a *marxism in transition*, a marxism that is critical, open-ended and creative? Today our task is to resolve, in what are different historical conditions, but *on the basis of certain instruments provided* by his work, the theoretical and political problem that is presented by the simultaneous development on the one hand of a certain form of passive revolution (that includes new features deriving from the present crisis of capitalism), and on the other, of a new type of democratic, pluralist, transitional state which can no longer be understood in terms of the classic state of parliamentary right with its eternal formal separation between political society and civil society.

In contrast to stalinism and social democracy – which are the two, strangely complicit, forms of passive revolution of the twentieth century – an anti-passive democratic transition must be based on non-bureaucratic expansion of the forms of political life within the totality of structures encompassed by the 'enlarged state' (from the base to the various hegemonic apparatuses). For as Gramsci rightly noted from 1930 onwards, the masses are no longer 'atomised', but are well organised and are dispersed throughout the entire complex of social institutions. Furthermore, this structure of modern democracy, so essential for the conduct of a war of position, has been shown to be inseparable from the existence of 'great mass political parties' and 'great economic trade unions'.[64]

This expansion of non-instrumental forms of politics means that the working class operates today in a relatively new political terrain – that of democracy as a form of class struggle and transition. But though this is a terrain somewhat different (because of the contemporary transformations of capitalism) from that examined by Gramsci, it nevertheless remains the locus of an internal confrontation between two 'wars of position'. What we need to define, therefore, is *the form* of a transitional state that is capable of offering, in opposition to the various passive revolutions immanent to the crisis, a new political dialectic between representative democracy and that democracy of the base which is central to gramscian thought. This *is* a dialectic; it is not a frontal opposition between the two that destroys the power of both or absorbs the one into the other as a result of some new reformist policy that would identify the transition simply with a change of government. In this perspective, the gramscian theory of passive revolution is more than a critical correlate of the marxian problematic of transition; it offers a theoretical and political instrument of relevance to our present situation.

Notes

This chapter was originally published in *Politica e Storia in Gramsci*, vol. 1, Rome, Editori Riuniti, 1977, and was translated into English by Kate Soper.

1 *Quaderni del Carcere*, ed. V. Gerratana, Turin, Einaudi, 1975, p. 1827. English translation in *Selections from the Prison Notebooks*, ed. and trans. Q. Hoare and G. Nowell Smith, London, Lawrence & Wishart, 1971, p. 114. Wherever the citation is of passages from the *Quaderni* which are included in the *Selections from Prison Notebooks*, the reference is given to both the Italian and the English translation.
2 *Quaderni*, p. 1774, *Prison Notebooks*, p. 106.
3 Ibid., *Prison Notebooks*, p. 107. The emphases in the quotations are usually mine.
4 Ibid., p. 1827, *Prison Notebooks*, p. 114 (author's italics).
5 Ibid., p. 1227, *Prison Notebooks*, p. 119 (author's italics).
6 Here and elsewhere I have followed normal English usage in translating *direzione* as 'leadership', but it should be kept in mind that Gramsci uses the group of words centred around the verb *dirigere* (*dirigente, direttivo, direzione*, etc.) to mark a crucial conceptual difference between power based on 'domination' (*dominio*) and the exercise of 'direction' or 'hegemony'. Cf. *Prison Notebooks*, pp. xiii–xiv, 55–6 n. (author's italics).
7 *Quaderni*, p. 41, *Prison Notebooks*, p. 59.
8 Ibid., p. 1827, *Prison Notebooks*, p. 114.
9 Ibid., p. 2140, *Prison Notebooks*, pp. 279–80.
10 Antonio Gramsci, *La costruzione del partito comunista*, Turin, 1971, p. 139; *Selections from Political Writings 1921–26*, trans. and ed. Q. Hoare, London, Lawrence & Wishart, 1978, p. 443.
11 *Quaderni*, p. 1767, *Prison Notebooks*, p. 109.
12 'Gramsci's general theory of marxism', translated in this volume, p. 151.
13 I shall not take up here themes that I have discussed elsewhere (cf. C. Buci-Glucksmann, *Gramsci et l'État*, Paris, 1975). It scarcely needs saying that Gramsci diverged not only politically but also *theoretically* from the line, and the 'marxism' it upheld, of the Third International in the years 1929–30.
14 *Quaderni*, pp. 2287–8, *Prison Notebooks*, p. 52.
15 Ibid., p. 2288, *Prison Notebooks*, p. 52.
16 Ibid.

17 Gramsci, *La construzione del partito comunista*, p. 347, *Selections from Political Writings*, pp. 418, 419.
18 *Quaderni*, p. 2156.
19 Gramsci, 'Produzione e politica', *L 'Ordine Nuovo*, no. 13, 1920.
20 *Quaderni*, p. 1818.
21 Ibid., p. 2288, *Prison Notebooks*, p. 52.
22 On the specificity of the gramscian concept of hegemonic crisis relative to Lenin's concept of revolutionary crisis or to the analysis of the Third International, cf. my contribution in *La Crise de l'État*, Paris, Presses Universitaires de France, 1976.
23 *La construzione*, p. 343.
24 *Quaderni*, p. 1325.
25 Ibid., p. 747.
26 Ibid.
27 Ibid., p. 1822, *Prison Notebooks*, p. 104.
28 Ibid., p. 937.
29 Ibid., p. 764, *Prison Notebooks*, p. 263.
30 Cf. *Gramsci et l'État*, especially the first part, 'L'État comme problème theorique'.
31 *Quaderni*, p. 1822, *Prison Notebooks*, p. 105.
32 *Quaderni*, p. 1823, *Prison Notebooks*, pp. 105–6.
33 Ibid., p. 747.
34 Ibid.
35 Ibid., p. 1823, *Prison Notebooks*, p. 106.
36 Ibid., p. 1139, *Prison Notebooks*, p. 189. Gramsci here explains bureaucratic centralism as the result of a lack of initiative at the base, which he connects with a political 'immaturity'. Compare this with his remarks elsewhere on the role of the police in political parties and their function in the bureaucracy (ibid., p. 1634).
37 Ibid., p. 1615. There is no point in dwelling here upon these remarks which are so frequently quoted; *Prison Notebooks*, p. 235.
38 Ibid., p. 1767, *Prison Notebooks*, p. 108.
39 On the relations between cultural revolution and historical bloc cf. *Quaderni*, p. 451. I shall not develop the point, which is already contained in the critique of Bukharin; I consider that it goes without saying that the modification of the relations leaders/led, rulers/ruled, intellectuals/people, and the transformation of habits, customs and norms, that is, of 'life-style', that takes in a cultural revolution are necessary features of any 'anti-passive' revolution.
40 *Quaderni*, p. 1228, *Prison Notebooks*, p. 120.
41 Ibid., p. 1089. The discovery of the affinity between fascism and passive revolution is the outcome of a critique of Croce's cultural position, which was the ideological representation in Italy of 'passive revolution'. For its French equivalent, Gramsci refers principally to Proudhon.
42 Ibid., p. 1089.
43 Ibid., p. 1228, *Prison Notebooks*, pp. 119–20.
44 Ibid.

45 Ibid., pp. 2139, 2140, *Prison Notebooks*, pp. 279–80.
46 Ibid., p. 2177.
47 Nicola Badaloni, *Il marxismo di Gramsci*, Turin, Einaudi, 1975, p. 152.
48 *Quaderni*, p. 2146, *Prison Notebooks*, p. 286.
49 On these direct relations between Gramsci and Marx, and for a reinterpretation of hegemony on the basis of *Capital*, see the work of Biagio De Giovanni, *La teoria politica delle classi nel 'Capitale'*, Bari, De Donato, 1976.
50 *Quaderni*, p. 1312.
51 Ibid.
52 Ibid., p. 1283. It is from this that Gramsci derives the political character and morphology of crisis: 'The morphology of the crisis is *political* because the contradictory process whereby organised labour can come to occupy a "fundamentally" different position in the exercise of the economy is itself political' (De Giovanni, op. cit., p. 303).
53 *Quaderni*, p. 1138. On the contemporary relevance of this gramscian problematic cf. Bruno Trentin, *Da sfruttati a produttori*, Bari, De Donato, 1977.
54 *Quaderni*, p. 1591, *Prison Notebooks*, p. 161.
55 Ibid., pp. 489, 2164, *Prison Notebooks*, p. 301.
56 Cf. 'Some Aspects of the Southern Question' in *Selections from Prison Writings*, pp. 441 ff.
57 *Quaderni*, p. 1571, *Prison Notebooks*, p. 247.
58 Ibid., p. 1615, *Prison Notebooks*, p. 234.
59 Ibid., p. 1493, *Prison Notebooks*, pp. 403–4.
60 Cf. M. Salvadori, 'Gramsci and the PCI: two conceptions of hegemony', in this volume, pp. 237–58.
61 *Quaderni*, p. 1567, *Prison Notebooks*, p. 243.
62 *La costruzione del partito comunista*, p. 145, *Selections from Political Writings*, pp. 429, 430.
63 *Quaderni*, p. 1827, *Prison Notebooks*, p. 114.
64 Ibid., p. 1566, *Prison Notebooks*, p. 243.

7 Gramsci and the PCI: two conceptions of hegemony

Massimo Salvadori

Hegemony and/or dictatorship of the proletariat

The original meaning of the term 'hegemony' is an amalgam of two elements: the idea of command on the part of whoever exercises hegemony and the idea that this command is enforced by whoever holds it. with the following objectives in view: 1 to 'lead' the allies; 2 to undertake with them violent action against one or several hostile groups. It would thus appear that, in its double meaning, the concept of hegemony implies on the one hand the attempt to achieve consensus within a bloc of alliances and, on the other, domination of hostile groups achieved by means of force. These two aspects are absolutely indissociable.

It is common knowledge that, in contemporary Italian political culture – and not only Italian – the debate on hegemony and its implications is linked with the work of Antonio Gramsci and, in particular, with the meaning of the concept of hegemony in the *Prison Notebooks*. And so it can be universally asserted that Gramsci today appears above all as the 'theoretician of hegemony'. The particular attention devoted to Gramsci's theory of hegemony is rooted in the research carried out by the Partito Comunista Italiano (PCI) on the forms of a route to socialism adapted to the complexity of the development of civil society and the state in the industrially developed countries. This in the full knowledge that the 'model' of socialism represented by the socialist countries of the bolshevist-stalinist type is nowadays no longer either attainable or desirable. The work of Gramsci, and more particularly the *Prison Notebooks*, is considered by communist theoreticians and ideologists as a central stage, a link between leninism and post-leninism. What might be called the most common

237

interpretations and those which are of a more directly political kind (that of Luciano Gruppi is a good example), tend to suggest a reading according to which Gramsci has accomplished a sort of theoretical 'rotation', at the beginning of which he was within the bounds of leninism and the leninist perspective. Yet ultimately, and specifically when he had completed the elaboration of the 'theory of hegemony', he opened the way to the current strategy of the PCI which is founded on an acceptance of 'pluralism', on political democracy, on a dialogue between different political forces, and on a strategy of reforms.

Of Gramsci's theory which is contained in the *Prison Notebooks* the elements which are now most in use concern:

1   the necessity, for a force which intends to found a new state, to be 'hegemonic' even before assuming power;
2   the necessity for the proletariat to form a 'bloc' of historical forces so as to be able to express the complexity of civil society;
3   the necessity to assign a crucial role to liaison with the intellectuals;
4   the necessity to undertake in the West a struggle which takes precise account of the differences between the forms of social revolution in Russia and the forms of a revolutionary process in the bourgeois developed countries, in short, to take account of the *lessons* stemming from the failure of the revolution in Central and Western Europe in the period immediately following the First World War.

A political problem

It is not only natural but also just that a force with the political weight of the PCI should tend to use its theoretical 'tradition' and above all those aspects of it which are linked with the person of its greatest thinker. But having said this, it seems to me that the debate must be carried on to a more fertile plane, that is on to the level of the modalities of this sort of usage.

A question of *method* ('comment') of such a kind may use as its starting-point two requirements which can remain separate yet which it is good to take in close conjunction. The first of these is historical in character and consists in determining the exact significance of Gramsci's theory, of its 'message' ('lettre') and inherent aims and nature. The second requirement is of a more strictly political kind and concerns elucidation of the relation between theory and policy. The required elucidation may be expressed in the following question: Is the attempt mounted so purposefully by the PCI to present its current strategy ('the historical compromise') as being founded on the implications of Gramsci's theory of hegemony legitimate or not? Let me explain in more detail. By raising a question of legitimacy at this point, it is by no means my intention to tackle a problem of the historiographic determination of concepts, but rather a political problem, since, depending on the 'authenticity' of the reference to Gramsci, a different judgement on the PCI of today will necessarily follow. There is a clear difference between a party whose policy is characterised by unity of theory and practice and a party which lives by the at least partly instrumental utilisation of the ideas of its greatest theoretician, whence the rupture – quite uncharacteristic of Gramsci – between a certain dimension of the theory (which consists in quoting Gramsci as justification) and its praxis. If it were possible to assert that in the theory and practice of the PCI there was a *fundamental* continuity with Gramsci's theory, this would mean that the actions of the communists are always what may be termed 'leninist-revolutionary' in inspiration, in a sense the historical roots of which go back to 1917; in the opposite case, the PCI would have to be asked to explain in more specific terms both the true nature of its relation to the bolshevik tradition and its 'nature' as a socialist force. It can, in my view, be asserted without contradiction that the absence of adequate elucidation of the relation between theory and practice leads not only to theoretical but also practical 'empiricism'.

To be more explicit, the PCI is the most important party of the Italian left and enjoys great popular success; much more so than the Partito Socialista Italiano (PSI) it has succeeded in conducting a very broad policy on the ideological front. In conclusion, it represents the central and decisive force of the Italian left and, at the international level, carries increasing weight. For this reason it bears the greatest responsibilities, for the problems with which it is confronted are inevitably, directly or indirectly, those encountered in Italy by the left as a whole.

The leaders of the PCI at various levels constantly invoke this force as an effective proof of a theoretical and practical capacity which alone ought to make its critics prudent. Two observations may be made on this point. The first is that history has already provided examples of socialist and workers' parties which, having attained the maximum of their power in terms of electoral consensus, solidity and the extent of their power base in the popular masses, find themselves in a strategic 'impasse', which is also characterised by a rupture between theory and practice (consider only German social democracy on the eve of the First

World War or the Italian Socialist Party in the 1920s). The second observation is that, at all events, the PCI ought – if it has not already done so – to give careful consideration to the fact that, to put it a trifle bluntly, to an appreciable extent its present strength stems, from the sort of rent that the '*malgoverno*' of the Democrazia Cristiana (DC) and the historical weaknesses of bourgeois domination have virtually offered to the principal opposition party (causing inter-classist heterogeneous forces to flock towards it), forces which had good reason to be disgusted with the DC and to be disillusioned by the incapacity or impossibility of the PSI to determine in a decisive way the reforming action of the governments of the period of the 'centre-left'. This explains the obscure, heterogeneous character of the passive discontent of a certain base of 'consensus' recently obtained by the PCI. Faced with a phenomenon of such a kind, it is of the greatest importance for all the left to 'settle its accounts' objectively with theoretical questions, with a view to elucidating the theoretical premises of practice in full knowlege of the facts. If this is not done, the strategic choices will be most precarious; without this knowledge, the base of broad consensus which the forces of the left enjoy today could, in the longer term, become an element of ruin. Indeed, only a clear theoretical perspective, or at least the determination of a clear problematic, can prevent one of the important components of this consensus from being subject to sudden changes of fortune.

All this being said, I believe that one of the ways of determining a theoretical problematic in correct terms resides in the answer to the question: is the present strategy of the PCI 'compatible' with that which is indicated by Gramsci? And, more specifically, is the line of 'hegemony' followed by the PCI comparable to the 'theory of hegemony' held by Gramsci? It is clear that if I reply – and let me state immediately that this is my own case – that there is neither political continuity nor intrinsic conceptual homogeneity between the two terms opposed, this does not mean that treason has been committed but, by thus raising the issue of ambiguity it becomes possible to establish pointers for a determination of the real nature of the present conception of hegemony held by the PCI, to conduct a realistic debate on the reasons which have lead the PCI to a different evolution, and to analyse the greater or lesser validity of one or the other conception of hegemony in relation to present tasks.

The orthodox interpretation of Gramsci

I think that all debate on the 'theory of hegemony' elaborated by Gramsci must take account of the following requirements:

1 an investigation of its origins and their relation to subsequent developments in order to reach some conclusions on the essential question of whether these developments introduced qualitative changes, with respect to the origins of the theory, which might open the way to different perspectives;
2 an examination of whether the developments of the theory have implications in Gramsci which could substantially modify the leninist theory of the dictatorship of the proletariat;
3 an examination of whether the final point of Gramsci's thought as it appears in the *Prison Notebooks* does or does not allow one, even if only *in nuce*, to consider hegemony as anything other than dictatorship of the proletariat, or whether for Gramsci hegemony always remains a means of adding to the meanings of the theory of dictatorship.

This is absolutely not a merely academic discussion for it is common knowledge that the PCI is today developing a theory of socialist power which can no longer be likened to a theory of dictatorship of the proletariat. Yet the ideologists of the PCI assert that its strategy is, so to speak, 'directly related' to the ideas of Gramsci.

Luciano Gruppi has gone furthest along this road, and with the utmost clarity.[1] His interpretation of Gramsci's 'theory of hegemony' is roughly as follows: Gramsci's starting-point is leninism; during the strictly leninist phase, hegemony represented for Gramsci a direct manifestation of dictatorship of the proletariat. Confronted with the defeat of the worker movement at the beginning of the 1920s, Gramsci embarked upon a phase of elaboration founded on the East/West dichotomy of which the *Prison Notebooks* are the finished conceptual expression. The end result for Gramsci is a reflexion on leninism which results in a conception of hegemony leading not explicitly but potentially, or better still methodologically, to what Gruppi terms an enrichment of the leninist conception of the state as state can no longer be regarded only as an oppressive machine which has to be 'broken'[2] (it is truly difficult to imagine a more ambiguous use of the term 'enrichment' than this).

In consideration of which Gruppi adds, significantly, a phrase which

conveys, even if a trifle hermetically, the 'essence' of his interpretation:
'The consequences this can entail in theory and practice are clear to see'
and he adds

> the whole conception of an Italian road to socialism would be
> inexplicable if the principle of hegemony was not the starting-point.
> ... The point of a complete strategy and tactic of alliances would be
> lost. ... The relation between reform and revolution would be lost. ...
> The conception of the *new party*, in short of a party which does not
> limit itself to negative opposition, to the propagandist expression of
> the solution offered by socialism, but which actively intervenes in
> order to determine and resolve the problems which are 'concretely
> posed' would also be lost.

It is impossible to show more clearly the elements of an interpretation of
the continuity of the line followed by Gramsci and that followed by the
present PCI (whose relevance is in no way diminished by Gruppi's
essay, dated 1967, to which I am referring).

The crux of the question is, therefore, whether Gramsci truly opened
the way to a conception in which the state (with all its consequences) is
no longer to be broken? Did Gramsci in essence pose the premises for
the transition from a conception in which the state as the expression of
dictatorship of the proletariat, 'proletarian democracy', is the opposite of
bourgeois parliamentary democracy and marxist ideology is an ideology
of 'total antithesis', to another conception in which the bourgeois state as
state is not to be 'broken', 'pluralist' democracy is the expression of
liberal parliamentary democratic institutions and 'ideological hegemony'
is a 'peaceful' confrontation between the ideologies produced by the
different social and political forces? Is Gramsci the father of a conception
of 'hegemony' as an 'enrichment of dictatorship of the proletariat',
which in fact lays the foundations for a rejection of such dictatorship?

The experience of the councils

When Gramsci wrote in 1926 that, during the period of the *Ordine
Nuovo*, 'the Turin communists had concretely posed the question of the
hegemony of the proletariat, in other words, of the social base of
proletarian dictatorship and the worker state', he was giving a correct
assessment of his own experience by seeing, in the strategy of the factory
councils, the origin of his conception of hegemony as an instrument

enabling the proletariat to 'mobilise the majority of the working population against capitalism and the bourgeois state'.

What was Gramsci's chief preoccupation during the period of the councils? He was fully aware that the simple use of force, while in exceptional circumstances permitting accession to power, could in no way serve as a base for a society moving towards socialism. The pages concerning the necessity for the party to be enveloped in a halo of 'prestige' deriving from its capacity to rule, and the necessity to avoid succumbing to the temptations of authoritarianism and bureaucracy, are too well known to refer to again. The full import of Gramsci's experience of the councils will never be appreciated unless, even more than as an attempt to indicate a 'technical' solution of proletarian power to the problems of production, it is viewed as the search for a terrain to provide a social hegemonic base for the projected dictatorship of the proletariat. His pithy assertion that 'the factory council is a model of the proletarian state' is no more than a brilliant and picturesque way of asserting that there can be no true political domination without social rule and it is also a way of denouncing the limitations of a party dictatorship which is passed off as dictatorship of the proletariat. At the same time it is evident that the strategy of hegemony during the period of the councils is the supreme instrument not of a 'broadening' of democracy, but of a reversal of the established order: the council is the antithesis of employers' power in the factory, and an attempt by the proletariat to form alliances with the peasantry and the intellectuals as a means to break the social bloc of the bourgeoisie; the 'intellectual and moral reform' of the masses being the desired objective in order to destroy bourgeois-capitalist hegemony over society and to render the domination of the state, which is the expression of it, impossible.

This series of antitheses remained at the root of Gramsci's political thought until its completion. But if this is true, it follows that *a theory of the state, of social alliances, of the role of the intellectuals, which culminated in a repudiation of the 'mobilisation against capitalism and the bourgeois state' instead of thinking this mobilisation in terms of the creation of a 'social base for the dictatorship of the proletariat and the worker state', cannot make any claim to be Gramsci's own.*

The steps of Gramsci's reasoning during the years 1919–20 can be rapidly retraced. He starts out from the hypothesis common to the revolutionary movement which takes bolshevism as its model, to the effect that in *general historical terms* the First World War had marked the demise of capitalism. By condemning this hypothesis, it was his concern to discover how a system of dictatorship of the proletariat could be achieved in Italy which would give that dictatorship an *expansive* character with the power to tackle two tasks positively, namely management of the productive machinery and the construction of a bloc of social forces which, as a whole, would be capable of mature and therefore successful opposition to the dominant bloc. *The germ of the theory of hegemony resided precisely in the awareness that the use of mere force against the hostile classes does not lead to the success of the revolution unless the revolution attains proper social maturity, in other words, unless a sufficient reserve of political consensus and technical and managerial capacity is built up.* For Gramsci, the council of workers and peasants was the melting-pot, the original and fundamental nucleus of the revolutionary party's rule over the mass of the producers and of dictatorship over the classes to be overthrown. As in a sense Gramsci took for granted the 'objective' maturation of the revolution, his problem was to construct its 'subjective' maturation.

The revolution in the West

When in 1923–4, after what we shall term the 'bordigan' period, Gramsci opposed his own line to that followed by Bordiga, he explained his theory of hegemony with new-found clarity. But this explanation is not a mechanical reiteration of the theories of the period of the councils, as the situation was new and somewhat complex. One should ponder for a moment the meaning of Gramsci's sudden realisation of this complexity and relate it to his objectives. In a letter of February 1924, Gramsci asserts that in the West[3]

> [the situation] is complicated by all these political superstructures, created by the greater development of capitalism. This makes the action of the masses slower and more prudent, and therefore requires of the revolutionary party a strategy and tactics altogether more complex and long-term than those which were necessary for the Bolsheviks in the period between March and November 1917.

Here Gramsci perfectly anticipates what he was later to write in the *Prison Notebooks* on the differences between East and West. But what other elements does he correlate with this aspect of his argument? In short, what is his purpose in emphasising the 'complexity' of the West? To initiate a 'new' discussion on the state and on the social components of the historical bloc? To elaborate a conception of hegemony which is expressed in a formula which modifies the projected building of dictatorship and permits the initiation of a policy of alliances of a 'democratic' type? On the contrary; his argument is entirely founded, on the one hand, on the awareness of the 'supplementary' difficulties created by the greater development achieved by capitalist society in the West and, on the other hand, on the search for a strategy which would make it possible to achieve a result identical to that achieved by the Russian Bolsheviks. The difference which he aims to establish between the West and bolshevism is based entirely upon a more complex and let us say more 'mature' conception of the dictatorship of the proletariat. This is why, when reflecting on the 'differences' between East and West, Gramsci is able to assert that the objective to aim for is the achievement of 'the conditions in which the Russian Bosheviks found themselves when their party was constituted'.

In short, the difficulty for Gramsci consists in overcoming all the obstacles which the complexity of bourgeois society in the West, with the creation of an 'aristocracy of the workers and its adjuncts, union bureaucracy and democratic social groups', opposes to the *bolshevisation* of the proletariat and, thanks to the deep-rooted existence of 'democratic' forces, to arrive at a policy of alliances which would permit the creation of a revolutionary 'historical bloc'. Consequently, the perspective which Gramsci aims to give to the worker movement and his conception of 'hegemony' are wholly determined by the idea of defeating: first, social democracy; second, the forces of bourgeois 'democracy'. Gramsci is aware that, by contrast with the Russian situation, the revolution and bolshevism cannot succeed in the West unless, *even before* the revolution, a displacement of forces in a revolutionary sense is provoked which would have the power to ensure an adequate foundation, on an 'autonomous' base, for the eventual running of the modern productive apparatus and the state.

The Theses of Lyons

If one reads the *Theses of Lyons* of 1926,[4] in order to see what they really contain, it will be seen that they are informed by the need for 'bolshevisation', in other words, for the struggle against 'tendencies which represented a deviation in relation to the principles and the practice of the revolutionary class struggle', against 'utopian democracies' as regards the state, against the 'chain of reactionary forces' which stretches from the fascist to the maximalist party, passing through the 'anti-facist groups' of the liberals, the democrats, the soldiers, the Popular Party, the Republican Party and the Social Reformist Party. Similarly, various regional 'democratic' parties, such as the Sardinian Action Party, represent an 'obstacle' to the creation of an alliance between workers and peasantry under the direction of the PCI. The attention devoted to 'sectorial struggles' serves the aim of dictatorship of the proletariat and the 'foundation of the worker state'. The final points of the *Theses*[5] (42–4) clearly indicate the relation between a form of tactics which purposely use 'democratic' slogans and a strategy which aims to exclude any solution which does not lead to the proletarian state founded on dictatorship. The role of the tactics of the single front 'as political action of the "movement" type', is the creation of the premises for the effective 'leadership' of the masses by the Communist Party and the winning over of the majority within them. It would fail if it did not make it possible to 'expose the so-called proletarian and revolutionary parties and groups'. Moreover, it is in relation to the question of the determination of an effective route towards dictatorship that Gramsci introduces his observation that the tactic of a single front and the tactical adoption of 'democratic' slogans have become necessary, for there does exist among the masses an adherence to the parties and groups which must be politically destroyed. This adherence makes the 'frontal struggle' inopportune in certain circumstances.

This problem must therefore be regarded as containing the origin of the assertion made in the *Prison Notebooks* that the 'war of movement' must be *delayed* until the 'war of position' has borne fruit. This is why there is no opposition between the two concepts of 'war', but rather a functional correlation. One cannot begin the assault on the seizure of power (worker state and dictatorship of the proletariat) until the struggle in the trenches has opened the way to success: yet the assault on the destruction of the adversary remains the supreme goal. So much so that the conclusion of the *Theses* (the expression of a cycle of thought of which the 'Alcuni temi sulla questione meridionale' are a particular clarification) is as follows: the formula 'workers' and peasants' government' (a slogan which to some extent can be labelled 'democratic')[6]

> is an agitational slogan, but only corresponds to a real phase of
> historical development in the same sense as the intermediate solutions
> dealt with in the preceding paragraph. The party cannot conceive of a

realisation of this slogan except as the beginning of a direct revolutionary struggle: i.e. of a civil war waged by the proletariat, in alliance with the peasantry, with the aim of winning power. The party could be led into serious deviations from its task as leader of the revolution if it were to interpret the workers' and peasants' government as corresponding to a real phase of development of the struggle for power: in other words, if it considered that this slogan indicated the possibility for the problem of the State to be resolved in the interests of the working class in any other form than the dictatorship of the proletariat.

Thus, at the same time as Gramsci arrives at a precise awareness (identical in all respects to that expressed in the *Prison Notebooks*) of the differences between East and West and at the same time as he expresses, in *Alcuni temi*, the conception of the maturity of the 'theory of hegemony' and the 'historical bloc', he also explains quite unequivocally the actual meaning of his strategy, namely dictatorship of the proletariat and the worker state. *What is it therefore which sets Gramsci apart from the most 'retrograde' partisans of dictatorship and the worker state? It is that he does not think to found dictatorship and the state on force alone, for he is convinced that this cannot resolve the problems related to the building of a new society. Such a task requires the active consensus of the working masses which must be expressed in the framework of the institutions arising from the revolution and the destruction of the apparatus of bourgeois government.*

Gramsci develops this aspect because it concerns not merely Italian and more generally Western strategy, but also the strategy of Russia. It is in this way – in the light of his theory of hegemony – that the assertion made to Togliatti can be read, to the effect that[7]

> Today, at nine years distance from October 1917, it is no longer *the fact of the seizure of power* by the Bolsheviks which can revolutionise the Western masses, because this has already been allowed for and has produced its effects. What is active today, ideologically and politically, is the conviction (if it exists) that the proletariat, once power has been taken, *can construct socialism*.

All the reservations expressed by Gramsci with regard to the methods of Stalin are motivated by the concern that a capacity for hegemony might fail to materialise in Russia and that *domination* might unilaterally triumph over *leadership*.

I am convinced that what characterises Gramsci and his theory of hegemony is not at all the fact that he introduced elements which are calculated to prepare the way for a conception of the state of the liberal-parliamentary type and to a national path, in the sense that the PCI uses this today, but rather the fact that this theory is the most elaborate and complex expression of his attempt to give dictatorship of the proletariat an adequate foundation, so that Gramsci is the most 'independent' and even the most autonomous disciple, but in all respects he is indeed the disciple of leninist doctrine. He was so, and it was fully his intention to remain so in 1926. Do the *Prison Notebooks* open a new phase, and in what sense?

Hegemony as foundations of dictatorship

There is no need to seek to minimise the meaning of the way Gramsci characterises Lenin in the *Prison Notebooks*, in the very place, that is, where the theory of hegemony attains 'philosophical' completion. On the subject of Lenin, he makes two fundamental assertions which must be examined in their conceptual unity:

1　Lenin must be regarded as having laid the foundation for the theory 'the theoretico-practical principle of hegemony has also epistemological significance, and it is here that Ilich's greatest theoretical contribution to the philosophy of praxis should be sought.'[8]

2　But Lenin 'did not have enough time to develop his formula'. Yet where does Gramsci find that Lenin 'falls short'? It is specifically in the indications concerning the transition in the West from a 'war of position' to a 'war of movement' in order, after all, to achieve dictatorship of the proletariat. It is a true distortion of the facts to imagine that the corollary of Gramsci's attempt to develop leninism on the base of an awareness of the differences between East and West is a 'shelving' of the leninist theory of the state and the objective of dictatorship of the proletariat.

When he states – in a formula which has become famous, and which for him possesses the value of a general principle in a science of politics – that 'the supremacy of any social group is expressed in two ways, as "domination" and as "intellectual and moral leadership",'[9] Gramsci expresses himself with exemplary clarity. It is in no way his concern to minimise the sense of the necessity for a dominant class to politically and socially destroy its enemies; on the contrary, he fully insists on this idea. What he aims to explain is that *force alone does not suffice*, far from it, for the use of force alone is a sign of the historical immaturity of those who claim to found a new state; a dominant class cannot govern unless, while it exercises its domination (dictatorship) over its enemies, it is at the same time able to obtain a consensus of allied social forces (which nevertheless need *a tendentially homogeneous social and economic base*), which is the object of its leadership. Hegemony is therefore the same as dictatorship, a dictatorship which, furthermore – and this is the decisive element – professes to be something other than the dictatorship of a political force which lacks the ability to direct the indispensable economico-social forces to the new type of operation of the material and intellectual production.

If one takes all this into account, the following becomes crystal clear: 'a social group is dominant in relation to the hostile groups which it aims to eliminate or to bring into submission even by the use of armed force and it is ruling in relation to kindred, allied groups'. Gramsci then adds: 'a social group can and must be ruling even before winning governmental power.' He pursues a line of reasoning which coincides perfectly with the views he held in 1926 regarding the impossibility of seizing power unless one has first won over leadership of allied groups by means of 'tactical' movements capable of destroying the influence which the 'chain of reactionary forces' has begun to exercise over the masses. In the West what this implies specifically is the destruction of the forms through which bourgeois hegemony is achieved, even if this is through the 'democrats' and the pseudo-socialists.

The whole theory of 'democratic centralism' in the *Prison Notebooks* is aimed at enforcing the principle of leadership from the top downwards in the revolutionary party and constitutes a specification of hegemony within the party of which one further specification is the relation between the party taken as a whole and the allies. Who are these allies? For Gramsci they are always, and solely, economic and social forces and not other parties which would remain in an autonomous and different perspective from that opened by dictatorship of the proletariat.

Marxism as total philosophy

Close consideration should be given to the way Gramsci returns again and again in the *Prison Notebooks* to the 'total' character of marxism and the impossibility, on account of the unity between theory and praxis, for it to form the object of a 'dialogue' with other world-views. On the contrary, marxism is merely a means of winning over enemy positions in order to substitute one hegemony for another. Lastly, it should be noted that the 'total' character of marxism is one of the dimensions of the projected dictatorship of the proletariat, in other words, of a democracy of a new type, because it is built within the institutions of the proletarian state as an antithesis to the bourgeois state. Regarding this 'total' character, Gramsci writes that the[9]

> Orthodoxy ... is ... to be looked for ... in the fundamental concept that the philosophy of praxis is 'sufficient unto itself', that it contains in itself all the fundamental elements needed to construct a total and integral conception of the world, a total philosophy and theory of natural science, and not only that but everything that is needed to give life to an integral and practical organisation of society, that is, to become a total integral civilisation. ... A theory is 'revolutionary' precisely to the extent that it is an element of conscious separation and distinction into two camps and is a peak inaccessible to the enemy camp. To maintain that the philosophy of praxis is not a completely autonomous and independent structure of thought in antagonism to all traditional philosophies and religions, means in reality that one has not severed one's links with the old world, if indeed one has not actually capitulated.

Gramsci continues by defining the conception of the party which splits the unity of theory and practice and which permits its 'members to regroup into idealists, materialists, atheists, catholics, etc.' as 'the most abject and vile opportunism'. It is only with this in mind that it is possible to understand the sense of Gramsci's valorisation of the cultural factor and the ethico-political aspect of hegemony, the aim of which is to seek an expansion of marxism in its struggle against all other conceptions of life and politics. When he writes that 'the most recent phase' in the development of the philosophy of praxis consists 'on the one hand precisely in this claim that the moment of hegemony is essential to his conception of the state and on the other hand in the "valorisation" of the cultural fact, of cultural activity, of the necessity for a cultural front as against the purely economic and political fronts,' he is merely affirming the necessity, for the state-power, of a proper base of consensus, obtained through victorious struggle against the other conceptions of the state, of politics and of life in general. It is a way of reaffirming the fact that since the simple moment of force is necessary yet does not permit the achievement of consensus, the limits of the extension of the consensus which is to be acquired depend on a determined conception of the state. It is not fortuitously that Gramsci traces the origin of the elaboration of the theory of hegemony he is seeking to develop back to Lenin:[10]

> the greatest modern theoretician of the philosophy of praxis, ... on the terrain of political struggle and organisation and with a political terminology, gave new weight – in opposition to the various 'economist' tendencies – to the front of cultural struggle, and constructed the doctrine of hegemony as a complement to the theory of the State-as-force, and as the present form of the Forty-Eightist doctrine of 'permanent revolution'.

The highest expression of leninism

A further aspect of Gramsci's idea of the meaning of hegemony and its relation to dictatorship is revealed when he examines the conceptions held by Croce and Gentile. Gramsci notes that:

1 for Gentile, 'History is entirely State history', 'hegemony and dictatorship are indistinguishable', and in this (unilateral) sense, 'force and consent are simply equivalent' and 'only the State, and of course the State-as-government, exists';
2 for Croce, history 'is on the other hand ethico-political', in other words, he 'seeks to maintain a distinction between civil society and political society, between hegemony and dictatorship'.[11]

How, on the basis of the above, can we synthesise Gramsci's position? In fact, in his conception of hegemony he sets himself apart from Gentile by refusing to identify dictatorship and hegemony (a characteristic peculiar to him), since his whole conception is aimed at explaining the existence of states which depend on dictatorship but are incapable of hegemony; similarly, he sets himself apart from Croce in the sense that he does not differentiate between 'hegemony' and 'dictatorship', 'civil society' and 'political society' in the same way as Croce. Synthesising the above, we can state that, according to Gramsci, *the system of hegemony can amount to the same as the system of dictatorship, but a system of dictatorship can exist which cannot express itself in terms of hegemony, whereas hegemony must intervene as a characteristic of a dictatorship capable of exercising both domination over the hostile classes and leadership of the allied classes and kindred groups.*

In conclusion, it seems clear that when he seeks to discover the sufficient mode of being (*mode d'être*) of the worker state, it is through his conception of hegemony that he finds it. There does, of course, exist a bourgeois hegemonic system founded on the capitalist mode of production and which is expressed in the bourgeois-democratic state. According to Gramsci, there must also exist *a hegemonic system*, based on a superseding of the capitalist mode of production. This system will find its expression in the state which, for the classes and groups belonging to the 'revolutionary historical bloc', will organise forms of 'proletarian democracy' and, for the classes and groups hostile to the worker state, forms of control and repression based on violence. What in any case seems inacceptable to Gramsci is a conception of the state as a 'general' expression of democracy (such as that which has been translated into the liberal-representative system), a conception of marxism as merely one of several possible ideologies, competing with them and integrated into the 'institutionalised pluralism' of a party in which marxism could exist side by side with religious beliefs and doctrines of various types.

In short it must, I think, be forcefully asserted that Gramsci's theory of hegemony is the highest and most complex expression of leninism. In no way can it be considered as a point of transition between leninism and a conception of the political struggle and the state which would oppose the system of hegemony to the system of dictatorship and the state as they are expressed in Lenin, whom Gramsci, as though wishing to avoid any possible ambiguity in the future, labels the Saint Paul of marxism. In Gramsci's view, the 'constantinian' moment was still to come.

The Third International

If one wishes to perceive the underlying motivation for Gramsci's 'structural' leninism, it must be stressed that it is closely linked to an interpretation of the nature of the historical epoch, which is that held by the Third International, and to the theoretical analysis of *imperialism* according to Lenin. Gramsci was totally convinced that socialism had long been objectively ripe. As Athos Lisa recalls in his *Memorie*,[12] summing up this conviction, Gramsci 'thought that the objective conditions for proletarian revolution had existed in Europe for more than fifty years'.

Only by taking account of this conviction can the real meaning of

Gramsci's opposition to the theory of social fascism and the adventurist political line which stemmed from it be fully appreciated. He was not opposed to the latter because he considered that the struggle against fascism should be undertaken in the name of a restitution of a system of democracy of liberal type in the framework of a '*Constituente*' of democratic type, like that which existed in Italy after the First World War; he was opposed to it because he considered that an 'intermediary' phase was necessary which, with the requisite differences, would enable the revolutionary party to accumulate the necessary forces for an Italian 'October'. His opposition to the social-fascist line resided in the fact that social fascism aimed to achieve an objective which was also his own, but without the appropriate tactical phase which he had already defined in 1924, that is to say, the search for a route which would make it possible to recreate the conditions of the Bolsheviks and to achieve dictatorship of the proletariat. In short, his opposition resided in the fact that he accused the PCI and the International of an oversimplified conception of the premises of dictatorship and of having failed to understand the importance of the construction of an equally indispensable 'hegemonic' dimension. An opposition therefore existed between two conceptions whose sole object was the basis of dictatorship of the proletariat.

Lisa states very precisely that '[Gramsci's] account of the question of the *Constituente* established the following two ideas: 1 the tactics required for the conquest of allies of the proletariat; 2 the tactics required for the seizure of power'.

The aim of the 'transitional' phase is to bring the masses to an understanding of the 'correctness' of the communist programme 'and the falseness of the programmes of the other political parties':

> the Party's objective is the seizure of power by means of violence and dictatorship of the proletariat, which it must bring about by using the strategy which best corresponds to a specific historical situation, to the relationship of forces between the classes, and to the various moments of the struggle.
>
> The '*Constituente*' represents an organised framework ['*forme*'] in which the most advanced claims of the working class can be made. It is in the bosom of the '*Constituente*' that the action of the Party, which consists in undermining all plans for peaceful reform and showing the Italian working class that the only possible solution in Italy lies in proletarian revolution, can and indeed must be undertaken through its representatives.

It is easy to understand how Gramsci, wishing to avoid all possible misunderstanding as to a 'democratic' reading of his conception of the role of the *'Constituente'*, recalls that in Russia Article I of the *Programme of Government of the Bolshevik Party* took account of the *'Constituente'*, and he concluded by saying that the slogan of the Party should be 'Republic of worker and peasant Soviets in Italy'.

Failure to take account of all these elements in a reading of the theory of hegemony put forward by Gramsci in the *Prison Notebooks* is to disfigure and exploit it for the purposes of a current political situation which has nothing to do with the situation and perspectives of Gramsci.

The abandonment of Gramsci's conception

It is impossible to understand Gramsci's points of view mentioned above unless they are replaced within the context of his more general analysis of capitalism and his more specific analysis of fascism. He did not succeed in thinking a future phase of the organic expansion of capitalism. And this is why he considered that fundamentally the class struggle was distinguished by the dialectic revolution-counter-revolution in a period which is essentially characterised by being a period of social revolution. Fascism represented a form of counterrevolution which was inherently incapable of being anything other than *passive*; this is why Gramsci believed that the end of fascism would coincide with a renewal of the relevance of proletarian revolution, even if the revolution should encounter tactical problems identical to those we referred to above.

The situation which actually arose with the end of fascism in the rest of the world and then in Italy was quite different, and Gramsci's strategy was set aside. World capitalism found its leadership in the USA under whose direction the capitalist reconstruction of Europe took place outside the soviet sphere. This meant that the bourgeois-democratic institutions and the states which were the expression of them became the milieu in which, for a whole new historical epoch (which is our own), the communist parties had to find their place. There was, therefore, a radical recasting of the situation as against Gramsci's hypothesis. Class relations were thereby modified above all as regards the relation of national and international forces, which made any plan to launch a struggle against the institutions in order to transform them in an anti-bourgeois sense, unrealistic. The 'war of position' was, so to speak, breaking its ties with the 'war of movement'.

It was in this new context that the PCI, undergoing contradictions and disagreements, gradually elaborated a conception of 'hegemony' which was later, and more and more rapidly in recent years, embraced definitively and which differs qualitatively from Gramsci's conception. Taking as base the acceptance of parliamentary institutions, the recognition of the pluralism of parties as a representation and organised form of the various groups and various social classes – nowadays included in the 'building of socialism' – a conception of ideologico-political 'pluralism' as an organic and necessary expression of democracy, and the hypothesis of participation in the government according to the modalities of the 'historical compromise', the PCI has arrived at its particular conception of hegemony. This has nothing in common with the conception of those who, like Gramsci, thought to make it the basis of the worker state and of the absolute supremacy, under the direction of the PCI of the industrial proletariat over its allies (allies limited to those social forces able to constitute an 'antithesis' to the social 'bloc' led by the bourgeoisie), of a conception of marxism as an element of differentiation and absolute separation with regard to all the other conceptions, of a vision of democracy internal to the revolutionary bloc alone.

For Gramsci, in keeping with his 'structural' leninism, democracy represented three things and three things only:

1   the means to a 'reflexion' between political equals 'that is to say between communists' on the presuppositions and modalities of their action;
2   the means to lead 'subaltern' social forces;
3   the means enabling the revolutionary party to muster the necessary energy to 'destroy' by rationality and persuasion the false idols which continue to dominate the consciences of the 'subaltern' allies and consequently to create the bases for a dictatorship upon the active supports of the old world.

Gramsci's 'pluralism' (if he ever used this term) had certainly nothing in common with the interpretation of it that the PCI gives today in relation to the problems posed by its insertion into the democratic-republican institutions of the liberal type, in which each conception of the world enters into 'free competition' with others, according to the idea 'that the best will win'.

Of course the evolution of the PCI was not originally doctrinal; it was, on the contrary and above all, the result of a precise social and economic reality. Confronted with the reality of international capitalism and the relations between the 'blocs' which, in the West and in Italy, had made it impossible to achieve a relatively rapid modification of the relation of forces between classes with a view to destroying capitalism and its institutions, and confronted with the hard reality of a conservatism which relied upon a broad mass political base, the PCI was obliged to set itself a new task, notably to insert itself into this context, to accept the techniques which govern relations between different classes and social groups and between the various mass parties, and to abandon the plan to modify these relations according to a dynamics which would lead to the worker state. Confronted with a bourgeoisie which, in Italy, had the means to enforce its state institutions, even if this took place in an advanced democratic constitutional framework, the PCI proposed to 'occupy' the institutions by a 'hegemonic' action which, on the one hand abandons the idea of the worker state and dictatorship of the proletariat, and on the other aims to assume direction of the parliamentary state. This is quite a different conception of 'hegemony' from that held by Gramsci.

Yet it is undeniable that the PCI also reached this new strategy by 'using' Gramsci. After reflecting on the crisis of the 'soviet model', the PCI might well have perceived a reference in the criticism which, in the light of his theory of hegemony, Gramsci had tirelessly addressed to every socialist project which imprisoned itself in a narrow conception of the state-power and which mechanically identified dictatorship of a party and dictatorship of the proletariat. But it subsequently 'muffled' the other aspects of Gramsci's theory of hegemony (precisely those which were associated with an expansive conception of dictatorship of the proletariat) which thus led it to confirm the interpretation that Gramsci's criticisms at least implicitly opened the way for the 'disjunction' between hegemony and dictatorship.

The 'catholic wisdom' of the PCI

I have tried to bring out the way in which the PCI, outlining its current strategy, has encountered new practical problems in relation to those encountered by Gramsci and to his particular hypotheses. Yet it is necessary that the PCI put an end to all theoretical opportunism, settle its accounts more decisively with theoretical tradition and abandon this 'catholic wisdom' for which all is 'adaptation' and nothing is 'mutation'. There is no possible doubt that its theory of hegemony is qualitatively different from Gramsci's. In its aims as in its means, Gramsci's theory, as I emphasised above, is the highest expression of the historical phase of the international communist movement which opens with the October Revolution and ends when stalinism sets itself up as a régime. The theory of hegemony, in the view of the PCI, expresses the attempt to elaborate a strategy on the fundamental base of acceptance of the existing institutions in the West and on the base of progressive liquidation of the historical phase of stalinism.

If we ask the PCI to base its practice on a less 'tactician' confrontation with the theoretical heritage of the past, this is not simply in response to a demand for 'truth'. It is above all a question of a political need. The entire Italian left, of which as is well known the PCI is an essential component, requires more truth if it is to achieve greater realism. The author is convinced that, in its essential aspects, the policy of the PCI is calculated to attach this party to a conception of the state, of relations between classes, of the 'road to power', and of the role of 'coalition governments' which has much more in keeping with social-democratic marxism than with leninist and even the gramscian conception. With one single exception, namely the very important leninist 'residue' of the criteria for the internal organisation of the party, which is a residue whose survival is uncertain to say the least. If this is the reality, then it must be discussed; if the reality is different, its elements need to be clarified.

It is never a sign of strength to establish a clerical and commemorative relation with the past (if there is strength in the past, it is for conservatives), unless one acts in a 'transformist' way in the facts. 'Transformism' occupies a considerable place in 'marxist clericalism'. When the social democrats adopted a liberal conception of the state, they claimed to do so by 're-interpreting' Marx; when Stalin undertook those actions we all know, he claimed to do so from pure leninism; and so on. Today, when socialism is confronted with difficult situations, it must fully accept its responsibilities and its theoretical responsibilities in the first place. It seems clear to me, in any case, that the strategy of the 'historical compromise', 'ideological pluralism', and the struggle for the 'democratic' transformation of the state, have nothing in common with the ideas of Antonio Gramsci, the greatest and most fertile interpreter of historical leninism, and mark a definitive turning-point with respect to Gramsci.

History is also interesting in so far as its permits no one to live beyond a certain level of income accumulated by the past. If need be, one can act in this way for a certain time, but sooner or later, we find ourselves 'naked', and it cannot be said in the last analysis that this is always a bad thing, for it enables us to see ourselves as we are.

Notes

This chapter was originally published in *Mondoperaio*, No. 2, 1976, and was translated into English by Hal Sutcliffe.

1 Luciano Gruppi, *Il concetto di Egemonia in Gramsci*, Rome, Editori Riuniti, 1967.
2 Quotation inadequately adapted to the text (translator's note).
3 Antonio Gramsci, *Selections from Political Writings 1921–26*, ed. and trans. Q. Hoare, London, Lawrence & Wishart, 1978, pp. 199–200.
4 *The Lyons Theses*, in ibid., pp. 340–75.
5 Ibid., pp. 373–5.
6 Ibid., p. 375.
7 Ibid., p. 440.
8 Antonio Gramsci, *Selections from the Prison Notebooks*, ed. and trans. Q. Hoare and G. Nowell Smith, London, Lawrence & Wishart, 1971, p. 365.
9 Ibid., p. 462.
10 Ibid., p. 56 n.
11 Ibid., p. 271.
12 Athos Lisa, *Memorie*, Milano, Fellrinelli, 1973.

8 Lenin and Gramsci: state, politics and party

Biagio de Giovanni

1 Lenin and the form of political mediation

In a passage of *What is to be Done?* a critical image of economism is established from which it is still valid to take up an argument, concerning the actual crisis and political structures, which it is necessary to construct in order to contribute to the supersession of this crisis, in view of a higher form of society. Lenin writes:[1]

> The manner in which the connection between, and interdependence of, legal criticism and illegal Economism arose and grew is in itself an interesting subject, one that could serve as the theme of a special article. We need only note here that this connection undoubtedly existed. The notoriety deservedly acquired by the *Credo* was due precisely to the frankness with which it formulated this connection and blurted out the fundamental political tendency of 'Economism' – let the workers carry on the economic struggle (it would be more correct to say the trade-unionist struggle, because the latter also embraces specifically working-class politics) and let the marxist intelligentsia merge with the liberals for the political 'struggle'. Thus, trade-unionist work 'among the people' meant fulfilling the first part of this task, while legal criticism meant fulfilling the second.

Stripped of the most immediate references to the reality which is the object of Lenin's analysis, that text is essential for the clearness with which it critically registers the way the strategy is divided along the two separate lines of the economic and the political. Within the text is a stringent reference to the 'containment' of the working class inside the economic struggle – even where the latter is presented as a 'specifically working-class politics' – and to the exclusive relationship between political 'struggle' and the 'struggle' by the intelligentsia for freedom. Behind this view, Lenin singles out an extremely reductionist and subaltern notion of the political, which renders itself, so to speak, visible either through *economic* conflict or through the *ideological* struggle. In a certain sense, Lenin's problem is how to achieve the autonomy and the primacy of the political. This autonomy and this primacy are perceived and, I would say, enclosed within the concept and famous expression which Lenin uses a few pages later:[2]

> Class political struggle can be brought to the workers *only from without*, that is, only from outside the economic struggle, from outside the sphere of relations between workers and employers. The sphere from which alone it is possible to obtain this knowledge is the sphere of relationships of *all* classes and strata to the state and the government, the sphere of the interrelations between *all* classes. ... To bring political knowledge to the *workers* the Social Democrats must *go among all classes of the population*: they must despatch units of their army *in all directions*.

This passage from Lenin's text is an integral part of the history and organisation of the communist movement, and I do not here want even briefly to run through the interpretative possibilities which it has developed of various moments.[3] I believe, however, that one may extract one point from the text which is important for the analysis, and quite evident already in the way in which the text is tied to the Kautskyan thesis of the determinate character of the relationship between intellectuals and the working class.[4] The reference to the *outside* certainly is a reference to the complexity and the capacity of the unification of the political (from here the reference to 'the field of relations of *all* classes': the discovery, therefore, of a field of 'productivity' for the relations between classes which coincides with the field of constitution of the state), but it also contains a discovery of the primacy of the political which is firmly tied to his 'centralism' and his 'specialism'. The political dimension is contracted into a determinate focus. Its determination shows up the surrounding reality, but does not penetrate it, reproducing to a certain extent the character of a type of state which Lenin is confronted with. The primacy of the political is above all to be grasped in its specificity, in the impossibility that it may be diluted between the economic and the ideological. For this reason it is essential to preserve a double level of analysis for *this* Lenin:[5] that which grasps the tremendous novelty of this neither economic nor ideological relationship between the working-class movement and political initiative (organisation), and that which makes evident the concentration of the primacy of the political in a form of specialism which is the principal guarantee that the political will not be subjected to spontaneity, nor confused with different levels of organisation.[6]

> We must have such circles, trade unions and organisations everywhere in *as large a number as possible* and with the widest variety of functions; but it would be absurd and harmful to *confound* them with the organisation of revolutionaries, to efface the border line between them, to make still more hazy the all too faint recognition of the fact that in order to 'serve' the mass movement we must have people who will devote themselves exclusively to Social-Democratic activities, and that such people must *train* themselves patiently and steadfastly to be professional revolutionaries.

But the specialism of the political in Lenin exists not only in relation to the problem of organisation. I mentioned before that we found his first reference to it when he refers to the concentration of the political in the enemy. We must carefully reflect upon this point. In Lenin the first aspect of the form of the political is linked to a specific dimension of Russian reality during the nineteenth and early twentieth century – to autocracy with the extreme restriction of the political domain to that of the repressive organisation of the state apparatus. But this is not the crucial point. Lenin's thesis does not have as its condition a political reality which is perhaps the most backward in Europe during the early twentieth century. If this were the case, the disrupting effect it had on the entire theoretical and practical history of the working-class movement and its ability to provide political and organisational direction for two complete historical phases of life of the communist International would be incomprehensible. The true link, the true relation lies elsewhere. We are thus immediately led to one of the high points of bourgeois political theory which broadly conveys the historical sense of a transformation of the political morphology in the West. 1918: *Politics as a Vocation* by Max Weber signals a quite determinate moment within this theoretical development.[7] The intricate relationship between state and capitalist development is defined by the progressive growth of the autonomy of the political, by the concentration of political power into a focal point determined by the unit of state power. Let's take a quick look at the two central points in Weber's argument:

1   Everywhere the development of the modern state is initiated through the action of the modern prince. He paves the way for the expropriation of the autonomous and 'private' bearers of executive power who stand beside him, of those who in their own right possess the means of administration. ... The whole process is a complete parallel to the development of the capitalist enterprise through gradual expropriation of the independent producers. In the end, the modern state controls the total means of political organisation, which actually come together under a single head.[8]

2   Let us confidently take the present as an example. He who wants to establish absolute justice on earth by force requires a following, a human 'machine'. He must hold out the necessary internal and external premiums, heavenly or worldly reward, to this 'machine' or else the machine will not function. Under the conditions of the modern class struggle, the internal premiums consist of the satisfying of hatred and the craving for revenge. ... The leader and his success are completely dependent upon the functioning of his machine and hence not on his own motives.[9]

I shall not engage here in a critique of some of the 'mystical' features in this weberian text. It is the meaning of the whole discource that points in an important and significant direction. The interpenetration, which becomes increasingly accentuated, between the economic and the political, may above all be managed, within the continuity of the capitalist socio-economic formation, through the progressive centralisation and concentration of the political and its apparatus of command. This leads to an ultimate theoretical development which must be carefully followed: the interpenetration of the political and the economic must be governed by an increasingly rigorous separation between these two fields specific to the organisation of domination. The primacy of the political is shown here in isolation, and I would say almost in the naked and schematic determination of its laws of operation. The gradual expropriation of the direct producers at the political level, at the moment when the apparatus of command becomes concentrated, in some way isolates from it its scheme of movement while it frees and enhances the *autonomous productivity of the political* precisely at the time when 'the whole process constitutes a perfect parallel with capitalist economic development'. Through the filter of Weber, we return to the modernity of Machiavelli. But behind the autonomy of the political, and the immense concentration of means which it now presupposes, there lies the specific organicity of the world of the economy which at this point is separated from the political level.

I believe that it is here where the 'tie' for Lenin and the theoretical guarantee for his 'modernity' lie. But let us look at the question in a more determinate way. The concentration of the means necessary for the exercise of political action 'into one single centre' which, if it is the solid basis on which the dominant classes may construct the unity of the political, more than ever excludes the fact that the answer on part of the working-class movement may not be a *political answer* which is capable of moving at the height of the most elevated level of practice of the enemy and his organisation of power. Lenin's whole critique of economism is read within the framework of a historically determined class antagonism and an organisation of the relations between classes which maintains itself on the basis of a form of the primacy of the political which corresponds to the mechanism of a determinate state. One must respond to the primacy of the political which operates for the dominant classes with a powerful concentration of the political within the working-class movement. It is here that we find the modern meaning of *What is to Be Done?* Here also lies the meaning of that consciousness that comes from the outside. Since this dimension also materially conveys a sense *of concentrated* origin of politics, of something which possesses its own laws of movement, these are not born out of the relationship based on workers and owners, but come from the outside, from a dimension set at the height of that unique centre in which the power of the capitalist state becomes unified.

Lenin's party responds to this structure of the state and to its theory.[10]

> The political struggle of Social-Democracy is far more extensive and complex than the economic struggle of the workers against the employers and the government. Similarly (indeed for that reason) the organisation of the revolutionary Social-Democratic Party must inevitably be of *a kind different* from the organisation of the workers designed for this struggle. ... In view of this common characteristic of the members of such an organisation, *all distinctions as between workers and intellectuals*, not to speak of distinctions of trade and profession, in both categories, *must be effaced.*

It is symptomatic how Lenin relates the political level to the organisational level. Corresponding to the vastness and complexity of political struggle, one finds a form of organisation which reconstitutes within itself the same level of homogeneity and autonomy leading to the political dimension. As the place of the homogenisation of political figures, organisation reflects within the domain of the real practice of the movement the concentration of politics into one single point as the specific point of confrontation between the dominant class and the working-class movement. Corresponding to the 'professional' (and in this sense 'scientific') level of revolutionary organisation there is, on the part of the state, a general theory of politics as a profession which accentuates the division precisely during that phase in which the state prepares to become the maximum point of organisation of the economic 'productivity' of classes. The two dimensions of politics (that of capital and that of the working-class movement) meet – without vanishing as would be the result following Weber, in the convergence of a 'technical' structure – inasmuch as they are enhanced at the point of their 'autonomy'. *The revolutionary party is, in this sense, the anti-state of the working class.* Until possible, thus until the specificity of the relationship between state and capital, and party and working class re-emerge, this comparison is valid and allows for the concentration of attention on one important point. The exclusivity of political organisation in 'centralising' the form in which the masses are present, coincides with the exercise of political monopoly, within the 'purely' political reality of the revolutionary party, as much as within the legitimacy of force, 'as a means of exercising sovereignty',[11] in the capitalist state. I am saying that the concentration of the political *outside* the social processes leads to determining in this central and precise point the recognition (the unification) of the whole comprehensive arch of the relationship between political forms and the masses. The concentration of politics (of its logic, and of a kind of continuity, along the lines of Machiavelli and Weber) into one single point sharpens and accentuates to an extremely high degree the relationship between political practice and the institutional apparatus by restoring the modern centrality of the interconnection between the 'massification' of the social processes and the instantaneous perception of their unification in a political form.

Naturally, having arrived at this point, the specificity of the party-working-class relation then emerges. By saying that the revolutionary party is the anti-state of the working class, a concept which exactly specifies the slope of confrontation between these two forms of politics, one already is describing this specificity. The point of reference for a conflict is still the weberian state, which is largely comprehensive (and in part anticipatory) of the new elements which are intervening in the capital-state relation. It is crucial to see *how* the relationship of the masses with the place where the unity of power and the consistency of its institutional form is constituted, becomes centralised. Most important is to focus on the politico-economic connection because, within the state-capital connection, the dilution of the political logic into forms which apparently ignore this logic is tied to it. The institutional forms of capital mediate the concentrated level of politics. The central point which accompanies the link between politics and the economy is the decomposition of the masses, the constitution of a fabric where forms of organisation appear which segment the life of the masses and which avoid the recognition of their history in a directly political practice.

The relation between party and working class centralises the historical life of the masses by attempting to enhance a historically determined level of their recomposition. In respect to the level of 'politics as a vocation' in Weber, Lenin's revolutionary political profession introduces that profoundly subversive element into capitalist society which is given by the effective attempt to centralise the life of the masses in real forms of political practice which is largely seen as *dominance + directly political hegemony*. It is not by chance that within the decisive pages of *What is to Be Done?* the problem of the relationship between working class and democracy should appear. How does Lenin pose this problem? It is rigorously defined from the standpoint of the working-class party, and is defined by the 'political' (revolutionary) necessity to set the party into relation with other forms of political organisation of the masses and other social classes. 'In order to bring the *workers* political knowledge, Social-Democrats must *go into all classes of the population*, must dispatch units of their army in all directions.'[12] 'For it is not enough to call ourselves the "vanguard", the advanced contingent; we must act in such a way that *all* the other contingents recognise and are obliged to admit that we are marching in the vanguard.'[13]

What emerges here in this double development of the problem is a fundamental need which permits a thorough investigation of the specificity of the operational form of the political; the way in which it appears concentrated in the party which is the advance detachment of the working class. The central point on which Lenin reflects on the eve of 1905 is how to define the relationship between the maximum 'external' concentration of politics, and the necessity of this 'external' dimension becoming the principle of a *mass line*, by introducing into this necessity the decisive contribution of the working class to the development of democracy. As Gramsci has understood, this certainly was the birthplace of the practical principle of hegemony and, one may add, of an extremely rich form of 'the primacy of politics'.

A quick return to the comparison with Weber will make the meaning of the development of this argument much clearer. Within the weberian form of 'politics as a vocation', the concentration of the material means in the hands of the 'leader' and his machine, the expropriation of social groups 'who formally controlled these means in their own right',[14] which accentuates and unifies the level of political domination, certainly does not neglect the problem of this complex organisation of the social 'mass' which is organised, so to speak, within the weft of scientific and juridico-institutional formalism running through all levels of modern capitalist society. The concentration and professionalism of political activity are determined in relation to the non-political level of the organisation of the social mass, and therefore to its specialism which has become very wide-spread within 'technique' and the connection between 'technique' and power. The recomposition of political power filters, in a reversed manner, through the 'pluralism' of the organised forms of the social.

In Lenin the process is completely different, and profoundly recalls the specificity of the party–working-class binomial. The point is clarified precisely by the relationship which the working-class party must establish with the other organised levels of society, in such a way that '*all* the other detachments should see and be forced to recognise that we are moving in the forefront'. Decisive here is the attempt to *politically* reconstruct society which must begin from the level of direction which the working-class party is able to express. The field of the relation is completely and directly political. It becomes essential to see how a plane which is able to reconstitute the masses, or rather 'unify' the various 'detachments' around the direction of the working-class vanguard, passes through a level which is purely political. Important to the concrete physiognomy which this problem assumes is the way in which the form of politics elaborated by Lenin for *What is to Be Done?* is critically modelled on the specificity of the relation between the state and the centre of the organisation of power during the phase of the transformation of the relation between the state and capital. I have already shown before how the 'external' character of the political dimension has, in an extremely determinate manner, before itself the concentration of politics – and, I would say, its expulsion from the social – in the way that it reveals itself in the real body of the bourgeois-capitalist state. The extreme difficulty and problems involved in the need of reconstitution, of which I spoke before, as an unrenounceable factor in the *democratic* relation between the party and society in its totality, lies precisely in the strong accentuation of the autonomy of politics and its 'external' character, in respect to the necessity of governing a 'mass line' within the whole fabric of society. This necessity is on the other hand intrinsic to the working class – party binomial, if the political consciousness of the class is precisely 'the field of relationships between *all* classes'.[15] But, because of the way in which politics becomes dimensioned, in its specific physiognomy, the field of this relationship is immediately *totally* political, and in this sense determines the level of direction for society. To put it more explicitly: having gathered politics in the sphere of consciousness – organisation which is constitute in its own subjective and objective space,[16] it becomes crucial to see in which way the 'unique centre' of direction *from above* can act as the decisive filter of recomposition and, in other words, how the mediation of direction from above and a mass line can occur during a phase in which *a particular morphology of politics* emerges as the fundamental field of recomposition. The two possibilities implicit in this state of affairs become clear, and I will outline them in the most schematic (and therefore also risky) brevity:

1   That politics concentrated at the highest level, i.e. the level which has the *separate* state before itself, in some way isolates itself into a forced logic of its own, and immediately articulates the recomposition as the instance embracing the 'autonomous' spheres in the 'political' and, in particular, as the subordination of all the other detachments to the working-class vanguard. Politics here continues to function in a kind of space which is separate and profoundly filled by a determinate 'practice'. In this sense, what exists is a modern jacobinism which renews, in new forms, the *old* jacobinism as the real form of political mediation. Here, in its modern form, its real solid base lies in the strong, pressing return of the autonomy of politics as it is constructed in the logic of the expropriation of the 'direct producers' (and of the social producers of politics) through the concentration of the political 'means'.

2   That the concentration of politics at the highest level carries to this level the whole scheme of the transformation of the relations between classes; that it, so to speak, uses that 'high' level as the place of effective re-unification of politics and the economy, thus offering a real measure to the mass-politics relation by overturning the way in

which politics and the economy manifest themselves as separate within the dominant formation.

We are not dealing with an immediately real alternative, nor with a real and proper *aut-aut*, at least from the moment in which the political movement organised by the working class appears on the historical scene. But the basis for the discourse and the fact, however, that it encounters real problems and difficulties, lies precisely in the critical link of the working-class movement to the high point of the transformation of the bourgeois-capitalist state, and with the extreme complexity and contradictory nature of the connection between politics and the economy. The 'modern' return of the primacy of politics may be determined in the reorganisation of the state and its 'functions' (Weber) and in the *political* organisation of the working class (Lenin). It is the complexity of this double knot – which is never less than this in Lenin – theoretically confronting leninism, which nevertheless finds reality objectively unbalanced by the slope of the political as the 'unique centre' and separated from the organisation of the social which is the focal point of the management of the separation of the producers from the means of production; and which therefore supplies an answer which largely appears conditioned by the historically determined form of politics which it has before itself.[17]

The main consequence of this interconnection, which comes about already with Lenin and not after him, is the direct confrontation between the state (which is to be overthrown) and the party; and the party's tendential posing of itself as the anti-state of the working class. The complexity of the function and the form of the state must be reflected in that unique centre which now becomes the state. There the whole life of politics becomes concentrated, not only in how the party determines the structure of 'political' domination, but also because of the way in which it functions as the place of unification of the subject (of the revolutionary 'cadres') who enter to become a part of it. To a certain extent, this situation signals of its own the same critique of economism developed by Lenin from which this argument has taken its momentum. That politics does in fact have its own specificity (and its own ability of unification) in respect to the *economic* and the *ideological* struggle, is a notion that, on the one hand opens a historical phase of extreme importance for the strategy of the working-class movement, but on the other hand, undergoes with Lenin a type of reading *which emphasises the autonomy of politics rather than its connections*. One point which is close to Lenin's heart, during this phase of development of his thought, is the specification of a structure (the party as the real organ of politics) in which 'all distinctions as between workers and intellectuals must be effaced'.[18]

This absence of distinction contains in itself the two possibilities of development described before: 1 politics as the effective concentration of the social (of the economy), the embryo of a form of state as the unity of the diverse; 2 politics (but more rigorously, the party) as the place of unification which forces the subjective figures, specified in the dimension of the political 'cadres', under the determination and government of an autonomous logic. This logic is the only general level of mediation through which the relation between 'leadership' and 'mass line' is filtered, for which the critique of economism is partly overturned into a historically determined form of primacy of politics as primacy of the party.

I believe that in *What is to Be Done?* it is the second of these directions of analysis that comes to dominate because of reasons to which I have already briefly referred − leading to the 'high' points of the form of politics of the enemy − reasons which converge into one central point: the form of the state, during the phase of development and construction of monopoly capital, leads to any authoritarianism of the apparatuses of power, against which one must concentrate as intensely as possible the capacity of the political impact produced by class antagonism. From here, the ultimate consequence to which I want to return from another angle: if it is not just the organising instrument, but also a 'political' one of the direction of the revolutionary process, the unification which occurs within it *is precisely that of a type of state* which in the autonomy of the socio-economic level sees the merit of decomposition − spontaneity into which it interpenetrates the mechanism of dominant power. Here, too, it would be interesting to follow the ambivalent meaning in Lenin's critique of 'spontaneity'.[19] But there is one point I believe one can understand in its totality: the places and forms of decomposition of the masses are seen as the overturned objectification of that 'unique centre' in which the 'political' focus of the apparatuses of the dominant power can be determined. In this sense, one cannot only begin from these to overturn the process − because politics is not found in them − rather it is necessary to move from the attack to the place where the dominant power is directly *state and politics*. There is a kind of immediate coincidence within this framework between the construction of power and the overthrow of the existing state.

From here the point on which I have already insisted: the positioning of the party directly against the state, as a state-party, as a structure which counterposes one form of autonomy of politics to another. Whatever the historically determined level of the passage of the social recomposition of the masses through the filter of leadership constituted by the party may be, this determination of politics poses a vertical system of mediations; a system of mediations, a system which is specified by the levels that move from the top to the bottom: party-class-society. The metaphor of this 'verticality' is to have a meaning which is full of possible implications. The rigorous closure of the form of politics within the practices of the party, and the hegemonic character of this practice in respect to the political constitution of the class – and even more in respect to the relationship between party and the class and all other classes of society – are elements which end in becoming an obstacle to a wider and diffuse collocation of the masses in the political domain because they restrict politics to one level only. This reductionist notion of politics, along with its primacy, in the moment in which it determines the indicated consequence, by renewing the effective possibility of a separation of politics from the masses,[20] hinders the development of a direct productivity of the productive forces within the field of their 'making politics' during the phase of transition, and therefore contributes to returning the same notion of 'productive forces' to economism. This weighs heavily on the determined working class-political relation.

This situation constitutes an effective antithesis to pluralism which from the start is excluded from a state which, as a political state, is measured on the form of the party and on a strong charge, so to speak, of syllogisms which ties the general 'productivity' to politics, politics to the party and the party to the concentration of consciousness and organisation in a determinate focus. In this certainly also partial sense, leninism and pluralism are historical antitheses, where by pluralism we mean the expansion of the relationship between the masses and politics in such a way that one may discern direct centres of political 'productivity' of the level of the social: centres which define themselves in relation to a form of state within which the recomposition of the masses is determined by an unknown relationship between (economic, social, ideological) 'productivity' of the masses and a diversified articulation of its political forms.

2 Gramsci

With the 1930s one specific aspect of the political mediation constructed by Lenin comes to an end, in the sense that the definite signs of crisis in the morphological conditions of one political form begin to gather. If this frame of reference has any foundation, then that means that it is possible to verify the following hypothesis: that the form of mediation examined by Lenin in *What is to Be Done?* is the fundamental historical experience of the working-class movement on a determinate stage in the organisation of financial capital, a stage which is distinguished – elliptically – from the weberian form of relation between the political structure and society. The prolonging of leninism beyond this time – when not a dogmatic hardening of theory and practice – is tied to the extreme complexity of its dimension on the one hand, and to the impossibility of restricting it to a rigid relationship with a phase in the history of the relation between capital and the state, on the other hand. Nevertheless, to use this rather neat periodisation, it would seem correct to me to pose at least one specific determination: it is not the same thing to say that today the problem is to apply – with all the necessary 'critical' distinctions – leninism to our present time, and saying, on the other hand that the characteristics of our present are to be *beyond* the political mediation which is dominant in leninism. It is the analysis of the present political form which leads to either one or the other choice.

Let us rapidly try and establish a few points of discussion for an analytical investigation. There is one conditioning circumstance to which one must pay attention and, again, one must keep in mind for its definition on the one hand the level of the 'revolution from above' operated by capital and, on the other, the ability and resiliance of the working-class movement, within the framework of a history still marked by the prevalence of a given socio-economic formation. The references will end by being pure 'titles' for a possible verification. I believe that the gramscian concept of 'diffusion' of hegemony is essential for societies characterised by advanced capitalism in the West at the beginning of the 1930s. The morphological transformation of which I spoke before, when seen as the level of change in the political forms, refers precisely to the way in which the dimension of the political breaks many 'chains' which determine their concentration into one single point. This transformation is not a simple morphological 'development' internal to historically determined moments of the capitalist socio-economic formation. The transformation is here radically tied to the crisis (to the capital-mass contradiction) and at least in part poses itself as an answer to an unknown phase of the crisis which transforms the world picture in an irreversible manner. The explicit passage is from a phase of restriction and concentration of hegemony (which is rigorously reflected in the weberian vision of politics, even if in this vision there are also elements capable of 'seeing' far ahead) to a progressive expansion of the necessity of a direct relation between masses and hegemony which through other mechanisms allows the interconnection between economico-social decomposition and political recomposition of society to function. Here only one of those possible passages from Gramsci:[21]

> The 'critical consciousness' was restricted to a small circle which was hegemonic but restricted: the spiritual 'government apparatus' has broken in two, and there is a crisis, but it is also one of diffusion, thus one that will lead to a new, more secure and stable 'hegemony'.

This quote from Gramsci does not refer to any type of forced transition. Meanwhile, it forms part of a complex discourse which Gramsci conducts from 1929 on the morphological transformation of politics during a historical phase dominated by 1 organised capitalism; 2 fascism; 3 the change in relations of forces produced by the October Revolution; 4 the specification of a new strategic framework for the working class in the West after its defeat between 1919 and 1921.[22]

What this reference to Gramsci is trying to indicate is nevertheless a precise and definite matter: Gramsci's answer is the only one, emerging from within the marxist camp, which is adequate to the political and economic transformations of capitalism around the years of the 'Great Crisis'. This clarification should not be understood in a 'closed' sense (and it would have to be verified through the reading of two theoretical 'continents' which are so wide apart yet singularly parallel, and expressed, in an abbreviated way, by the Gramsci-Keynes binomial), but nevertheless it should be taken as a possible criterion for an analytical reconstruction. I shall now try and clarify only one direction in which this hypothesis may be taken. The point to insist on is precisely *the gramscian consciousness of the 'morphological' transformation of politics*. Essential to this transformation is the way in which the new relationship between the state and the economy determines the relationship between the masses and the state at a totally different level. This can already be seen at the level of the elementary stratum of the *economy*, which forcefully breaks away from the rigidity of the old nineteenth-century dichotomies, thus breaking the relative stasis of the equilibrium. Gramsci's attention focuses on the tremendous increase of unproductive labour as the emerging sign of the crisis with the coming of the 1930s. It would be useful to remember here a not very short text which is quite important:[23]

> What is the excess of consumption to be attributed to? Can one prove that the working masses have raised their living standards to such an extent that it can be seen as an excess of consumption? Thus, that the relationship between salaries and profits has become catastrophic for profits? Statistics could not even show this for America ...: has it not happened that within the distribution of national income especially through commerce and the stock exchange a category of 'withdrawers' has introduced itself after the War ... which fulfils no necessary and indispensable productive function, while it absorbs an impressing part of the income? ... After the war, the category of the unproductive parasites has in absolute and relative terms grown enormously, and it is them who devour all savings. ... The causes for the crisis are thus not 'moral' (enjoyment, etc.) nor political ones, but socio-economic, thus of the same nature as the crisis itself: society creates its own poisons, it must let the masses (not only unemployed wage-earners) of the population live that hinder saving and thus break the dynamic equilibrium.

The increase in unproductive 'masses' and the shift of equilibrium in the relation between income and productive work meanwhile specified the important changes in the social stratifications. Along with the increase in unproductive income, entire social groups become dislocated which have no direct contact with production. The fact is this: given the general conditions, huge profit created by the technical progress of work creates new parasites, that is people who consume without producing, who do not 'exchange' work for work, but other people's work for personal 'aims',[24] and which already in this elementary state of their collocation establish a generalised relation with 'functions' which are mediately or immediately of the state. It is thus above all the relationship between the state and the economy which, if one may say so, changes the class structure and the form of their 'productivity'. But this elementary fact is still not sufficient. Especially in the sections of the *Prison Notebooks* dedicated in 1934 to 'Americanism and Fordism', Gramsci is careful − in a unique way, I believe, within the marxist thought of those years − to individualise a central knot in the morphological transformations of politics, precisely in the shift of great human masses to a *direct* relationship with the state. I shall provide only one central point of reference for the development of the argument. It is in the paragraph on 'Shares, Debentures and Government Bonds', included in the section entitled 'Americanism and Fordism'. The analysis is above all concerned with the place of convergence of the mass of savings which emerges from the wide band of unproductive income:[25]

> It could be said that the mass of savers wants to break off any direct connection with the *ensemble* of private capitalism, but that it does not refute its confidence to the state: it wants to take part in economic activity, but through the state, which can guarantee a modest but sure return on investment.

This simple economic relationship sets complex categories and relations into motion. The centralisation of savings around the state forces the state into a more intense relationship with productive organisation[26] within the framework of a 'functional' dislocation of income which is also parasitic *vis-à-vis* the reproductive organism. But, at this point one level of the gramscian description which escapes from the determination of the purely economic stratum is released in order to place itself in the domain of the organisation of the new 'politico-social basis' of the state where what is decisive is a new political relationship between the masses and the state. It is worth quoting the passage in full:[27]

> This complex of demands, not always acknowledged, is at the origin of the historical justification of the so-called corporate trends which manifest themselves for the most part in the form of an exaltation of the state in general, conceived as something absolute, and in the form of diffidence and aversion to the traditional forms of capitalism. The result of these phenomena is that in theory the state appears to have its socio-economic base among the ordinary folk and the intellectuals, while in reality its structure remains plutocratic and it is impossible for it to break its links with big finance capital.

> That a state can exist politically based simultaneously on the plutocracy and on the 'ordinary folk' is not in any case entirely contradictory, as is proved by the example of France, where the rule of finance capital could not be explained without the political base of a democracy of petit-bourgeois and peasant *rentiers*. For complex

reasons, however, France still has a relatively healthy social composition. .... In other countries, on the other hand, the savers are cut off from the world of production and work.

There are two elements in particular which require attention:

1 The political determination of the relationship between the masses and the state, tied to the development of the 'unproductive' sector, but above all connected with the inclusion of this sector into a more complex relationship of the state with social 'productivity'. The productivity of the 'masses' thus becomes 'political' *lato sensu* because it is an integral part of the function and organisation of the state. Gramsci explicitly draws this consequence, whenever he sees in these 'masses' the politico-social base of a state organically linked to big financial capital.

2 The determination, therefore, of the non-contradictory character of the political unification between the mass basis and the state of big capital. Or, rather, more than that, not only the non-contradictory character, but also the forced connection between state intervention in the economy and the diffusion of politics, in the form of a *clear leak of 'productivity' from the immediate level of the economy* and of a new relationship between social 'masses' and the political organisation of the state. This, rather, becomes the central development of Gramsci's discourse. The transformation of the relationship between masses and politics within a form of state which maintains and develops its organic relationship with finance capital, implies a particular type of diffusion of politics which bases itself on the organisation of the 'ordinary folk' and the 'intellectuals' as the mass nuclei of a specific form of reproduction.

I shall end this analytical point of departure here, in order to rapidly come to a conclusion which returns us to the initial point of the outlined hypothesis. This radical diffusion of politics, which follows the way in which the 'Great Crisis' forces the dominant classes to rearticulate the relationship between politics and the economy, does not correspond to the collapse of that 'unique centre' of which Weber spoke, but certainly to the diffusion of political forms (moving from those emerging from the immediate economic level, but also far beyond them), and of the masses organised along the whole spectrum of society, even in their reference to a restricted political state, the structure of which 'remains plutocratic'.

'The spiritual "government" apparatus has broken in two and there is a crisis, but this crisis is also one of diffusion which will lead to a new, more secure and stable "hegemony".' The strong chain of 'casemates' dislocated in various strata of civil society, by overcoming the levels – not only the direct ones – of social atomisation, and by introducing elements of politics into the forms of economico-social life, provides a real basis for the classical gramscian hypothesis on the strategy of the passage from the 'war of manoeuvre' to the 'war of position'. In this framework, what is questioned *is the morphology of the state*. Here lies the radical change of the 1930s. No preceding theoretical and political form is more adequate for the complex phenomenology of this change. The interconnection between politics and the economy by affecting the character of the productivity of classes, the link between productivity and unproductivity, and the forms of organisation of the masses, introduces elements which break up a frame of reference where the scientific and juridico-formal organisation of the levels of the organisation of the social runs parallel to the concentration of power. Increasingly, the masses put themselves directly into the domain of the state, and confront the state within the very 'immediacy' of their productive position. The new attention that the state (from the fascist state to the state of the New Deal) paid towards the forms of political organisation of the masses[28] is largely a response to the expansion of the level of the political 'productivity' of the latter.

This determines a centrally new element for the strategy of the working-class movement, and constitutes, so to speak, new 'chains' for its articulation in Western society. The multiplication of 'centres' to 'hit', changes above all the *theoretical* character of the political struggle, and introduces this dimension into society as soon as it is expropriated from politics. The answer by the working-class movement should not be at this level of the problem, even when it is evident that the duration of the diffusion of this process is quite long and tenacious, the continuation of the efforts at corporate 'decomposition' of society and at the discovery of the 'antidotes' – even if it is in the form of a specific 'making politics' – to the diffusion of politics in the real practice of the socialised masses.

Above all, the object of thought again becomes – and with Gramsci in a singularly rich way – *the party* as the political instrument of strategy for the working-class movement. The point is to smooth out its ability of direction over a process which in itself contains the contradiction between a tendency towards expansion of politics and an equally 'tense' necessity of concentrating the forms of power. In order to define itself and act within the space of this contradiction, the party no longer functions as an *anti-state apparatus* – and in this sense as the anti-state of the working class – but rather restricts itself to a point where, at a very high density, the impact of the political becomes concentrated. It is the entire knot between party and state that enters the discussion here, on the slope of the conflict between the capitalist bourgeois state and the communist party, as much as on the slope of the state dimension internal to the physiognomy and initiative of that same party. Gramsci is the thinker who on this subject reaches a level of elaboration nearest to the awareness of the fact that the transformation of politics involves transformations of its own morphology, and of the level of the great shifts of the masses. His reflections on the party are moved by an attention which is very much determined by the necessity that the initiative of the party should *really* let the political productivity of the masses filter through its own work of direction. The main risk is seen in the collapse of this relationship.[29]

This order of phenomena is connected to one of the most important questions concerning the political party – i.e. the party's capacity to react against force of habit, against the tendency to become mummified and anachronistic. ... The bureaucracy is the most dangerously hidebound and conservative force; if it ends up by constituting a compact body, which stands on its own and feels itself to be independent of the mass of members, the party ends up by becoming anachronistic, and at moments of acute crisis it is voided of its social content and left as though suspended in mid-air.

This 'separate' character of the party can be tied to and be a specific form of a mechanical and 'fetishistic' vision of history, capable of becoming mass common sense, according to which 'the organism' has a distinct life from the 'individual' within a real abstract centralisation of initiative:[30]

What is surprising and characteristic is that fetishism of this sort should reproduce itself through 'voluntary' organisms, which are not 'public' or of the state, such as the parties and the unions. One tends to think of the relationship between the individual and the organism as a dualism, and one tends towards a critical attitude which is external to the individual in relation to the organism (if the attitude is not an acritical enthusiastic admiration). Whatever, it is a fetishistic relationship. The individual expects the organism to do something, even if it does not work and reflect that precisely – its attitude being very diffuse – the organism is necessarily inoperative.

The possibility that such an analysis could be the principle of a new tie between the party and the masses is closely linked to the fact that the different stratifications where the masses move already imply profound and elementary levels of organisation. The accent is now above all on this 'link', on the relations which force the 'political' dimension on to the most elementary strata of economico-productive life. The political activation of the masses must, in order not to be an 'unfounded' mechanism, organically adhere to economico-productive life inasmuch as the general tendency lies in the fact that this stratification of social life already sets the masses into a *general* dimension which is penetrated by the structure of productivity: Gramsci writes:[31]

> It should be observed that political action tends precisely to rouse the masses from passivity, in other words to destroy the law of large numbers ... with the extension of mass parties and their organic coalescence with the intimate (economico-productive) life of the masses themselves. The process whereby popular feeling is standardised ceases to be mechanical and casual ... and becomes conscious and critical. ... In this way a close link is formed between the great mass, party, and leading group; and the whole complex, thus articulated, can move together as 'collective-man'.

It is important here to go straight to the central problem which emerges from this problematic. What in effect radically changes is *the relationship between the party and the state* because the determinate place of their confrontation changes. The expansive diffusion of politics does not leave either of the two terms of that relationship unchanged because the field of constitution and movement for both, the party and the state, changes. The elements of recomposition in the relationship between the masses and the state give rise to new forms which pose the problem of *unification* as the historically determined dimension of the communist party in different terms. To put it more explicitly: *it is the form of state internal to the party* which 'suffers the effects' of the first signs of contradictory expansion of politics beyond the limits set by the restrictiveness of a separation which is objectively preconstituted and blocked. A state dimension in the party develops outside the simplification – concentration of the party as the anti-state of the working class.[32]

> When does a party become historically necessary? When the conditions for its (triumph), *for its inevitable progress to state power,*

*are at least in the process of formation, and allow their future
evolution* – all things going normally to be foreseen.

What is introduced into the party is the 'processual' dimension of the
state which is the most visible result of the morphological transformation of politics. But this dimension which in its decisive elements
penetrates the party-state 'in process of formation', leaves its mark
above all on that type of unification taking place within the party which
clarifies the continuity and rupture from the old relationship of the
vanguard with the rest of society. Meanwhile, 'this unification' has a
contradictory expansion of the political before itself. Within the domain
of the political practice of the dominant state this contradiction becomes
explicit through the effort – which is a real and true general and
objective 'tendency' – to contain diffusion and overwhelm the senses by
distancing, so to speak, the political dimension from the *real practice* of
the masses, while at the same time preserving the general levels of
'unification' of the mass movements. The working-class movement and
the communist party must come to terms with this contradictory
expansion of politics and bring within their own structures a type of
unification which can be the first practico-theoretical answer to 'this'
specific form of the contradiction.

This ensemble of problems involves within itself the transition from
What is to Be Done? to the *Prison Notebooks*. Above all it is the
determinate 'chain' of the transformation of politics (the answer to the
crisis, and the revolution from above by capital) which developed in the
West after the 1930s, that renders necessary the central idea *of a new
way in which the party becomes state*. The concentration of politics,
having changed at the state level, the way in which the party meets the
political domain changes too. Its being a 'state' in process of formation
implies that in it the moment of unity and harmony becomes
concentrated, although the accent on the 'process' (state-process, party-
process) and on hegemony as leadership-unity as the levels inherent in
the complex lives of the masses, leads to setting the logic of politics (of
the party) into close relation with the domain of the extension of the old
civil society. The function of the unification of politics is not in
discussion, but the specific manner of its movements as a moment of
unity is.[33]

The political party, for all groups, is precisely the mechanism which
carries out in civil society the same function as the state carries out,
more synthetically and over a larger scale, in political society. In other

words, it is responsible for welding together the organic intellectuals of a given group – the dominant one – and traditional intellectuals. The party carries out this function in strict dependence on its basic function, which is that of elaborating its own component parts – those elements of a social group which has been born and developed as an 'economic' group – and of turning them into qualified political intellectuals, leaders and organisers of all the activities and functions inherent in organic development of an integral society, both civil and political.

The 'external' consciousness of *What is to Be Done?* is no longer the adequate form of political mediation for the 'massification' emerging from the social processes, and for the paths which make the party the real filter of a mass line. From *What is to Be Done?* one can preserve the essential point on the generality of political mediation,[34] but the politico-intellectual 'function' is seen by Gramsci as the place of the construction of the unity between civil society and political society. This unity must run through the effective life of the party, thus giving to the 'primacy of the political' a fullness which is capable of involving the transformation of the relations of forces (material, economic, ideological, of hegemony) between classes. The unification which is realised through the party sets the political morphology of the class into motion in the same way as the transformation of the state–masses relation introduces elements of change into the 'class' structure of the state and therefore – within the unity of a historically determined development – into the relationship between the state and the working class. One may not think very much of the way in which Gramsci returns to rethink the party-class relation ('every party is the nomenclature of a class'),[35] if one does not completely understand that the process of *political* constitution of the class and its alliance is formed within the fabric specified by the dominant classes – state relation. The entire thematic of the expansion of the unproductive classes, set into relation with the relationship between the state and the distribution of income, specifies the objective scheme of an introduction of the 'productivity' (*lato sensu*) of classes into the domain of a hitherto unknown relationship with the state. The new morphology of the state redefines, within its limits, the morphology of the classes and the internal relations with each other. The party–class link thus becomes dynamic, and the elements of 'universalisation' which the party introduces into the class ('if it is true that parties are only the nomenclature for classes, it is also true that parties are not simply a mechanical and passive expression of those classes, but react energetically upon them in order to develop, solidify and universalise them')[36] reveal another feature of that 'process' which hinders the strong determination of the class as external to the state (anti-state) until the moment in which its 'vanguard' 'overthrows' the 'old' state.

With the coming of the 1930s in the West, one may witness the exhaustion of the 'classical' hypothesis tied to the dichotomous opposition of party and state. Gramsci is the thinker who, in the communist movement, within the drama and contradiction of the European experience of those years, has seen through and analysed those elements of transformation which were destined to act for a long time as the nuclei of a profound change in strategy.

3 The theoretical basis of pluralism

I believe that one must retrace the theoretical basis of pluralism within this framework. The gramscian 'modern prince' is not the origin of a theory of hegemony closed within itself. Attention should be conclusively paid to the way in which Gramsci constructs the relationship between the party and the state. One text of particular significance establishes the levels of the mediation.[37]

> If the state represents the coercive and punitive force of juridical regulation of a country, the parties – representing the spontaneous adhesion of an elite to such a regulation, considered as a type of collective society to which the entire mass must be educated – must show in their specific internal life that they have assimilated as principles of moral conduct those rules which in the state are legal obligations. In the parties necessity has already become freedom, and thence is born the immense political value (i.e. value for political leadership) of the internal discipline of a party and hence the value as a criterion of such discipline in estimating the growth potential of the various parties. From this point of view the parties can be considered as schools of state life. Elements of party life: character (resistance to the pressures of surpassed cultures), honour (fearless will in maintaining the new type of culture and life), dignity (awareness of operating for a higher end), etc.

The point on which to briefly concentrate the analysis is the character of 'organicity' of the 'free' mediation of the party. I believe that it may be interpreted as the registration of the 'necessity' of the political forms as the general domain of the movement, as the passage of the masses through the fabric of society. The thesis should, therefore, be seen as a historically determined specification of the morphological transformation of politics. The expansion of politics, which in a certain way continues to break away from the separateness of the state, redefines the mediation which inheres at the different levels of the life of the masses, by introducing elements of unification there where the social decomposition tended to make itself felt in its immediacy. The organicity is therefore, to a certain extent, a necessary character of the forms of mediation. Now, this measure and physiognomy tends to redefine on the one hand the relationship leadership-masses ('the process of development is tied to a dialectic between the intellectuals and the masses. The intellectual stratum develops both quantitatively and qualitatively, but every leap forward towards a new breadth and complexity of the intellectual stratum is tied to an analogous movement on the part of the mass of the "simple", who raise themselves to higher levels of culture and at the same time extend their circle of influence ...')[38] and on the other hand, and above all, the contents which pass through the filter of political mediation. The accentuation of the 'collective' character of the mediation which immediately penetrates the mechanism of the party ('a complex element of society in which a collective will, which has already been recognised and has to some extent asserted itself in action, begins to take concrete form'),[39] already gives the sense of a very strong enrichment of the primacy of political mediation. The collective dimension which passes through it relates its primacy to the transformation of the ensemble of hegemonic relations between classes, in such a way that that which runs through is loaded with references to the diffuse forms of organisation of social life. This passage is important. The 'diffuse' character of hegemony, as the specific referent of political action in the developed West, transforms and enriches the content of political mediation of class relations (a decisive element for the 'transition') is realised around a progressive overcoming of the separateness of politics. For Gramsci this does not mean to deny politics as 'centralised' leadership ('But innovation cannot come from the mass, at least at the beginning, except through the mediation of an elite for whom the conception implicit in human activity has already become to a certain degree a coherent and systematic ever-present awareness and a precise and decisive will'),[40] but rather to intuit in a determined sense, that this same leadership is something which remains 'unfounded' in the realm of pure political mediation if it does not pass through the forms of elementary change of the political morphology, and if it does not introduce this change in the precise process of posing itself as leadership.

If we turn for one moment to the text quoted just before in which Gramsci talks of parties as features of society where 'the necessity has already become liberty' and which function 'as schools of state life', one can see that their level of mediation organises and, so to speak brings to the light of social life, the feelings, the culture, forms of consciousness, knowledge of the general ends and, altogether, an organic process of unity between theory and practice in which the specific existence of a social group is not only preserved and objectified, but also defines its 'collective' relation to the whole of society. The plurality of the points of organisation of social life is the solid basis so that the 'political' mediation of the party may become the moment of real unification between the masses and politics. In this framework, the relation between the state and the party begins to take shape. To limit ourselves to only one of the possible directions for analytical development which are present in Gramsci, the mechanism of the party poses for itself as a historical task that of transforming the 'necessity' of the state into 'liberty' of the state by supplying the levels with 'continuity' in the fabric which divides the masses from the state. If the decisive point is producing a crisis of the separate state, of the state-coercion, in order to start off a 'process', at the end of which the 'state will be identified with civil society',[41] then what becomes essential is constructing a political practice – and a corresponding theory – which specifies *the lines* of flow between the state and the fabric of the ensemble of civil society. *It is in this sense that the state passes through the party*, and that the 'state' finality of the party (of that party which is 'rationally and historically founded on this end')[42] contains its own organic function. At this point we are within a theoretical position which is quite different from that in which the immediate coincidence between party and state reduces the entire institutional dimension of politics to the way in which the party immediately incorporates the function of the 'state'. Together, it becomes evident that the organicity of the relationship, state-political society-civil society handed over to the diffusion of politics as the decisive principle which breaks the organic decompositions and the reciprocal strangeness of the planes of movement of the 'social', throws out the old forms of pluralism as the sanction and celebration of a divided society. But basic-ally, was it not already the weberian theory of the concentration of the pol-itical that constituted the awareness, within the dominant form of state, that the age of the liberal state had ended without any possibility of return?

4 Starting points for a conclusion

The realm in which the political struggle in Italy took place from 1944, prolongs and develops the analytical horizon which was perceived by Gramsci during the 1930s. This does not mean that Gramsci is sufficient, and that our efforts should be exhausted in 'interpreting' him. Things have moved fast, and the tasks of the Italian working-class movement have grown so much that they have also become radically new. Today rather one is aware of the great difficulties within the development of a theory of these themes, and at times a kind of difficulty on our part in respect to the way in which the problem is posed by the liberal-democrats.

On this point all the merit certainly goes to someone like Norberto Bobbio – a longstanding, acute speaker for the working-class movement – who has allowed for a re-opening of the debate around pluralism, after the publication of his very polemical essay in *Mondoperaio*, (1976). It should also be said that, while looking back at things calmly, the nucleus of the contributions provoked by that debate is something that has disturbed our indifference, and that today we are faced with rigour and the effort of free reflection between the old state of the question and the way in which we have been forced to return to it. But I also ask myself: are the problems posed by Bobbio really relevant to our present? As they have been put, does the theoretical link which conditions us begin from those problems? Do they really convey the high and also critical point (but these two things seen *together*, as they are revealed to us, today in real history) which our history has arrived at? On this point my answer is: very doubtful. My impression is that in Bobbio one finds the stubbornness of the great intellectual who, held by his own old but serious reasonings, has turned the history which has contested and contradicted these reasonings into a history of 'errors' and filled by the 'negative' (both theoretical and practical). But the framework of the problems he poses still looks backwards, to a form of state which is more residual of a passed experience than a way of seeing and opening up our present. It is not enough to say to ourselves that we are behind (and also much more), to push ourselves to return to forms of experience which today live more in isolated reflection than in the same institutions of the dominant state. The rapid and dramatic emergence of great multitudes in the history of the twentieth century has posed to the working-class movement in the West the problem of democracy in a way unknown to the liberal state as the problem of the 'necessity' of organising an '*institutional relationship between these great masses and the general world of politics and the state. Hic Rhodus, hic salta.*' Here, in this extremely defined point, lies the theoretical root and also the enormous practical difficulty of pluralism. There is nothing to look for in the hidden folds of Marx's thought in order to give a polish to our foundation to this theoretical point. One cannot go *beyond* that problem, and if one does, then one will find dangerously empty forms which are dangerously adaptable to different effective contents of domination. The fact is that the basis of pluralism (at least in Italy) has been largely constructed by the historical experience of the working-class movement, at the moment in which its effort has gone towards determining a wide 'political' scheme in civil society. Pluralism is not necessarily foreign to the history of the working-class movement; on the contrary, today – and for us, I would say, for Gramsci onwards – *it has necessarily become an organic part of it*. The party, the mass movement for the improvement of work, the readjustment of the relation between intellectual labour and the finality of development, have created a structural multiplicity, organic in points of aggregation, organised, unified by the return into the forefront of the use value of the productive forces and of social wealth. All this has changed, and continues to change in Italy in a realm full of political implications, tensions and ideological differences, and within a fabric riddled by crisis but nevertheless still full of those sentiments which the intensity of political life until today has posed. All this *must, therefore, express itself through differentiated political forms*, if it is the domain of politics which establishes (or at least is destined to establish) the continuous scheme of our interconnection between the masses and the state. But it should be very clear that the struggle for social recomposition remains at the centre of the strategy. Outside it, the working-class movement loses its own identity and its own *political raison d'être*. Only if the working class disappears *politically* will the need of recomposition disappear with it. The particularity of the task and, so to speak, its strategic possibility, is given by the extent to which the political mass movement *today is within the morphology of the state*. Within this post-gramscian framework the ability of the party to 'internalise' the state in no way implies that the party makes itself into a state. The Third International is a closed experience in the West. The morphology of this state in transformation is such that, inasmuch as it is not 'unique', it may not be blocked, closed or defined according to some forced verse. The state may exist in a multiplicity of particular political forms, precisely because it experiences the progressive collapse of its separateness, and because this suppression occurs through the exaltation of ways of using social subjectivity, and the creation of a number of differentiated forms of life and political control.

This whole process already implies a period of transition, and the idea of the transition as a 'process'. Here one can hardly arrive at a more precise determination. The process excludes and suppresses the old rigidity of the 'two times': the before and the after. In effect what goes is the static relationship between hegemony and state power according to the classical scheme: *first* the conquest of the state, *then* the construction of socialism. The two things become interconnected, first in the organisational redefinition of the instruments of political struggle, and above all, in all those elements that move, even a little, towards a regulated economy. The contact of the masses with the entire network of the state makes the drastic and simple alternative between elements of socialisation and the form of the old state disappear as it also introduces a multiplicity of centres inside the fabric of society from which one must move so that the viscious and ahistorical state bureaucracy does not become the future political 'subject' of socialisation. At this point, all of this can also be seen in the radical contradiction of a crisis which may be – and in part is – the occasion for establishing hegemony, but which concretely already is a possible reply by the dominant bloc to the hypothesis of a political recomposition of the productive forces.

In this light, the party also becomes a great problem of which one must speak. These morphological transformations cannot leave the party aside, as if the party itself was not an element of this situation, and had not contributed in a decisive way to make it such. Pietro Ingrao has written:[43]

> Has all of this also left a mark on the way of conceiving and organising the life of the working class party, or the various working class parties, including our own? Absolutely yes. It means that there are still inedited pages to write on that too, which concerns the role and the mode of existence of the modern political party.

The invitation for an open and diffused debate should be accepted.

Notes

This chapter was originally published in *Critica Marxista*, 3: 4, 1976 and was translated into English by Suzanne Stewart.

1. V. I. Lenin, *What is to Be Done?*, *Selected Works*, vol. 1, Moscow, Progress Publishers, 1971, p. 104.

2 Ibid., p. 152. An extremely acute reading – which will have to be discussed – of *What is to Be Done?* and particularly of the way in which the theory of the party and the theory of the state are intimately linked in Lenin, is that by M. Montanari, 'La teoria leniniana del partito', *Lavoro critico*, no. 8, 1976.

3 Important references, within the framework of a complex new setting of the problem, are found in the Introduction by L. Paggi to Max Adler, *Il socialismo e gli intellettuali*, Bari, De Donato, 1974, pp. 9–134.

4 Lenin, op. cit., vol. 1, p. 121. Lenin quotes a famous text of Kautsky's where, amongst other things, he writes: 'The vehicle of science is not the proletariat, but the *bourgeois intelligentsia*. ... Thus socialist consciousness is something introduced into the proletarian class struggle from without.'

5 The reference to *What is to Be Done?* poses a strictly defined relationship with a determinate phase of the leninist elaboration of politics. The complexity of Lenin's work (which confines itself, or almost, to those writings dedicated to 'On Co-operation' – in V. I. Lenin, *Collected Works*, 4th edn., vol. 33, London, Lawrence & Wishart, 1966 – which are a lucid contribution to the elaboration of a mass democracy) is such to render reductions impossible. The richness of these reflect on the phase of advanced capitalism and imperialism constitute fundamental pages in relation to the phase which today crosses through the history of the world. *What is to Be Done?* nevertheless, and the theory of the party described there, remains a decisive historical pivot for both leninist theory of the political and for the complex history of the communist movement. I thus believe it legitimate to take it as a reference point for the discussion, without exposing myself to the easy objection of wanting to 'reduce' or concentrate Lenin at this level of his reflections.

6 Lenin, *Selected Works*, vol. 1, p. 189.

7 I refer to the Appendix of 'La forma borghese della politica' included in my book *La teoria politica delle classi nel 'Capitale'*, Bari, De Donato, 1976, pp. 125–39, for the relationship between Lenin and Weber in relation to the problem of a critique of 'spontaneity' I refer to F. Cassano in his essay *Max Weber: Razionalita e capitalismo* to be published by De Donato.

8 Weber, 'Politics as a Vocation', in H. H. Gerth and C. W. Mills, *From Max Weber*, London, Routledge & Kegan Paul, 1970, p. 82.

9 Ibid., p. 125.

10 Lenin, *Selected Works*, p. 178.

11 Weber, op. cit., p. 82.

12 Lenin, *Selected Works*, p. 152.

13 Ibid., p. 156.

14 Weber, op. cit., p. 83.

15 Lenin, *Selected Works*, p. 153.

16 For an example of this, see ibid., pp. 193–4.

17 It is in this direction that it seems legitimate to me to insist on the analytical comparison between Lenin and Weber. The subject matter, in quite different

ways, is at the centre of attraction in M. Tronti, *Operai e capitale*, Turin, Einaudi, 1971, in particular pp. 279–89, and in M. Cacciari in his Introduction to G. Lukacs, *Kommunismus 1920–1921*, Padova, Marsilio, 1972, pp. 7–66, in particular pp. 52 ff.

18 Lenin, *Selected Works*, p. 178.

19 Cf. especially ibid., pp. 112–24.

20 Naturally, what remains open is the problem of a definition of the 'sign' that this separation takes on, and thus its determinate historicity, and its relation to the structure of a social formation. In this sense, the analysis of stalinism and its relation to leninism constitutes a wide subject which largely has not yet been covered.

21 A. Gramsci, *Quaderni del Carcere*, ed. V. Gerratana, Turin, Einandi, 1975, I, p. 89.

22 A more precise definition of these elements is in the above cited book, *La teoria politica delle classi nel 'Capitale'*, pp. 295–311.

23 Gramsci, op. cit., p. 793.

24 Ibid., p. 1348.

25 Gramsci, *Selections from the Prison Notebooks*, ed. Q. Hoare and G. Nowell Smith, London, Lawrence & Wishart, 1971, p. 314.

26 'But once, through unavoidable necessity, the state has assumed this function, can it fail to interest itself in the organisation of production and exchange? ... If this were to happen, the crisis of confidence that has struck private capital and commerce would overwhelm the State as well ...' (ibid., p. 314).

27 Ibid., pp. 315–16.

28 The book by G. L. Mosse, *The Nationalisation of the Masses, Political Symbolism and Mass Movements in Germany* (1812–1933), New York, Howard Fertig, 1975, constitutes a noteworthy contribution to this problem even if the categories used are largely debatable.

29 Gramsci, *Selections from Prison Notebooks*, p. 211.

30 Ibid.

31 Ibid., p. 429.

32 Ibid., p. 152 (my emphasis).

33 Ibid., pp. 15–16.

34 A tradesman does not join a political party in order to do business, nor an industrialist in order to produce more at lower cost. ... In the political party the elements of an economic social group get beyond that moment of their historical development and become agents of more general activities (ibid., p. 16).

35 Ibid., p. 152.

36 Ibid., p. 227.

37 Ibid., pp. 267–8.

38 Ibid., p. 334.

39 Ibid., p. 129.

40 Ibid., p. 335.

41 Ibid., p. 263.

42 Gramsci, *Quaderni del Carcere*, p. 1601.

43 P. Ingrao, 'Il pluralismo', *La Stampa*, 7 October 1976.